THE ASHTRAY

THE ASHTRAY

(Or the Man Who Denied Reality)

Errol Morris

THE UNIVERSITY OF CHICAGO PRESS
CHICAGO AND LONDON

The University of Chicago Press, Chicago 60637
The University of Chicago Press, Ltd., London

Published 2018
Printed in China

27 26 25 24 23 22 21 20 19 18   1 2 3 4 5

ISBN-13: 978-0-226-92268-3   (cloth)
ISBN-13: 978-0-226-92270-6   (e-book)

DOI: https://doi.org/10.7208/chicago/9780226922706.001.0001

Designed and typeset by Laura Lindgren

Library of Congress Cataloging-in-Publication Data
Names: Morris, Errol, author.
Title: The ashtray (or the man who denied reality) / Errol Morris.
Description: Chicago ; London : The University of Chicago Press, 2018.
    | Includes bibliographical references and index.
Identifiers: LCCN 2017038261 | ISBN 9780226922683 (cloth : alk.
    paper) | ISBN 9780226922706 (e-book)
Subjects: LCSH: Kuhn, Thomas S. | Paradigm (Theory of knowledge)
Classification: LCC Q175 .M8685 2018 | DDC 501—dc23
LC record available at https://lccn.loc.gov/2017038261

♾ This paper meets the requirements of ANSI/NISO Z39.48-1992
(Permanence of Paper).

Contents

Illustrations

Illustrations are listed by page number.

I don't want to die in a language I cannot understand.
—Jorge Luis Borges
(quoted in Alberto Manguel, *With Borges*)

Preface

It came hurtling across the room, spewing butts and ash. A cut-glass ashtray thrown by Thomas Kuhn, one of the most prominent intellectuals of the twentieth century. Was it thrown at my head? I'm not sure, but I remember it was thrown in my direction. With malice. You could imagine this occurred in some benighted place—perhaps in distant times—but you would be wrong, completely wrong. The assault occurred at the Institute for Advanced Study in Princeton, New Jersey—an independent center for theoretical research and intellectual inquiry founded in 1930; the academic home of Albert Einstein, John von Neumann, and Kurt Gödel, among others. The disparity between the act and the location of the act gives the event added piquancy. The home for some of the greatest intellectuals of the twentieth century, fleeing the intolerance of Nazi Germany, and yet the setting for an act of intolerance. Well, not just intolerance—actual violence.

INTRODUCTION

*Reality is a question
of realizing how real
the world is already.*
　　　　—Allen Ginsberg, "The Terms
　　　　　in Which I Think of Reality"

It has now been over fifty years since the publication of Thomas Kuhn's *The Structure of Scientific Revolutions*, a book considered by many to be one of the seminal works of the twentieth century. I do not regard it as such. Although it has spawned thousands of worshipful articles and books, it remains for me, at best, like Pet Rocks—a fad.[1] When I first wrote this, I received instant criticism

1. Developed in 1975 by Gary Dahl, an advertising executive, Pet Rocks sold for four dollars a piece. Dahl quickly sold over a million and a half of them. *Structure*, which celebrated its fiftieth anniversary in 2012, has sold roughly the same number of copies.

from my editor and others: fads are short-lived, while enthusiasm for Kuhn's book has persisted for half a century. And unlike Pet Rocks, *Structure* was never sold as a comforting companion, a solution to urban loneliness in a post-industrial society. So not *exactly* Pet Rocks. Maybe what emerged was more of a cult. With Kuhn as leader, dispensing his own brand of pernicious intellectual Kool-Aid.

(In John Milius's movie *Conan the Barbarian*, a peddler tells Conan about the cult of Set: "Two, three years ago, it was just another snake cult. Now you see it everywhere.")

A cult, then: misplaced admiration for a particular person or thing. Or maybe it's the Emperor's New Clothes, a case of community madness, an almost inexplicable desire to believe in something nonsensical because others are doing so. *Structure* itself feasts on the offal of innuendo and vagueness. It is, at best, an inchoate, unholy mixture of the work of others—Ludwig Wittgenstein, Charles Darwin, Rudolf Carnap, Norwood Russell Hanson, Alexandre Koyré, Jerome Bruner, and more. At worst, it is an assault on truth and progress.

Some philosophers and historians of science who are familiar with the controversies that have swirled around Kuhn's work believe that most of the issues have been put to rest. I would argue otherwise. But just what are these controversies and why should anyone care? Why should *you*, the reader, care? I suppose it depends on whom you ask, but for me, they point to big questions—about how language attaches to the world, the nature of truth, reference, realism, relativism, progress. Questions that continue to demand answers. Can we have knowledge of the past? Does science progress toward a more truthful apperception of the physical world? Or is it all a matter of opinion, a sociological phenomenon that reflects consensus, not truth? Unfettered emission of greenhouse gases promotes global warming. Species evolve through natural selection. Can we meaningfully assess the truth of these assertions? I will discuss many aspects of Kuhn's work—indeterminacy of reference, incommensurability, scientific change triggered by anomalies, Darwinian evolution as a model for the development of science, the relativism of truth, the social construction of reality, his philosophical idealism, and more. In each of these aspects, I have found it to be wanting and, more often than not, false, contradictory, or even devoid of content.

And then there's the specter of skepticism. Kuhn was a great skeptic, but like Des Esseintes, the antihero of Joris-Karl Huysmans's novel *Against Nature* ("Lord, take pity on the Christian who doubts, on the skeptic who would fain believe . . ."[2]), he both

2. Huysmans, *À Rebours* (1972), p. 206.

believed in something and, at the same time, hoped to undermine it. His skepticism fed on childhood doubts. Haven't we all wondered whether the world really exists? Whether we are just figments of someone's imagination or artifacts of some infernal computer program, like in a Philip K. Dick novel or *The Matrix*? It could be. Why not? But on the other hand, don't we all have a strong predilection for realism? We perambulate in the real world. Let's consult an authoritative source. *The Stanford Encyclopedia of Philosophy* defines realism as the belief that there are things that exist "independent of anyone's beliefs, linguistic practices, conceptual schemes, and so on."[3] Chairs, tables, rugs. The furniture of the world.[4] On a Victorian table, a well-thumbed copy of William Makepeace Thackeray's *Vanity Fair*, a red checked tablecloth, a vase of irises. The furniture of the world may *be* furniture—or the printed letters that form the first (prolonged) sentence of Thackeray's novel:

> While the present century was in its teens, and on one sunshiny morning in June, there drove up to the great iron gate of Miss Pinkerton's academy for young ladies, on Chiswick Mall, a large family coach, with two fat horses in blazing harness, driven by a fat coachman in a three-cornered hat and wig, at the rate of four miles an hour.

In fiction, we are often given an imaginary world with seemingly real objects—horses, a coach, a three-cornered hat and wig. But what about the objects of science—positrons, neutrinos, quarks, gravity waves, Higgs bosons? How do we reckon with their reality?

And truth. Is there such a thing? Can we speak of things as unambiguously true or false? In history, for example, aren't there things that actually happened? Louis XVI guillotined on January 21, 1793, at what has become known as the Place de la Concorde. True or false? Details may be disputed—a more recent example: how large, comparatively, was Donald Trump's victory in the electoral college in 2016, or the crowd at his inauguration the following January?[5] But do we really doubt that Louis's bloody head was held up before the assembled crowd? Or doubt the existence of the curved path of a

3. Alexander Miller, "Realism."

4. "Furniture of the world" is a phrase used in ontology, the branch of philosophy concerned with the question of what *things* exist. What is real. I tried to track down the origins of the phrase, with limited success. I vaguely remembered reading it in Bertrand Russell. And my researcher Josh Kearney did find a reference in Russell's *Introduction to Mathematical Philosophy* (1920), p. 182. Addressing the question of whether classes of things exist, Russell remarks, "The first thing is to realize why classes cannot be regarded as part of the ultimate furniture of the world." Kearney also located Barry Sandywell's entry "Furniture of the World," in *Dictionary of Visual Discourse* (2016): "The phrase 'store and furniture' applied to the world can be found in John Ray's *The Wisdom of God Manifested in the Works of Creation* (1717 . . .). The closest relative of this expression applied to philosophical topics makes a classical appearance in George Berkeley's *The Principles of Human Knowledge* (§6). . . . It is notable that the expression 'furniture of the world' is a hybrid phrase of Berkeley's 'furniture of the earth' and 'the mighty frame of the world.'"

5. Members of the Trump administration have denied the relevance of truth and suggested that there are such things as "alternative facts"—in short, that history is up for grabs and can be defined by those in power. This book, I hope, will serve as an antidote to those poisonous views. Truth and the apperception of truth, in my view, are what make civilization and progress possible. The denial of these things ultimately, perhaps irrevocably, undermines civilization.

Many may see this book as a vendetta. Indeed, it is. I find Kuhn's advocacy of the social construction of knowledge to be deeply disturbing, even pernicious. He was certainly not the only person to propound such ideas. But I am still possessed by the image of Kuhn cloistered in his office at the Institute for Advanced Study, writing about the absence of progress in science while bombs were dropping over Southeast Asia. The reader may think the two have nothing to do with each other. For me, they are inseparably connected.

6. "An invisible high-energy electrically-neutral light particle (photon) travels down from the top of the image and scatters off an invisible neutral hydrogen atom that is located near the middle of the figure, where the three curves meet at a cusp. The collision of the photon with the atom causes four particles to appear: a positively charged proton (not visible), a negatively charged electron knocked free from the hydrogen atom (this corresponds to the nearly straight track continuing downwards), and the *creation* of two new particles, a negatively charged electron and a positively charged antiparticle called a positron, whose paths trace out the two spirals." (Henry Greenside, "Creation and Conservation of Charge during Electron-Positron Particle Production from a Photon" [2015].) Such images illustrate one of the most important results of modern physics, the direct conversion of energy into matter.

positron in a bubble chamber?[6] Even though we might not know the answers to some questions—"Was Louis XVI decapitated?" or "Are there positrons?"—we accept that there are answers.

And yet, we read about endless varieties of truth. Coherence theories of truth. Pragmatic, relative truths. Truths for me, truths for you. Dog truths, cat truths. Whatever. I find these discussions extremely distasteful and unsatisfying. To say that a philosophical system is "coherent" tells me nothing about whether it's true. Truth is not hermetic. I can't hide out in a system and assert its truth. For me, truth is about the relation between language and the world. A *correspondence* idea of truth. Coherence theories of truth are of little or no interest to me. Here's the reason: They're about coherence—not *truth*. We are talking about whether a sentence or a paragraph or group of paragraphs is true when set up against the world. Thackeray, introducing the fictional world of *Vanity Fair*, evokes the objects of a world he is familiar with—"a large family coach, with two fat horses in blazing harnesses, driven by a fat coachman in a three-cornered hat and wig, at the rate of four miles an hour." Were Thackeray describing a real scene, his sentence would be true if (and only if) the horses and coachman were fat, the hat three-cornered

and sitting atop a wig, and the coach indeed moving at a rate of four miles per hour.

We're approaching a nasty problem: the relation between meaning, truth, and reality. Words and worlds. How do the words we use relate to things in the world? What links the beliefs and associations I attach to words—buzzings in the ball of electric jelly inside my skull—to objects in the world around me? Strictly speaking, it's not mind-body; it's language-world. At the end of the nineteenth century, the philosopher Gottlob Frege addressed these questions, distinguishing between sense and reference in a landmark essay.[7] When we use a word, what is the relation between that word and the world? Can words mean different things but refer to the same thing?

7. The title of Frege's 1892 essay—"Über Sinn und Bedeutung"—has traditionally been translated as "On Sense and Reference." For one detailed discussion, see Saul Kripke, "Frege's Theory of Sense and Reference."

Take the seemingly simple category of proper names. For example, "Mark Twain" and "Samuel Clemens"—the two names refer to the same person but have, according to Frege, different senses. Similarly, "Hesperus" and "Phosphorus," as the Evening Star and the Morning Star were known in the ancient world, both refer to the same object, the planet Venus, but have different senses. (The Pre-Raphaelite painter Evelyn de Morgan painted the brothers as separate individuals. If they're both fictitious, why not?[8])

Here is where the real trouble begins—think of it as Frege's curse: Does language connect us to the world or lead us back to ourselves? Is there a relation between things in our head (e.g., the beliefs we have about things) and things in the world (e.g., the furniture of the world)? Or are we hopelessly trapped inside our skulls?

We are now good to go.

8. Hesperus and Phosphorus were sons of Eos, the goddess of the dawn. The De Morgan Foundation website provides the following description of the painting: "Phosphorus is rising, his pale torch held aloft, its flame strong and reflecting off his golden hair, heralding the morning which is lightening the sky behind him. Hesperus's evening starlight is fading, as his flame in its dark torch weakens and gutters, his eyes are closing, his dark head anticipating the relaxation of sleep."

1. THE ULTIMATUM

*What song the Syrens sang, or what name Achilles assumed
when he hid himself among women, although puzzling questions,
are not beyond all conjecture.*

—Thomas Browne, *Urn-Burial*
(quoted in Edgar A. Poe,
"The Murders in the Rue Morgue")

"Under no circumstances are you to go to those lectures. Do you hear me?"

Thomas Kuhn, the author of *The Structure of Scientific Revolutions* and the head of the Program in the History and Philosophy of Science at Princeton, where I was a graduate student, issued an ultimatum. The philosopher Saul Kripke had given a series of three lectures—later published as *Naming and Necessity*—at Princeton in 1970. He planned to lecture at Princeton again in the fall of 1971, and I wanted to attend.[1]

The Structure of Scientific Revolutions, first published almost a decade earlier, in 1962, had been attacked by a number of philosophers. Kripke was not among them. I don't believe Kuhn had much awareness of Kripke's work at the time. His opposition to my attending the lectures reflected a desire to control what courses I could and could not take rather than a rejection of Kripke's ideas.[2] Meanwhile, Kuhn was becoming more and more famous. He would become not just a major figure in the history and philosophy of science but an icon. His terms "paradigm" and "paradigm shift" would become ubiquitous in the culture at large. A physicist and rock-climbing friend from Princeton,

1. Saul Kripke has subsequently told me that the lecture he delivered in the fall of 1971 was not a reprise of *Naming and Necessity* but another, related lecture—in all probability, a version of "Identity and Necessity," published in 2011 in his *Philosophical Troubles*.

2. Kuhn eventually became aware that Kripke (and Hilary Putnam, a philosopher at Harvard) had ideas that differed from his own. He discusses Kripke and Putnam in Kuhn, "Dubbing and Redubbing: The Vulnerability of Rigid Designation" (1990). Many more responses to critics are included in Kuhn, *The Road since Structure: Philosophical Essays, 1970–1993* (2000). The secondary literature includes, e.g., Rupert Read and Wes Sharrock, "Thomas Kuhn's Misunderstood Relation to Kripke-Putnam Essentialism" (2002), and Alexander Bird, "Kuhn on Reference and Essence," (2004).

3. While looking for information on Saum's whereabouts, I learned that he had died in 2000 of brain cancer. It is a terrible loss. I spent a good part of my year at Princeton climbing with him—on the buildings of the university and in the Shawangunk Mountains. This picture was taken in the Shawangunks, near the Uberfall.

4. One way to think about possible worlds is in the context of love. For example, you might ask, Would you still love me if I were poor? Would you still love me if I had no arms? What if I had no arms or legs? These questions are about possible worlds: the possible world in which you are poor; possible worlds in which you lack limbs; perhaps even the possible world in which you are poor *and* have no arms or legs.

5. One of the first popular articles about Kripke, written by Taylor Branch for the *New York Times Magazine* in 1977, was filled with stories of Kripke's youthful genius, though this one was not among them.

6. Connections between Kuhn and Wittgenstein abound. James F. Conant, philosopher and grandson of Kuhn's mentor at Harvard James B. Conant, writes, "Kuhn was . . . utterly mystified by the fact that most of his colleagues in the M.I.T. Philosophy Department either did not take Wittgenstein seriously or else took someone whom they called 'Wittgenstein' seriously whom he was unable to recognize as Wittgenstein. . . . What Kuhn had in common with [Hilary] Putnam . . . was that they were both interested in Wittgenstein as someone whose ideas they could use to do philosophy, without either of them being (at least at that time) in the slightest degree interested in remaining faithful to Wittgenstein's conception of philosophy." Conant, "On Wittgenstein" (2001), pp. 102–3.

Dick Saum, later sent me a picture of a bumper sticker that said, "Shifts happen."[3]

Kripke was slight, bearded, and in his early thirties. He was not widely known, but in academic circles had a reputation as a genius. While still a teenager, he had published a semantics and a completeness proof for modal logic (which deals with questions of necessity and possibility)—and in the process reinvigorated Leibniz's ideas about possible worlds.[4] There is an amusing but apocryphal anecdote about Kripke being offered a chair at Harvard when he was sixteen. He wrote back, "Thank you, but my mother thinks I should finish high school first."[5]

It was hard to see how Kripke's theories had much to do with Kuhn, at least in the early 1970s. Modal notions have been with us since ancient times. They are central to Leibniz's philosophy and his belief, satirized by Voltaire in *Candide*, that our world is the best of all possible worlds. But Kripke's theories, expressed in *Naming and Necessity*, in *Wittgenstein on Rules and Private Language*, and in many journal articles, concern meaning, reference, rule-following, and so on—issues at the heart of Kuhn's theories of normal science and scientific change.[6]

I ignored Kuhn's ultimatum and went to Kripke's lecture. My relationship with Kuhn ended badly. But more about that later.

Kripke addressed the twenty or so graduate students and professors assembled in a small seminar room, at one point looking at them through an empty glass as if it were a telescope. The glass created all sorts of optical distortions, making Kripke's left eye distend like that of a flounder. I assume that the glass had a similar effect for him, rendering his seminar audience into an aquarium of flat-faced academics.

I didn't really understand Kripke then. It was only a year or so later, at Berkeley, that I began to grasp his ideas, thanks to the efforts of my friend and fellow graduate student Charles Silver. But there is, at the heart of Kripke's work (though never explicitly stated), a simple idea. What he propounds is a thoroughgoing realism: There is a world outside of our language and us. Language is not just about us and our thoughts; it *directly*—unmediated by our opinions and beliefs—connects us with the world.

For me, Princeton was sort of a consolation prize. I had not been accepted into Harvard's history of science program, but Erwin Hiebert, a professor at Harvard, had written a letter of recommendation to Kuhn on my behalf. I should have known there would be trouble. I had imagined graduate school as a shining city on a hill, but it turned out to be more like an extended visit with a bear in a cave.[7]

Kuhn in those days was a chain-smoker, alternating unfiltered Camels with True Blues (a low-tar, low-nicotine brand). First one, then the other. Six, maybe seven packs a day. No need for matches.

The burning stump of one cigarette lighting the next. Deposited in a massive cut-glass ashtray, soon filled with a mountain of burnt-out ends. A latter-day alchemy of fire, smoke, and ash.

7. I had come to the history and philosophy of science enthralled by the work of Alexandre Koyré—*Études galiléennes* (1939), *From the Closed World to the Infinite Universe* (1957), *Newtonian Studies* (1965), *Metaphysics and Measurement* (1968). Koyré wrote about the scientific revolution of the sixteenth and seventeenth centuries, but for him the history of science was not sociological but rather a history of *ideas*.

Kuhn was offering a two-part seminar on nineteenth-century theories of electricity and magnetism. Michael Faraday, Lord Kelvin (William Thomson), and James Clerk Maxwell were the principal figures discussed. I was attending the second part—primarily on Maxwell. The seminar was filled with an odd assortment of people. Some of his graduate students and a couple of visiting sociologists. Kuhn had already attracted the interest of social scientists around the world, and each year several made the pilgrimage to Princeton (and later to MIT) to attend his lectures. One particularly enthusiastic acolyte came all the way from Tokyo, and although I don't think he understood much English, he was enthralled. Philosophers stayed away. Kuhn had been appointed to what was called "the Program in the History and Philosophy of Science," but I can't remember a single philosopher attending any of the seminars or lectures. Philosophers had already begun to articulate their difficulties with his work, while nascent historians of science were unaware they were being fed a hefty portion of poorly masticated philosophical ideas.[8] Kuhn's antipathy to philosophers, and vice versa, in the end damaged the profession—leading to a generation of historians of science with a limited background in philosophy.

What I hated most about Kuhn's lectures was the combination of obscurantism and dogmatism. On one hand, he was extremely dogmatic. On the other, it was never really clear about *what*. Kuhn's seminar was a forum for his pet peeves and obsessions. In particular, his unending complaints about "Whiggishness." This is Whiggish; that is Whiggish; everything is Whiggish. The term comes from Herbert Butterfield's *The Whig Interpretation of History*, written when the future Regius Professor of History at Oxford was only thirty-one years old.[9] Butterfield defines Whiggishness as "the tendency in many historians to write on the side of Protestants and Whigs, to praise revolutions provided they have been successful, to emphasize certain principles of progress in the past and to produce a story which is the ratification if not the glorification of the present." Or more simply, "the study of the past with direct and perpetual reference to the present." For Butterfield "real historical understanding" can be achieved only by "attempting to see life with the eyes of another century than

8. In a paper presented at a 1965 conference in London, eventually published as "Falsification and the Methodology of Scientific Research Programmes" (1970), Imre Lakatos worried that Kuhn's theory reduced the history of science to "mob psychology" (p. 178).

9. The Whigs, advocates of the power of Parliament, are distinguished from the Tories, advocates of the power of the king. As English historian E. H. Carr wrote:

> The reader [of Butterfield's book] was left in no doubt that the Whig interpretation was a bad thing; and one of the charges brought against it was that it "studies the past with reference to the present." On this point Professor Butterfield was categorical and severe: "The study of the past with one eye, so to speak, upon the present is the source of all sins and sophistries in history. . . . It is the essence of what we mean by the word 'unhistorical.'" (*What Is History?* [1961], p. 50)

But just how do you go about avoiding this error? How do you blot out all knowledge of the present while writing about the past?

our own."[10] For Kuhn this meant that a historian, particularly a historian of science, should write with blinders on—and possibly a feedbag, to avoid modern influences lurking in the refrigerator.

As a historian writing about Galileo, you should *never* look at anything written *after* Galileo. Limit yourself to the first half of the seventeenth century and earlier. A historian writing about James Clerk Maxwell in the 1860s must take care not to apply ideas from the 1870s or further into the future. Kuhn weaponized Butterfield's concept as a fundamental principle in the history of science—although it is clear that Butterfield never embraced it in quite the same way. Butterfield's *The Origins of Modern Science, 1300–1800*, produced almost twenty years after *The Whig Interpretation of History*, is, ironically, Whiggish in nature.[11]

Historian and philosopher of science Nick Jardine writes about Butterfield's impact:

> By the mid-1970s, it had become commonplace among historians of science to employ the terms "Whig" and "Whiggish," often accompanied by one or more of "hagiographic," "internalist," "triumphalist," even "positivist," to denigrate grand narratives of scientific progress. . . . In particular, they were suspicious of the grand celebratory and didactic narratives of scientific discovery and progress that had proliferated in the inter-war years.[12]

10. Butterfield, *Whig Interpretation of History* (1931), pp. v, 11, 16. For more on the Whig theory of history, see David Hackett Fischer, *Historians' Fallacies* (1970). Fischer's book is one of my favorites—a compendium of historical mistakes and misconceptions.

11. "Twelve years elapsed. . . . Professor Butterfield's country was engaged in a war often said to be fought in defence of the constitutional liberties embodied in the Whig tradition, under a great leader who constantly invoked the past 'with one eye, so to speak, upon the present.' In a small book called *The Englishman and His History* published in 1944, Professor Butterfield not only decided that the Whig interpretation of history was the 'English' interpretation, but spoke enthusiastically of 'the Englishman's alliance with his history' and of the 'marriage between the present and the past.' To draw attention to these reversals of outlook is not an unfriendly criticism. It is not my purpose to refute the proto-Butterfield with the deutero-Butterfield, or to confront Professor Butterfield drunk with Professor Butterfield sober. . . . My purpose is merely to show how closely the work of the historian mirrors the society in which he works. It is not merely the events that are in flux. The historian himself is in flux. When you take up a historical work, it is not enough to look for the author's name in the title-page: look also for the date of publication or writing—it is sometimes even more revealing. If the philosopher is right in telling us that we cannot step into the same river twice, it is perhaps equally true, and for the same reason, that two books cannot be written by the same historian." Carr, *What Is History?*, pp. 50–52.
12. Jardine, "Whigs and Stories" (2003), pp. 127–28.

13. Weinberg, "Eye on the Present" (2015), p. 82. Weinberg has often defended Whiggishness: "A historian of science who ignores our present scientific knowledge seems to me like a historian of U.S. military intelligence in the Civil War, who tells the story of McClellan's retreat from the Virginia peninsula in the face of what McClellan thought were overwhelming Confederate forces, without taking into account our present knowledge that McClellan was wrong. Even the choice of topics that attract the interest of historians has to be affected by what we now know were the paths that led to success. What Herbert Butterfield called the Whig interpretation of history is legitimate in the history of science in a way that it is not in the history of politics or culture, because science is cumulative, and permits definite judgments of success or failure." "Sokal's Hoax" (1996), p. 15.

14. When Maxwell invented the concept of the displacement current, he was wedded to a mechanical model of electromagnetism—vortices, stationary idle wheels, etc. But the term means something different to modern-day physicists. In many ways, this makes it an ideal focus for a discussion of reference and belief. Our *beliefs* about the displacement current have changed since Maxwell's time, but does that mean we are *referring* to something different? Or that we cannot discuss the differences between Maxwell's early ideas and modern non-mechanical models of electromagnetism? See Daniel Siegel, *Innovation in Maxwell's Electromagnetic Theory* (2003), pp. 85f.

15. In an article precursory to his book on Maxwell, Siegel writes, "The fantasy has been entertained of having the history of science written by individuals who do not know the modern histories, and who will therefore be able to enter into the spirit of past theories unprejudiced." The historian of science as Kaspar Hauser, locked away in a cave or a vault, educated up to some point (for historians of Maxwell, up to 1865) but no further. Siegel continues:

> Such individuals, however, would be ill situated to interpret the theories

And more recently, physicist Steven Weinberg has written in the *New York Review of Books*:

> Butterfield's strictures were fervently taken up by later generations of historians. Being called "whig" came to seem as terrifying to historians as being called sexist, or Eurocentric, or Orientalist. Nor was the history of science spared. The historian of science Bruce Hunt recalls that when he was in graduate school in the early 1980s, "whiggish" was a common term of abuse in the history of science. To avoid that charge, people turned away from telling stories of scientific progress or from giving "big picture" stories of any kind, and shifted to accounts of small episodes, tightly focused in time and space.[13]

———

I had written a final paper on Maxwell's displacement current. The paper might have been thirty or so double-spaced pages. Kuhn's reply, on unlined yellow paper, was thirty pages, single-spaced, with Courier type marching all the way from the left to the right edge of the paper. No margins. It looked like something written by a mental patient. He was angry—very angry.

The comments were mostly *ad hominem*. He concluded, "You have long since passed the end of the road on which you began." I asked for an explanation. He said that I was a "good" first-year graduate student but would be "less good" in subsequent years. Our discussion took place in the West Building, a new building at the Institute for Advanced Study. Kuhn had taken a leave of absence from Princeton to write the book *Black-Body Theory and the Quantum Discontinuity, 1894–1912*.

We soon began arguing. Kuhn had attacked my supposedly Whiggish use of the term "displacement current." I had failed, in his view, to understand the historical context of Maxwell's first theories. In particular, Maxwell's reluctance to abandon mechanical explanations.[14] On the other hand, I felt that Kuhn had not just misinterpreted my paper, he had refused to even read it.[15] I felt that he, not I, had provided a Whiggish interpretation of Maxwell. I said, "You refuse to look through my telescope." And he said gravely, "It's not a telescope, Errol. It's a kaleidoscope."[16]

The argument turned ugly. I wondered, Was my problem with his philosophy or with *him*?

For me, the argument was exacerbated by the use of the term "incommensurability"—a cornerstone of Kuhn's *Structure*, without which, his philosophy of scientific change is little more than warmed-over sociology. You cannot objectively compare the terms of one theory with those of another, Kuhn argues, because they are incommensurable. Think of it as an emendation of John Donne's *Meditation XVII*. "Every *theory* is an Island, entire of it self . . ."

I asked him, "If paradigms are really incommensurable, how is history of science possible? Wouldn't we be merely interpreting the past in the light of the present? Wouldn't the past be inaccessible to us?"

I thought, "How can any of us know what Maxwell was thinking?"

I said, ". . . except for someone who imagines himself to be God?" A megalomaniac who creates a philosophy but doesn't believe he has to abide by it.

He put his head in his hands and muttered, "He's trying to kill me. He's trying to kill me."

Then he looked up and threw the ashtray at me. And missed.

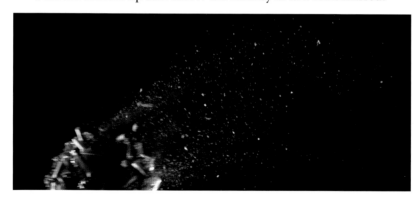

I saw the arc, the trajectory. As if the ashtray were its own solar system. With orbiting planets and asteroids (butts) and interstellar gas (ash). I thought, "Wait a second. Einstein's office is just around the corner. *This is the Institute for Advanced Study!*"

I call Kuhn's reply "The Ashtray Argument." If someone says something you don't like, you throw something at him. Preferably

of the past for audiences acquainted with modern theories, and would be ill equipped to discern patterns of development leading from the past to present. It is just as well, then, that there are historians of science who are conversant with modern science. These historians face the task of learning to transcend the prejudices inherent in their knowledge of modern science, in order to perceive the past without distortion. . . . The result of this sort of endeavor, one hopes, will be a coherent modern scientific culture, in which past and present will be seen as part of a continuous human endeavor, and will be mutually illuminating. ("The Origin of the Displacement Current," [1986], p. 101)

16. A version of this story appears in "Predilections," Mark Singer's 1989 profile of me in the *New Yorker*. Although I would happily agree that there is a kaleidoscopic approach in some of my thinking, there is an unintended irony here: Kuhn's multiple paradigms and paradigm shifts are much closer to a kaleidoscope than anything I have ever conceived.

something large, heavy, and with sharp edges. Perhaps we were engaged in a debate on the nature of meaning and reality. Maybe we just wanted to kill each other.

Was Kuhn blind to the problems with incommensurability? I doubt it. Indeed, I believe he was haunted by them. Perhaps he was antagonized by my suggestion of megalomania. The end result was that Kuhn threw me out of Princeton. He had the power to do it and he did it. God only knows what I might have said in my second or third year. At the time, I felt that he had destroyed my life. Now, I feel that he saved me from a career I was not suited for.

2. SHIFTING PARADIGMS

The hero of my tale, whom I love with all the power of my soul, whom I have tried to portray in all his beauty, who has been, is, and will be beautiful, is Truth.

—Leo Tolstoy, *The Sebastopol Sketches*

Philosophers endlessly debate the importance and content of Saul Kripke's *Naming and Necessity*. There are hundreds, if not thousands, of journal articles devoted to these *three* lectures.[1] Lectures that

realigned our ideas about how language "connects" to the world. And affirmed a decidedly un-postmodern (or, if you prefer, non-relativistic) idea of meaning, reference, and truth. In Kripke's view some words are attached to things *in the world* through a causal (or historical) chain of reference.[2] And although the first part of Kripke's *Naming and Necessity* is devoted to proper names, like "Julius Caesar" or "Kurt Gödel," in the third part of his essay he extends these ideas to scientific concepts and to mass terms—like "water" and "gold."

Kripke's picture of proper names provides an alternative to what had become known as description theories, an amalgam of ideas

1. The lectures were delivered at Princeton on January 20, 22, and 29, 1970. They were tape-recorded, transcribed, edited, and published in 1972 as part of a collected volume. I first saw them as a set of stapled, xeroxed and re-xeroxed copies. Eventually, they were published as a separate book, *Naming and Necessity* (1980), with a preface that discusses some criticisms of the original version and includes nine pages of "addenda" and footnotes. Kripke inscribed the copy he sent me, "With thanks for your appreciation of my work, and with mutuality, February, 2009."

2. Kripke's friend John Burgess, a philosopher at Princeton, has written, "Kripke's picture has for obvious reasons been called the 'historical chain' picture. It has also sometimes been called the 'causal chain' picture, but this label is inappropriate. For . . . there need not on Kripke's view be any causal link between the initial baptist and the object baptized. Any object that can be described can be named, and this includes, for instance, causally inert mathematical objects, which figure in a couple of Kripke's examples." "Saul Kripke: Naming and Necessity" (2006), pp. 172–73. The square root of 2 ($\sqrt{2}$), discussed in subsequent chapters, is an example of a "named" mathematical object.

3. Kripke does not claim to have provided a theory of reference, only a "picture" of how reference works. See Kripke, *Naming and Necessity*, p. 93. Not to be quarrelsome, but I look at it as a theory and refer to it as such.

proposed by Gottlob Frege, Bertrand Russell, Ludwig Wittgenstein, P. F. Strawson, and John Searle—in which reference is determined by a definite description or a cluster of descriptions.[3] (A definite description is an expression that takes the form "*the* so-and-so": "*the* author of *Waverley*" [Sir Walter Scott], or "*the* man who brought the Ten Commandments down from Mt. Sinai" [Moses].) Modern description theories are variants of the descriptivist program proposed by Bertrand Russell in his 1905 paper "On Denoting" and taken up by Wittgenstein in paragraph 79 of *Philosophical Investigations*:

> According to Russell, we may say: the name "Moses" can be defined by means of various descriptions. For example, as "the man who led the Israelites through the wilderness," "the man who lived at that time and place and was then called 'Moses'," "the man who as a child was taken out of the Nile by Pharaoh's daughter" and so on. . . . But when I make a statement about Moses—am I always ready to substitute some *one* of these descriptions for "Moses"? I shall perhaps say: By "Moses" I mean the man who did what the Bible relates of Moses, or at any rate much of it. . . . And this can be expressed as follows: I use the name "N" without a *fixed* meaning. (But that impairs its use as little as the use of a table is impaired by the fact that it stands on four legs instead of three and so sometimes wobbles.)

The four-legged table may cause me more trouble than it caused Wittgenstein.

Here's one way to distinguish between Kripke's picture of how reference works and the various description theories that preceded it:

You have two goldfish in a fishbowl. *Carassius auratus auratus*. One of them is gold in color; the other one is green. The golden fish you name "Goldie." The other fish you name "Greenie." Perhaps you use the *description* "the gold fish" and point to the one that is gold in color. When you say "Goldie," you are *referring* to this same golden fish. Over time, however, Goldie starts to change color. Six months later, Goldie is no longer gold. Goldie is now green. Greenie, meanwhile, has turned gold. Goldie is no longer "the golden fish." Greenie is. But Goldie is still Goldie. The description theory would have it that Goldie *means* "the fish that is gold in color." If that's true,

then when we say "Goldie," we are now referring to the other fish. But clearly, Goldie hasn't become a different fish; Goldie has merely changed his (or her) appearance.[4]

4. This example comes from Seymour "Sandy" Cohen, by way of my friend, Charles Silver. Cohen's unpublished paper was written in 1967.

If the description theories are correct, then Goldie is the formerly green fish on the right. If Kripke's historical chain theory of reference is correct, then Goldie *remains* Goldie no matter what color Goldie is.[5]

This idea is often traced back to John Stuart Mill, who writes, in *A System of Logic*:

> A man may have been named John, because that was the name of his father; a town may have been named Dartmouth, because it is situated at the mouth of the Dart. But it is no part of the significa-tion of the word John, that the father of the person so called bore the same name; nor even of the word Dartmouth, to be situated at the mouth of the Dart. If sand should choke up the mouth of the river, or an earthquake change its course, and remove it to a dis-tance from the town, the name of the town would not necessarily be changed. . . . *Proper names are attached to the objects themselves, and are not dependent on the continuance of any attribute of the object.*[6]

Mill tells us that names are attached to the *things* themselves but never tells us exactly how this is done. It might be like a gummy label: "Hello, my name is John Stuart Mill."

Kripke's central intuition is this: A description can *fix* a refer-ence, but it does not *determine* the reference. Descriptions can help

5. The example is not perfect. Warren Goldfarb has suggested to me that it is misleading—that the appropriate definite description of "Goldie" would be "the fish in the bowl that is gold *at such-and-such a time*." But appending a timestamp is purely an ad hoc way to save descriptivism, like adding epicycles to make the Ptolemaic view of the universe comport with the evi-dence. This misses the point. If "Goldie" means the fish that at such-and-such a time is gold-colored, then Goldie couldn't possibly be green. And that is clearly contrary to Kripke's way of thinking.

Kripke would most likely invoke possible worlds. He would ask, Is there a possible world in which Goldie could be green and still be Goldie? His answer (and mine) is yes. At the heart of Kripke's analysis of proper names are his notions of necessity. It's not that Goldie could turn green. It's that Goldie could be green and still be Goldie. In Kripke's parlance, "Goldie" is a rigid designator. "Goldie" refers to Goldie in all possible worlds.

6. Mill, *A System of Logic* (1881), p. 36 (emphasis mine).

us attach a name to a thing. We can use a description to pick out a specific fish—for example, the gold fish swimming around in the bowl. Our subsequent descriptions of Goldie or beliefs about Goldie could be *all* wrong, but we can still *refer* to Goldie. We can grab ahold of Goldie independent of any belief or theory we have about him. And we can say true or false things about him. (Is it true that Goldie is green? Or gold? Or red?) This is because of a causal (or historical) chain that links words back to things.[7]

Here's another way of looking at it. Many of us, like John Stuart Mill, have a powerful intuition that we can reach outside our beliefs, our minds, and grab ahold of things in the world. As Mill argued, names are attached to things themselves.

Kripke's arguments can also be framed using counterfactuals. Ask yourself a counterfactual question—a question involving conditions contrary to fact. Goldie is gold, but could Goldie be green and still be Goldie? For me, the answer is yes. Counterfactuals can also be thought of in terms of possible worlds. Is there a possible world in which Goldie is green (and is still Goldie)? Is it possible for Goldie to be a different color (pick any color) and still be Goldie? (An unpleasant experience at O'Hare International Airport provides a similar example. "Mr. Morris, please pick up the white courtesy telephone." There was only a red one in the vicinity. The customer service representative explained to me, as if she were talking to a moron, "The white courtesy telephone isn't white, it's red.")

7. Kripke's theory of reference should be thought of as a theory of the *preservation* of reference, grounded in his theories of modality—of possibility and necessity. In this view, proper names are thought of as *rigid designators*. That is, in all possible worlds "Goldie" refers to Goldie. The troublesome element in Kripke's theory involves the historical (or causal) chain. What keeps the chain intact? What keeps the links from being broken? For Kripke it is *intentions*. The intention to refer. If Speaker Y intends to refer to the same thing to which Speaker X intended to refer, there is an unbroken chain of intentions that takes us back to, for example, Goldie.

The relation between names, things, and descriptions takes us deeply into several areas of philosophical inquiry, each with its own entrenched concepts about the world:

Metaphysics considers the concepts of the *necessary* (it couldn't be otherwise) and the *possible*, or contingent (it could be otherwise).

Epistemology distinguishes the *a priori* (before experience) and the *a posteriori* (after experience).

And semantics categorizes sentences as *analytic* (true by the definitions of the words and the rules of grammar used to express it) and *synthetic* (true by recourse to experience).

Take a triangle. The sentence "A triangle has three sides" is true by definition. It is analytic. It is also necessarily true; there is no possible world in which a triangle has fewer (or more) than three sides. And we know this *a priori*, without looking at the world. You don't have to look out a window to know that a triangle has three sides.

But there are instances where you *do* have to look out a window. The sentence "It is raining today" could be true or false, depending on whether it is, indeed, raining today. It is possibly true but not necessarily true. It is synthetic—not true by definition. And it is known only *a posteriori*—after experience. I have to look out a window and observe the inclement weather.

Kripke realigned these concepts.[8]

Immanuel Kant writes in *Critique of Pure Reason*, "Experience teaches us that a thing is so and so, but not that it cannot be otherwise." As John Burgess expresses it, "Experience *can* teach us that a necessary truth is true; what it is not supposed to be able to teach is that it is necessary."[9] Contrary to much received philosophy, Kripke embraces the idea of the necessary *a posteriori*—something that could not be otherwise but that we learn from experience. For Kripke, this includes necessities of identity. Something is necessarily identical to itself. How could it be otherwise? Take Frege's example of Hesperus and Phosphorus. We *learn* that the Evening Star is the Morning Star, that Hesperus is Phosphorus. And we learn it from experience. It took observation to show that they are one and the same. It is synthetic. But it is also necessary. If Hesperus is Phosphorus, then necessarily Hesperus is Phosphorus.

Kripke provides a laundry list—necessities of origin (e.g., Elizabeth II's biological parents were Elizabeth Bowes-Lyon and

8. John Burgess calls this realignment Kripke's greatest contribution to analytic philosophy, in *Saul Kripke: Puzzles and Mysteries* (2013), pp. 1–7.

9. Kant, *Critique of Pure Reason*, p. 43; Burgess, "The Origin of Necessity and the Necessity of Origin" (2012).

George VI), necessities of natural kind membership (e.g., Aristotle was a man; tigers are animals; and, as we shall see, glyptodons are armadillos), necessities of constitution or composition (e.g., water is H_2O; gold is *the* element with atomic number 79). Kripke refers to these as *metaphysical* necessities. If gold really does have atomic number 79, there is *no* possible world in which that is *not* the case.[10]

Kuhn would not approve.

———

Kuhn's *Structure of Scientific Revolutions* was far more influential than Kripke's *Naming and Necessity*, possibly because it fit the pop culture of the moment—the idea that things are culturally determined and depend on your "frame of reference."[11] It produced a cottage industry around itself and became a kind of postmodernist bible.[12]

Kuhn's book introduced its own nomenclature—normal and revolutionary science, paradigms, paradigm shifts, anomalies, incommensurability, and so on. Here is a brief description of his mechanism of scientific change: Science is parsed into normal and revolutionary science. In normal science a group of "practitioners" has settled on a way of defining and solving problems—a *paradigm*, a conceptual scheme. They have a way of looking at the world and are by and large happy with it. But then there are *anomalies*—things that don't fit neatly into the conceptual scheme.[13] An anomaly could be an unexpected experimental result or an internal contradiction—something that happens that prevents things from going on as before.[14] One or two anomalies can perhaps be ignored, but as they accumulate they shatter the tranquility of the paradigm. Unexplained anomalies lead to a crisis, a crisis leads to a revolution, and a revolution leads to a shift to a new paradigm.

The most significant and most controversial aspects of Kuhn's theory involve his terms "paradigm shift" and "incommensurability." In a paradigm shift, the scientific terms of one paradigm are said to be *incommensurable* with those of the paradigm that replaces it. Paradigms shift, and meanings shift with them. A revolution occurs.[15] Much scholarship on Kuhn concerns these two terms, but the word "paradigm," like the word "incommensurable," is used by Kuhn in multiple ways. One article identifies "not less than twenty-one different senses."[16] Even Kuhn seemed frightened at the prospect of his concept endlessly metastasizing.[17] James B. Conant, a past presi-

10. One could imagine a hierarchy of necessities: physical necessity, logical necessity, metaphysical necessity. They might all amount to the same thing. Or not. Physical necessity is the necessity of physical laws. Our physical laws tell us that gold has an atomic number of 79, but could we live in a universe with different physical laws? Could the atomic number 79 be a physical necessity but not a metaphysical necessity?

11. *Structure* has been named in several "top 100" lists, including Martin Seymour-Smith's *The 100 Most Influential Books Ever Written* (1998) and the *Times Literary Supplement*'s "The Hundred Most Influential Books since the Second World War" (October 6, 1995), p. 3.

12. The essence of postmodernism, for me, is the social construction of meaning: If there are such things as reality and truth, they are, at best, socially constructed.

13. Kuhn writes, "Discovery commences with the awareness of anomaly, i.e., with the recognition that nature has somehow violated the paradigm-induced expectations that govern normal science" (*Structure* [1962], pp. 52–53).

14. "Anomalous" experimental results like the precession of the perihelion of Mercury or the negative results of the Michelson-Morley experiments are often cited in the history of general and special relativity, but it is unclear what historical role they played in the development of Einstein's theories. Kuhn was particularly fond of examples from the discovery of oxygen; see *Structure* (1962), pp. 53f.

15. Hovering over all of this is the ghost of Paul Feyerabend, Kuhn's colleague at Berkeley. He was also my teacher. Oddly, ironically, they both came up with the idea of "incommensurability" at roughly the same time—around 1960. They provide their own recollections. First, Feyerabend:

> I do not know who of us was the first to use the term "incommensurable" in the sense that is at issue here. It occurs in Kuhn's *Structure of Scientific Revolutions* and in my essay "Explanation, Reduction, and Empiricism" both of which appeared in 1962. I still remember marveling at the pre-established harmony that made us not only defend similar ideas but use exactly the same word for expressing them. The coincidence is of course far from mysterious. I had read earlier drafts of

Kuhn's book and had discussed their content with Kuhn. ("Consolations for the Specialist" [1970], p. 219)

Then Kuhn:

I think I remember a talk with Feyerabend. He was sitting behind his desk and I was standing at the door of his office, which was very close to mine. Now, I'm not sure this is right, I mean this is the sort of thing I could easily have constructed. I said something to him about my views including the word *incommensurability*, and he said, "Oh, you are using that word too." And he showed me some of the things he was doing, and *Structure* came out at the same year as his big article in *Minnesota Studies*. We were talking about something which was in some sense the same thing. (*Road since Structure*, pp. 297–98)

Although both emphasize similarity, their views come from different places.

And radically different temperaments. Kuhn was often humorless, completely lacking in irony. Feyerabend was an absurdist—displaying a complete contempt for everything, including himself. Injured while serving in the Wehrmacht during World War II, he was left partially paralyzed and got about with the help of crutches, like the defense attorney in Orson Welles's *The Lady from Shanghai*. My friend Charles Silver, who served for a time as Feyerabend's teaching assistant, recalls a story in which Feyerabend, just for fun, brought in a self-described warlock to deliver several of his lectures. A visiting academic from Russia was absolutely convinced that it was Feyerabend giving the lecture.

16. Margaret Masterman, "The Nature of a Paradigm," p. 61.
17. From Kuhn's 1995 interview with Aristides Baltas, Kostas Gavroglu, and Vassiliki Kindi:

One of the people who had been invited to participate in this further discussion was Margaret Masterman—whom I'd never met, but of whom I'd heard, and what I'd heard about her was not altogether good, and it was largely that she was a madwoman. She got up at the back of the room in the discussion, strode toward the podium, turned to face the audience, put her hands in her pockets and proceeded to say, "In my sciences, in the social sciences" (she was running something called the Cambridge Language Lab), "everybody is talking about paradigms. That's the word." And she said, "I was recently in hospital and I went through the book and I think I found twenty-one," twenty-three, whatever, "different uses of it." And, you know, they are there. But she went on to say, and this is the thing that people don't know, although it's more or less in her article, "And I think I know what a paradigm is." And she proceeded to list four or five characteristics of a paradigm. And I sat there, I said, my God, if I had talked for an hour and a half I might have gotten these all in, or I might not have. But she's got it right! And the thing I particularly remember, and I can't make it work quite but it's very deeply to the point: a paradigm is what you use when the theory isn't there. (*Road since Structure*, pp. 299–300)

Radical principles often spawn multiple versions of themselves—the cosmological anthropic principle; the Sapir-Whorf hypothesis; the Turing test; incommensurability. In *The Anthropic Cosmological Principle* (1986), John D. Barrow and Frank J. Tipler provide no fewer than five distinct versions of incommensurability. In *Rhetoric and Incommensurability* (2005), Randy Allen Harris lists another four. My guess is, the strongest versions make no sense, but there is enough ambiguity in their presentation to allow for almost anything. These strong principles, although often wrong, are interesting. The weaker variants tell us less and less and quickly become platitudinous or devoid of content.

18. Conant, letter to Kuhn, June 5, 1961, in Daniel Cedarbaum, "Paradigms" (1983), p. 173.
19. In a postscript to the second edition of *Structure* (1970), Kuhn suggested that

dent of Harvard, an early mentor to Kuhn, and one of the fathers of modern history of science, warned his protégé in 1961, "Those who react negatively to your point of view will brush you aside, I fear, as the man who grabbed on to the word 'paradigm' and used it as a magic verbal wand to explain everything!"[18]

Kuhn made various attempts to clarify his concepts, changing and modifying them along the way.[19] In *Structure*, incommensurability is perceptual. People in different paradigms *see* things differently. He likens it to a Gestalt-switch—the famous duck-rabbit illusion.

Welche Thiere gleichen einander am meisten?

Kaninchen und Ente.

the problem was with philosophers. "A number of them, however, have reported that I believe the following: the proponents of incommensurable theories cannot communicate with each other at all; as a result, in a debate over theory-choice there can be no recourse to *good* reasons; instead theory must be chosen for reasons that are ultimately personal and subjective" (pp. 198–99). In his effort to refute these complaints, Kuhn often equivocated, sometimes changing nomenclature (e.g., "paradigm" became "disciplinary matrix").

20. Hanson crashed in a storm while piloting his Grumman F8F-2 Bearcat, the fastest prop-driven fighter ever built, from Yale to Cornell.

21. Hanson, "A Note on Kuhn's Method" (1965), pp. 371–72.
22. *Structure* resembles a rag doll stitched together from diverse pieces into an inchoate whole. The conservatism of ordinary science might have come from Pierre Duhem; tacit knowledge from Michael Polanyi; "seeing as" from Norwood Russell Hanson; the indeterminacy of translation from Quine; and the social construction of knowledge from Wittgenstein. In his magisterial *The Invention of Science* (2015), David Wootton details how Kuhn expropriated the use of "paradigm" from Hanson (pp. 585–86).
23. They were also an enormous influence on my book about photography, *Believing Is Seeing* (2011).

The example comes straight out of Wittgenstein (from "Philosophy of Psychology—A Fragment," printed as part of *Philosophical Investigations*) and makes a subsequent appearance in *Patterns of Discovery* by Norwood Russell Hanson, a neglected and brilliant philosopher of science who died in a plane crash while still in his early forties.[20] Curiously, Hanson served as an early reader for the University of Chicago Press of the manuscript of *Structure*. His prepublication remarks concern what he saw as an inherent problem in Kuhn's reasoning. If revolutions are defined as a change in paradigm, and a change in paradigm is defined as a revolution, how is any of this falsifiable? He repeated many of his early criticisms in a published article:

> Allow a Martian scholar to interrupt Professor Kuhn's studies late some night. The Martian historian asks "What is a paradigm?"
>
> Kuhn's answer: "A paradigm is that conceptual commitment which is such that if challenged seriously, a 'Scientific Revolution' will ensue."
>
> Martian: "And what is a Scientific Revolution?"
>
> Kuhn: "A Scientific Revolution is that shock to the metabolism of an established science which results when one of its paradigms is challenged."
>
> The Martin historian will surely perceive some circularity in this presentation. He will observe the ideas of "paradigm" and "Scientific Revolution" to be *so* interlocked semantically that to understand either one must first understand both.[21]

Hanson concludes, "If I had been correct in this early reaction [in 1961], then Kuhn's thesis would not be a genuine *historical* thesis at all. . . . [I]t would not even have been informative—but only an elaborate set of definitions."

Clearly Hanson had reservations about Kuhn's *Structure of Scientific Revolutions*. Ironically, Kuhn borrowed many of Hanson's central ideas.[22] Hanson's Gestalt-switch example, described as "there is more to seeing than meets the eye," and his belief that observation is theory-laden were an enormous influence on Kuhn.[23] But there are important differences between Hanson and Kuhn. Hanson tells us that observation is theory-laden. He does *not* tell us that because observation is theory-laden there is no reference, no reality, no progress, no truth. There's a big difference between saying that a theory *influences* how we see the world, and saying that a theory *determines* how we see the world.

Think about the Gestalt-switch. In looking at the drawing we never lose our ability to see the rabbit or the duck, even if we can't see both at the same time. We see a rabbit, then a duck. Or a duck, then a rabbit. Rabbit, duck. Duck, rabbit. But Kuhn in *Structure* writes, "What were ducks in the scientist's world before the revolution are rabbits afterwards."[24] What? This comes in a chapter titled "Changes in World View," but it seems it could be titled "Changes in the *World*."[25] Peter Godfrey-Smith, a philosopher of science at CUNY, writes:

> [Some] think that this whole side of Kuhn's work is a mess. When paradigms change, ideas change. Standards change also, and maybe, the way we experience the world changes as well. But that is very different from claiming that the *world itself* depends on paradigms. The way we see things changes, but the world itself does not change . . . the X-rated Chapter X is the worst material in Kuhn's great book. It would have been better if he had left this chapter in a taxi, in one of those famous mistakes that authors are prone to.[26]

Most of Kuhn's fans will argue that he doesn't really mean that ducks turn into rabbits. There are ducks and there are rabbits, but there are no transmutations between one and the other, no genie in a bottle. But many passages in *Structure* suggest otherwise. For example, "We may want to say after a revolution scientists are responding to a different world."[27] So which is it? Do scientific revolutions change the world or just our *beliefs* about the world? And if all we have are our beliefs, how are we to distinguish them from reality? As W. B. Yeats wrote in "Among School Children," "How can we know the dancer from the dance?"

Kuhn writes, "Consider . . . the men who called Copernicus mad because he proclaimed the earth moved. They were not either just wrong or quite wrong. Part of what they meant by 'earth' was fixed position. Their earth, at least, could not be moved. . . . The proponents of competing paradigms practice their trades in different worlds."[28]

24. *Structure* (1962), p. 110.

25. Occasionally, a commonsense realism peeks through Kuhn's miasma of nomenclature: to be fair, he also tells us that "nothing in the environment has changed," that we "are looking at the world, and the world has not changed" (*Structure* [1962], pp. 113, 149). The reason he vacillates—or says seemingly contradictory things—is simple. His worldview does not allow for a fixed, unchangeable real world. It does not allow him to talk about reality at all, fixed or changeable.

26. Godfrey-Smith, *Theory and Reality* (2003), p. 96.

27. Kuhn, *Structure* (1962), p. 110.

28. Ibid., pp. 148–49.

29. The new editions have not brought many changes. David Wootton tells me, "I've never seen an account of what the differences are between the 1962 and 1970 editions—whenever I've checked there weren't any, apart from the addition of the postscript. Kuhn says there are some minor changes, and I think they must be very minor. It's a myth, for example, that the reference to Polanyi was added in the 1970 edition—it was always there. And I don't think there are any changes after 1970, apart from the addition of an index." Email to author, January 31, 2016.

30. Ironically, Noam Chomsky does not believe in reference in ordinary language but, unlike Kuhn, does believe in reference in science. (This is explored in chapter 7, "The Furniture of the World.") I believe that reference in science is *not* theory-laden. It's one thing to say that observation (or perception) is theory-laden. It's altogether different to say that reference—that is, referring to something in the physical world—is theory-laden. This may be confusing, and one could raise objections to my claim. Isn't referring to a positron or an omega minus particle theory-laden? No. These particles exist in the real world. Kripke would tell us that we refer to them independent of our beliefs about them.

31. Hanson, *Patterns of Discovery*, p. 20.

32. Kuhn, *Structure* (1970), p. 200.

33. Kuhn writes, "After discovering oxygen Lavoisier worked in a different world" (*Structure* [1962], p. 117). I would amend that slightly. It was only after the application of the guillotine that Lavoisier worked in a different world.

Structure has gone through four editions over fifty years (1962, 1970, 1996, and 2012)—but there are still ducks and rabbits.[29] The moon remains as it was over a million years ago, with the exception of an American flag or two.

Kuhn tells us that observation is theory-laden. As I've mentioned, I regard this as one of Hanson's deep insights. But then Kuhn goes off the rails and essentially tells us that *reference* is theory-laden too. In this regard, I believe, he is dead wrong.[30]

This is one of Kuhn's central errors. Conflating perception with reference. I can *see* a duck or *see* a rabbit, but that doesn't mean that I am *referring* to a duck or to a rabbit. Hanson imagines Johannes Kepler and Tycho Brahe sitting on a hill at dawn looking at the rising sun. Two different conceptions of the solar system are at work here. For Kepler, a mobile earth revolves around the fixed sun. For Brahe, the sun revolves around a fixed earth. Hanson asks, *Do Kepler and Tycho see the same thing in the east at dawn?* His conclusion is that they do not. Observation is a theory-laden undertaking. Hence his distinction between "seeing," "seeing as," and "seeing that": "Seeing the dawn was for Tycho . . . to see that the earth's brilliant satellite was beginning its diurnal circuit around us, while for Kepler and Galileo it was to see that the earth was spinning them back into the light of our local star."[31] But Hanson does not conflate the distinction between what Kepler and Brahe see (or perceive) as a result of their beliefs about the solar system with the *things* they refer to. Their perceptions may differ, but when they speak of the earth, they refer to the earth, and when they speak of the sun, they refer to the sun.

Kuhn writes, "Two men who perceive the same situation differently but nevertheless employ the same vocabulary in its discussion must be using words differently. They speak, that is, from what I have called incommensurable viewpoints."[32] People use the same name (e.g., "Earth") but are talking about different things (e.g., Copernican-earth versus Ptolemaic-earth). Same words, different worlds.[33]

In 1980, in a series of three lectures delivered at the University of Notre Dame, Kuhn discussed the transition from Ptolemaic to Copernican astronomy:

Consider the compound sentence, "In the Ptolemaic system planets revolve about the earth; in the Copernican they revolve about

the sun." Strictly construed the sentence is incoherent. The first occurrence of the term 'planet' is Ptolemaic, the second Copernican, and the two attach to nature differently. For no univocal reading of the term 'planet' is the compound sentence true.[34]

34. Kuhn, "What Are Scientific Revolutions?," p. 15.

But do the two occurrences (first the plural "planets," then the pronoun "they") attach to nature differently? Not in Kripke's philosophy. "Earth" means the planet Earth, regardless of whether we believe it revolves around the sun, stands fast at the center of the

35. Kuhn, *Structure* (1962), p. 101.

36. What should we make of the claim that Newtonian mass and mass in special relativity are incommensurable? Steven Weinberg argues:

> In defending his position, Kuhn argued that the words we use and the symbols in our equations mean different things before and after a scientific revolution; for instance, physicists meant different things by mass before and after the advent of relativity. It is true that there was a good deal of uncertainty about the concept of mass *during* the Einsteinian revolution. For a while there was talk of "longitudinal" and "transverse" masses, which were supposed to depend on a particle's speed and to resist accelerations along the direction of motion and perpendicular to it. But this has all been resolved. No one today talks of longitudinal or transverse mass, and in fact the term "mass" today is most frequently understood as "rest mass," an intrinsic property of a body that is not changed by motion, which is much the way that mass was understood before Einstein. Meanings can change, but generally they do so in the direction of an increased richness and precision of definition, so that we do not lose the ability to understand the theories of past periods of normal science. ("Revolution That Didn't Happen," p. 49)

Einstein himself weighed in on this issue on a number of occasions in his correspondence, such as these five instances quoted by Arthur Fine in the appendix to Earman and Fine, "Against Indeterminacy" (1977), p. 538:

> I find it not very good to say that the mass of a body in movement is increased by the speed. It is better to use the word mass exclusively for rest mass. This rest mass is, f.i. for a molecule of copper, always the same, independent from the speed of the molecule.
>
> It is not good to introduce the concept of a mass which depends [on] its velocity, for this is not a clear concept.
>
> One should always introduce as "mass" m a quantity independent of motion.

solar system, or inhabits some Bizarro World out of Superman comics. Kuhn, not content to take on fifteenth-century science, shifts to the twentieth century. Considering the concepts of mass articulated by Newton and Einstein, he writes:

> The physical referents of these Einsteinian concepts are by no means identical with those of the Newtonian concepts that bear the same name. (Newtonian mass is conserved; Einsteinian mass is convertible with energy. Only at low relative velocities may the two be measured in the same way, and even then they must not be conceived to be the same.)[35]

Einstein and many others thought otherwise.[36]

It turns out that reference is at the heart of many of Kuhn's arguments. When we use a word, does that word refer to something in the real world? Specifically, a name? Or a scientific term? And how does this relate to the philosophy of Saul Kripke? Several philosophers and historians of science have cautioned me that Kripke and Kuhn were addressing unrelated questions—call it "the apples and oranges objection." What, they ask, do Kuhn's paradigms, incommensurability, and so on have to do with Kripke's possible worlds and rigid designators? Wasn't Kuhn writing about scientific change? And Kripke about the reference of proper names and names of natural kinds, such as gold?

Let me try to explain. Often, Kuhn uses the term "meaning" in disparate ways. (He is not alone in this regard.) For many philosophers, meanings are in the head. Reference is out there in the world. But how are they related? Ask Frege and you get one answer. Ask Bertrand Russell, you get another. Ask Wittgenstein, a third. Ask Saul Kripke and you get a clear answer (although many would argue with it). For Kripke, proper names have *no* meaning; they have *only* reference.

Kuhn, on the other hand, assumes that when words have different meanings (that is, we have differing beliefs about them), they cannot be referring to the *same* thing. This is clearly untrue. The Ptolemaic and Copernican models of the solar system provide an obvious example. I can believe that the sun orbits the earth or that the earth orbits the sun and still be referring to *the earth* and to *the sun*. It doesn't matter what my beliefs are. I am still referring to that *thing*—the earth.[37]

It will be helpful to provide some context about the origins of these concerns. The descriptivists linked the meaning of a name to a description or to a cluster of descriptions and the *reference* of a name to objects that satisfy those descriptions. "Scott" means "the man who wrote *Waverley*." In this view, meaning determines reference. In Kuhn's theory, descriptions and clusters of descriptions multiply without end—one set of descriptions in one paradigm, another set in another paradigm. We mean something different when we use the phrase "the earth" in a Copernican paradigm than what we meant in a Ptolemaic paradigm. And there is no way to compare the two meanings. We are trapped inside a fog of language with no way out.

For Kripke, proper names and mass terms, like "gold" or "water," have no meaning, but they refer. For Kuhn, scientific terms have incommensurable meanings and *no* meaning-independent reference. Reference and truth are relative. For Kripke, there are necessary truths (and essential properties). The atomic number of gold is an *essential* property of gold. (If it is *true* that gold has an atomic number of 79, can we imagine a world in which gold does not have the atomic number 79?) For Kuhn, meaning is paradigm-dependent. There are no essential properties. "Goldie" in Kuhn's view means "the beliefs I have about Goldie *in my paradigm*." On such a view, Galileo's retort to the Inquisition would be "And yet it moves—in my paradigm."

There is a real problem here. A serious one. A problem about truth. Kuhn's ideas promote a denial of truth, and that is dangerous. This is not an empty intellectual claim. It is not a matter of indifference whether God or natural selection produced the complexities of life on earth. Or whether CO_2 emissions and other greenhouse gases are producing global warming. These arguments are not just about heuristics—disciplinary matrices, problem solving, puzzle sets, trading zones, and the like. They are not just about social conventions. They are about truth and falsity. As Steven Weinberg has said, "To put it simply, if scientists are talking about something real, then what they say is either true or false."[38] The devaluation of scientific truth cannot be laid solely on Kuhn's doorstep, but he shares some responsibility for it.

I wish to add that the—unhappily—often mentioned concept of a mass depending from speed is quite misleading.

It is also preferable not to introduce a dependence of mass from the speed. The concept mass should be restricted to "rest mass."

37. Kripke offers the example of the Holy Roman Empire, which is neither holy nor Roman nor an empire (*Naming and Necessity*, p. 26). J. D. Norton, a historian and philosopher of science at the University of Pittsburgh, supplies an example of three *contradictory* descriptions that pick out the same thing: "The city that we otherwise know as Jerusalem is described variously as: 'the city in which the Temple was built' by Jews; 'the city in which Jesus, son of God, was crucified' by Christians; and 'the city from which Mohammed, God's true prophet, ascended to heaven' by Muslims. Each of the three religious groups harbor contradictory background assumptions. While the contradictions are not immediately apparent, they are there. Christians, for example, would contradict the Muslim's description of Mohammed; and Muslims would return the favor with Jesus. Yet they all refer to the same city. If temperature is like these proper names, then the term can still refer to the same thing, even though the term may appear in two different theories, thermodynamics and statistical mechanics, with contradictory background assumptions" ("Dense and Sparse Meaning Spaces").

38. Weinberg, "Sokal's Hoax," p. 14.

Kuhn writes:

> One often hears that successive theories grow ever closer to, or approximate more and more closely to, the truth. . . . Perhaps there is some way of salvaging the notion of 'truth' for application to whole theories, but this one will not do. . . . Einstein's general theory of relativity is closer to Aristotle's than either of them is to Newton's. Though the temptation to describe that position as relativistic is understandable, the description seems to be wrong. Conversely, if the position be relativism, I cannot see the relativist loses anything needed to account for the nature and development of the sciences.[39]

39. Kuhn, *Structure* (1970), pp. 206–7.

This paragraph contains much of what I find frustrating—and wrong—about Kuhn and about his attempts to defend himself from his critics. If scientific theories are not moving closer to the truth, then *that* claim in and of itself leads to relativism. Einstein's general theory is closer to Aristotle's than either of them is to Newton's? Perhaps if Aristotle had possessed a working knowledge of tensor calculus and covariance he would have developed general relativity two thousand years earlier?

At the end of *Structure* Kuhn writes, "We may, to be more precise, have to relinquish the notion, explicit or implicit, that changes of paradigm carry scientists and those who learn from them closer and closer to the truth."[40] In *Structure*, truth and reference do not just have to be relinquished. They are banished from the kingdom.

40. Kuhn, *Structure* (1962), p. 169.

No progress. No objective truth. No real world. In a Rothschild Lecture delivered at Harvard in the final decade of his life, Kuhn asserted or reasserted "a tripartite conviction. First, the Archimedean platform outside of history, outside of time and space, is gone beyond recall. Second, in its absence, comparative evaluation is all there is." Does one follow from the other? I would think not. Third, truth: "Truth cannot be anything like correspondence to reality."[41] OK, then what is it? Kuhn trots out the idea that the development of science is Darwinian—presumably because there is no fixed endpoint.[42] "Scientific development is like Darwinian evolution, a

41. Kuhn, "The Trouble with the Historical Philosophy of Science," p. 115.
42. "*The Origin of Species* recognized no goal set either by God or nature. Instead, natural selection, operating in the given environment and with the actual organisms presently at hand, was responsible for the gradual but steady emergence of more elaborate, further articulated, and vastly more specialized organisms." Kuhn, *Structure* (1962), p. 172.

Chapter 2

process driven from behind rather than pulled towards some fixed goal to which it grows ever closer."[43] I call this view "The Origin of the Specious." Is the discovery of America a "process driven from behind rather than pulled towards"? Not really.[44] To be sure, there are historical exigencies. America could have been discovered in 1392 or 1592. It could have been discovered by a European other than Christopher Columbus. (It was.) But it was *discovered* by someone because it exists. It was *not invented*. Just like the positron or the omega minus particle.

43. Kuhn, "The Trouble with the Historical Philosophy of Science," p. 115.
44. Of course, we can characterize discoveries in many ways. Norwood Russell Hanson has laid out what he calls a taxonomy of discovery activities, distinguishing between trip-over discoveries, back-into discoveries, puzzle-over discoveries, and so on and so forth. But the essential ingredient is that the thing discovered in the physical world has always been there, even when we didn't know it. Hanson, "An Anatomy of Discovery" (1967).

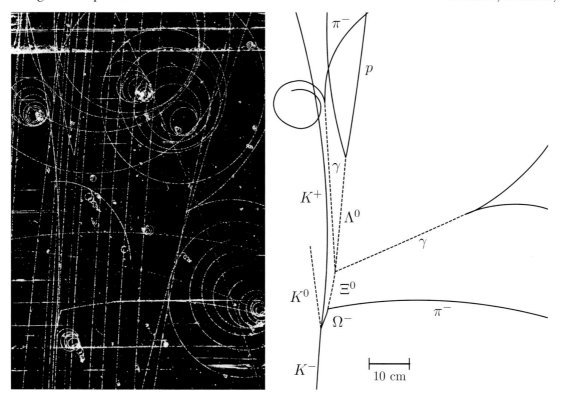

Imagine a group of islands—say, the Andaman Islands in the Bay of Bengal. By some accounts, there are 572 islands. Someone counted them. Presumably, they counted correctly. Maybe they even made a map. In the early fifteenth century a French *livre des merveilles* (book of marvels) depicted the islands as inhabited by wolf-headed people. Explorers, in the process of "discovering" the Andaman Islands, were *pulled* toward the realization that wolf-headed people, the cynocephalic, were nowhere to be found.

Discovery versus invention. The idea of invention lends itself to a sociological view of science. And yet, in his lecture, Kuhn tries to distance himself from practitioners of the purely sociological "strong program," which he characterizes as follows:

> Nature itself, whatever that may be, has seemed to have no part in the development of beliefs about it. Talk of evidence, of the rationality of claims drawn from it, and of the truth or probability of those claims has been seen as simply the rhetoric behind which the victorious party cloaks its power. What passes for scientific knowledge becomes, then, simply the belief of the winners.[45]

45. Kuhn, "The Trouble with the Historical Philosophy of Science," p. 110.

But how is this different from the beliefs expressed in Kuhn's "tripartite conviction"? How is his "comparative evaluation is all there is" different from "what passes for science knowledge becomes . . . the belief of the winners"? Can you have it both ways? Kuhn wants his system to privilege "reason" and "evidence," or at least he argues that it should. But he provides us with no reason *why* it should and many reasons to doubt that we can even determine what constitutes either "reason" or "evidence."

This sociological conception of science surfaces again and again in *The Structure of Scientific Revolutions*. Relativism, social construction . . . To some this is Kuhn's most important contribution. To me it is anathema. Take what John Earman, a philosopher of science, calls Kuhn's "purple passages":

> Like the choice between competing political institutions, that between competing paradigms proves to be a choice between incompatible modes of community life. . . . When paradigms enter, as they must, into a debate about paradigm choice, their role is necessarily circular. Each group uses its own paradigm to argue in that paradigm's defense. (P. 94)

> As in political revolutions, so in paradigm choice—there is no standard other than the assent of the relevant community. (P. 94)

> In these matters neither proof nor error is at issue. The transfer of allegiance from paradigm to paradigm is a conversion experience that cannot be forced. (P. 151)[46]

It's not surprising that, along with truth, the very notion of *reality* comes under attack in *Structure*. Here is Kuhn once again. "I am not suggesting, let me emphasize, that there is a reality that science fails to get at. My point is rather that no sense can be made of the notion of reality as it has ordinarily functioned in philosophy of science."[47]

Good God. Readers may wonder, haven't Kuhn's views been discredited? No. Not at all. People see paradigms and paradigm shifts everywhere.[48] Relativism has almost become the law of the land. For those who believe that Kuhn and Kripke are addressing unrelated problems, I would argue that it's all about reference and truth. Reference and truth are everything.

46. Earman, "Carnap, Kuhn, and the Philosophy of Scientific Methodology," p. 19.
47. Kuhn, "The Trouble with the Historical Philosophy of Science," p. 115. Like Ulrich, Robert Musil's protagonist in *The Man without Qualities*, whose aim is to abolish reality.
48. My favorite explanation of a paradigm shift occurs in DBC Pierre's novel *Vernon God Little*, which in 2003 won the Man Booker Prize:

> Ledesma hangs back. "Don't underestimate your general public, Vern—they want to see justice being done. I say give them what they want."
> "But, like—I didn't do anything."
> "Tch, and who knows it? People decide with or without the facts—if you don't get out there and paint your paradigm, someone'll paint it for you."
> "My *what*?"
> "Pa-ra-dime. You never heard of the paradigm shift? Example: you see a man with his hand up your granny's ass. What do you think?"
> "Bastard."
> "Right. Then you learn a deadly bug crawled up there, and the man has in fact put aside his disgust to save Granny. What do you think now?"
> "Hero." You can tell he ain't met my nana.
> "There you go, a paradigm shift. The action doesn't change—the information you use to judge it does. You were ready to crucify the guy because you didn't have the facts. Now you want to shake his hand."
> "I don't think so." (pp. 33–34)

3. A PARLIAMENT OF FEARS

"I'm so glad I don't like asparagus," said the Small Girl to a Sympathetic Friend.
"Because if I did, I should have to eat it—and I can't bear it!"
                                        —Lewis Carroll (as quoted by W. W. Bartley III,
                                                "Lewis Carroll's Lost Book on Logic")

For Kuhn the meaning of words is endlessly in flux. Changing your paradigm is not like changing your oil. You end up with a completely different set of meanings—except maybe you can't know it, because the meanings are inaccessible to you. To me, this is a nightmare, a real nightmare. Like one of Jorge Luis Borges's infernal allegories. Indeed, Kuhn resembles an addled version of Borges—without the irony, without the humor, without the playfulness.

In "The Library of Babel," Borges writes about the "feverish Library, whose random volumes constantly threaten to transmogrify into others, so that they affirm all things, deny all things, and confound and confuse all things, like some mad and hallucinating deity."[1] Kuhn created his own Library of Babel, his own self-defeating argument—though he never saw it as such.[2] If meanings are changing and paradigms cannot be compared, why not imagine each and every person in his or her own island universe? (Like Hamlet, he could be bounded by a paradigm and count himself a king of infinite space. But would he have bad dreams?) And indeed, Kuhn, at least in one instance, seems to embrace this possibility:

> I am tempted to posit the existence of two Thomas Kuhns. Kuhn No. 1 is the author of this essay and of an earlier piece in this volume. He also in 1962 published a book [*The Structure of Scientific Revolutions*]. Kuhn No. 2 is the author of another book by the same title. . . .

1. Borges, *Collected Fictions*, p. 117.
2. The argument that Kuhn's philosophy is self-defeating has been made by many philosophers, most notably by Donald Davidson, whose essay "On the Very Idea of a Conceptual Scheme" appeared in 1973, around the time Kuhn threw the ashtray (though I became aware of it only later). Davidson writes, "The dominant metaphor of conceptual relativism seems to betray an underlying paradox. Different points of view make sense, but only if there is a common coordinate system on which to plot them; yet the existence of a common belief system belies the claim of dramatic incomparability." He continues, "Conceptual relativism is a heady and exotic doctrine, or would be if we could make good sense of it. . . . Instead of living in different worlds, Kuhn's scientists may, like those who need Webster's dictionary, be only words apart" (pp. 5–6). See also Hilary Putnam, *Reason, Truth and History* (1981). The criticisms come down to a simple point: if conceptual schemes are incommensurable, how can you write about them?

That both books bear the same title cannot be altogether accidental, for the views they represent often overlap and are, in any case, expressed in the same words. But their central concerns are, I conclude, usually very different. As reported by his critics (the original is unfortunately unavailable to me), Kuhn No. 2 seems to make points that subvert essential aspects of the position outlined by his namesake.[3]

For Kuhn, this multiplicity of Kuhns and Kuhn-authored books-with-the-same-title provides further proof of his core belief that people with incommensurable viewpoints can't talk to each other. That they live in different worlds. He writes, "This collection of essays [*Road since Structure*] . . . provides an extended example of what I have elsewhere called partial or incomplete communication—the talking-through-each-other that regularly characterizes discourse between participants in incommensurable points of view."[4] But isn't this a misuse of words? Is it incommensurable points of view or an incoherent philosophy?

It reminds me of another Borges parable, "Pierre Menard, Author of the *Quixote*." I first read it in the early 1970s, in the New Directions paperback edition of *Labyrinths*. I talked about it at length with my then-girlfriend, the artist Sherrie Levine. The story deeply

3. Kuhn, "Reflections on My Critics," pp. 123–24. Freeman Dyson, a theoretical physicist at the Institute for Advanced Study, writes, "A few years ago I happened to meet Kuhn at a scientific conference and complained to him about the nonsense that had been attached to his name. He reacted angrily. In a voice loud enough to be heard by everybody in the hall, he shouted, 'One thing you have to understand. I am not a Kuhnian.'" Dyson, *The Sun, the Genome, the Internet* (1999), p. 13.

4. Kuhn, "Reflections on My Critics," p. 124.

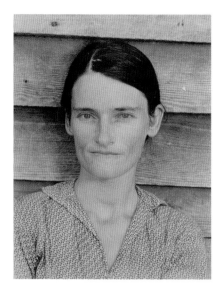  

affected both of us, and it is arguable that it became a basis for some of her subsequent artistic work. Among other themes, the question of authorship.

The story involves *two* writers. Borges imagines a second, fictional author, Pierre Menard, who, approximately three hundred years *after* Cervantes, sets out to replicate (or rewrite) portions of *Don Quixote* word for word. Borges cautions:

> Those who have insinuated that Menard devoted his life to writing a contemporary *Quixote* besmirch his illustrious memory. Pierre Menard did not want to compose *another* Quixote, which surely is easy enough—he wanted to compose *the* Quixote. Nor, surely, need one be obliged to note that his goal was never a mechanical transcription of the original; he had no intention of *copying* it. His admirable intention was to produce a number of pages which coincided—word for word and line for line—with those of Miguel de Cervantes.

The author immerses himself in the project:

> [Menard] resolved to anticipate the vanity that awaits all the labors of mankind; he undertook a task of infinite complexity, a task futile from the outset. He dedicated his scruples and his nights "lit by midnight oil" to repeating in a foreign tongue a

book that already existed. His drafts were endless; he stubbornly corrected, and he ripped up thousands of handwritten pages. He would allow no one to see them.[5]

In Borges's story—an elaborate literary conundrum—Menard has created an entirely new work of art. Take these two passages. First, from the *Quixote* by Cervantes:

> . . . truth, whose mother is history, rival of time, depository of deeds, witness of the past, exemplar and adviser to the present, and the future's counselor.[6]

Then, from the *Quixote* by Menard:

> . . . truth, whose mother is history, rival of time, depository of deeds, witness of the past, exemplar and adviser to the present, and the future's counselor.

They are lexically the same. But according to Borges, they have radically different meanings. In Cervantes's version, "this enumeration is a mere rhetorical praise of history." In Menard's, history is the "*mother of truth*":

> Menard, a contemporary of William James, defines history not as a *delving into* reality but as the very *fount* of reality. Historical truth, for him, is not "what happened"; it is what we *believe* happened. The final phrases—*exemplar and adviser to the present, and the future's counselor*—are brazenly pragmatic.[7]

The contrast in Borges concerns the nature of historical truth. Cervantes is a realist ("what happened"); Menard, a relativist, a social constructivist ("what we *believe* happened"). Truth versus belief.[8]

What is being argued here? That every text is endlessly reinterpreted? That each reader rewrites (or at least reinterprets) the book they are reading? Like Edmund Wilson's remark in the foreword to "The Triple Thinkers"—that "one can never read the book that the author originally wrote, and one can never read the same book

5. Borges, "Pierre Menard, Author of the *Quixote*," in *Collected Fictions*, pp. 91, 94–95.

6. Here's the extended passage: "For it should be the duty of historians to be exact, truthful, and dispassionate, and neither interest nor fear nor rancor nor affection should swerve them from the path of *truth, whose mother is history, rival of time, depository of deeds, witness of the past, exemplar and adviser to the present, and the future's counselor. In this work, I am sure, will be found all that could be desired in the way of pleasant reading; and if it is lacking in any way, I maintain that this is the fault of that hound of an author rather than the subject." Cervantes, *Don Quixote*, p. 83 (emphasis mine).

7. Borges, "Pierre Menard," pp. 91, 94. A different version of the Menard-Cervantes "conflict" is embodied in a quote attributed to Karl Rove, which pits those who are influenced by facts against those who (take your pick) create them or make them up:

> The aide [later identified as Rove] said that guys like me were "in what we call the reality-based community," which he defined as people who "believe that solutions emerge from your judicious study of discernible reality." I nodded and murmured something about enlightenment principles and empiricism. He cut me off. "That's not the way the world really works anymore," he continued. "We're an empire now, and when we act, we create our own reality. And while you're studying that reality—judiciously, as you will—we'll act again, creating other new realities, which you can study too, and that's how things will sort out. We're history's actors . . . and you, all of you, will be left to just study what we do." (Ron Suskind, "Faith, Certainty, and the Presidency of George W. Bush" [2004])

Are we products of history or do we create it? And if we (I) create history, why bother to study it? Rove's relativism, of course, has now been superseded by that of Donald Trump and his rotating cast of apologists, for all of whom truth has little allure.

8. There is yet another way to look at Menard v. Cervantes—as a version of Kuhn (or Wittgenstein) v. Kripke. For

Chapter 3

twice"? And how does Borges fit into this? Is Borges Menard? Cervantes? Neither? Both?[9]

Borges writes about *both* versions—Cervantes's and Menard's. And he compares the two. As such, "Menard" becomes an essay on translation. And interpretation. Not only do we translate one language into another, one theory into another; we also often translate one text into itself. It may all come down to translation. Translation and more translation. Cervantes's *Quixote* into Menard's *Quixote*, and vice versa. Maybe not an *exact* translation. But close enough. And we can describe in considerable detail how that translation succeeds and fails.[10]

ι   "A world of disorderly notions, picked out of his books, crowded into his imagination."—*p. 3.*

Kripke, reference is historical—there is a historical chain that leads back into the past to the *fact* of an initial baptism. For Kuhn, as for Wittgenstein, reference is a matter of social agreement, an agreement among language users as to what the reference of a term might be. For Kripke, meanings can change but the reference remain the same; for Kuhn and Wittgenstein, the reference (whatever reference is in such a scheme) changes.

9. Borges's biographer Alberto Manguel elaborates:

> In "Pierre Menard, Author of *Don Quixote*," [Borges] argued that a book changes according to the reader's attributions. . . . Pierre Menard is, of course, an invention, a superb and hilarious imagining, but the notion of a text that changes according to the reader's assumptions is old. . . . Once, after noting that we read now Dante in ways he couldn't have imagined . . . Borges recalled an observation by the ninth-century mystic, Scotus Eriugena. According to the author of *On the Divisions of Nature*, there are as many readings of a text as there are readers. (*With Borges*, pp. 63–66)

One more tidbit. Later in life, the story goes, Scotus Eriugena went to England to continue teaching. There he was stabbed to death by his pupils with their *styli*. Ah, violence against teachers as well as violence against students.

10. Borges writes about the Gothic novel *Vathek*, "William Beckford required only three days and two nights in the winter of 1782 to write the tragic story of his caliph. He wrote in French; Henley translated it into English in 1785. *The original is unfaithful to the translation*; Saintsbury observes that eighteenth century French is less suitable than English for communicating the 'undefined horrors' (the phrase is Beckford's) of this unusual story." "On William Beckford's *Vathek*," in *Selected Non-Fictions*, pp. 238–39 (emphasis mine).

Borges creates a linguistic nightmare. Words whose meanings are constantly in flux. Words, books, and libraries that disappear. Infinite libraries. "Menard" appeared in May 1939—shortly after Madrid fell to Francisco Franco's forces. Borges had written movingly against the fascist powers overtaking Europe—particularly, against anti-Semitism. "In vain I quoted the wise words of Mark Twain: 'I have no race prejudices. . . . All that I care to know is that a man is a human being—that is enough for me; he can't be any worse.'"[11] And he had written against the denial of reality. In Borges's review of *Citizen Kane*, first published in 1941, he called the movie

> a kind of metaphysical detective story. . . . Forms of multiplicity and incongruity abound in the film: the first scenes record the treasures amassed by Kane; in one of the last, a poor woman, luxuriant and suffering, plays with an enormous jigsaw puzzle on the floor of a palace that is also a museum. At the end we realize that the fragments are not governed by any secret unity: the detested Charles Foster Kane is a simulacrum, a chaos of appearances.[12]

Borges concludes by quoting G. K. Chesterton—"there is nothing more frightening than a labyrinth that has no center." (The quote is

11. "Two Books," in *Selected Non-Fictions*, p. 208.

12. "An Overwhelming Film," in *Selected Non-Fictions*, p. 258. *Citizen Kane* may or may not be the greatest movie, but this review is the greatest movie *review*. Ostensibly, Borges is writing about *Citizen Kane*, but he could be writing a review of his own work. Metaphysical detective stories about language, time, and memory—haunted by the fear that his own personal labyrinths may have no center, that it may all be but a simulacrum.

from Chesterton's story, "The Head of Caesar": " 'What we all dread most,' said the priest in a low voice, 'is a maze with *no* center. That is why atheism is only a nightmare.' "[13])

The labyrinth with no center. For the religious Chesterton, it is the nightmare of atheism, a universe without God. For the secular Borges, it is the chaos of appearances—jigsaw puzzle pieces that can never be assembled into a meaningful picture of reality. For me, a secular Jew from Long Island, it is the mystery without a solution. A murder without a murderer. A world without answers. It is the nightmare offered by a philosophy without objective truth. What are the answers to the questions, What really happened? When did it happen? Who really did it? There *are* no answers.

———

One of my favorite books is Bertrand Russell's *Nightmares of Eminent Persons*. It is imaginative fiction, written at a time when he was struggling to make alimony payments.[14] "The following 'Nightmares' might be called 'Signposts to Sanity,' " Russell writes:

> Every isolated passion is, in isolation, insane; sanity may be defined as a synthesis of insanities. . . . The man who wishes to preserve sanity in a dangerous world should summon in his own mind a parliament of fears, in which each in turn is voted absurd by all the others.[15]

Among Russell's many nightmares, his personal parliament of fears, were "Stalin's Nightmare," "The Psychoanalyst's Nightmare," "The Metaphysician's Nightmare," "Dr. Bowdler's Nightmare"—a catalogue of what-ifs. And "The Existentialist's Nightmare." What if existence precedes action and the existentialist exists no matter what? He exists even if he is sitting in a dark room doing nothing. At the end, the existentialist is screaming, "I don't exist. I don't exist." Poe's raven appears, speaking in the voice of the French poet Stéphane Mallarmé: You *do* exist. You *do* exist. It's your *philosophy* that doesn't exist.

Russell never got around to writing "The Postmodernist's Nightmare," but it is not difficult to imagine what it would be. The postmodernist is seated in a chair. A disembodied voice repeats over

13. Chesterton, *The Wisdom of Father Brown*, p. 150. Borges presumably translated Chesterton into Spanish, and it was translated back into English in a slightly different form. The passage remains perfectly intelligible. I even prefer Borges's Chesterton *after* the two translations.

14. Russell recounts the financial difficulties he had around Christmas of 1953: "The financial burden was heavy and rather disturbing: I had given £10,000 of my Nobel Prize cheque for a little more than £11,000 to my third wife, and I was now paying alimony to her and to my second wife, as well as paying for the education and holidays of my younger son. Added to this, there were heavy expenses in connection with my elder son's illness; and the income taxes which for many years he had neglected to pay now fell to me to pay. The prospect of supporting and educating his three children, however pleasant it might be, presented problems." *The Autobiography of Bertrand Russell*, vol. 3, *1944–1969*, p. 89. See also *The Collected Stories of Bertrand Russell*, p. 211.
15. Russell, *Nightmares* (1955), introduction.

and over again, "Truth exists. Reality exists." The postmodernist screams, "No, they don't." The voice sternly replies, "Oh, yes, they do. And if you don't believe it, how about jumping out that window over there? We're on the thirty-ninth floor."

And then there's my favorite, "The Mathematician's Nightmare." Professor Squarepunt falls asleep after a day of studying Pythagoras (something I'm not unfamiliar with). A strange drama visits his sleeping thoughts. As Russell describes it, the numbers in this nightmare "were not the bloodless categories that he had previously supposed them. They were living, breathing beings endowed with all the passions which he was accustomed to find in his fellow mathe-maticians." The odd numbers were male, the even numbers female. But at the center, masked, stood Pi. The master of ceremonies. Pierc-ing eyes looking out from inexorable cold. It was understood that, like the Gorgon, no one could behold it and live. "The numbers danced around Professor Squarepunt and Pi in a vast and intricate ballet." A ballet of integers. And then the numbers start arguing with each other. The mathematician looks to Pi for assistance. Pi proclaims in a sten-torian voice, "Silence! Or you shall all become incommensurable."[16]

16. *Nightmares*, pp. 42, 45.

———

Lewis Carroll—one of the great logicians of the nineteenth cen-tury—creates his own allegory of language and an examination of meaning, language, and truth.[17] The themes run throughout much of his work. In a conversation between Alice and Humpty Dumpty in *Through the Looking-Glass*, Humpty Dumpty—rotund, perched precariously on a wall, an egg—poses the question, Can words mean anything we want them to? And if not, who—if anyone—decides what words mean? His answer comes immediately. If you want to know what a word means, check with Humpty Dumpty. Words mean whatever Humpty Dumpty wants them to mean. It is easy to see it as an earlier version of the Ashtray Argument:

17. If I were to offer an introductory course in philosophy, my syllabus would include only four books: by Russell, *The Nightmares of Eminent Persons* and *The Problems of Philosophy*, and by Carroll, *Alice's Adventures in Wonderland* and *Through the Looking-Glass*.

"I don't know what you mean by 'glory,' " Alice said.

Humpty Dumpty smiled contemptuously. "Of course you don't—till I tell you. I meant 'there's a nice knock-down argument for you!' "

"But 'glory' doesn't mean 'a nice knock-down argument,' " Alice objected.

"When *I* use a word," Humpty Dumpty said, in a rather scornful tone, "it means just what I choose it to mean—neither more nor less."

"The question is," said Alice, "whether you *can* make words mean so many different things."

"The question is," said Humpty Dumpty, "which is to be master—that's all."

Alice was too much puzzled to say anything; so after a minute Humpty Dumpty began again. "They've a temper, some of them—particularly verbs: they're the proudest—adjectives you can do anything with, but not verbs—however, *I* can manage the whole lot! Impenetrability! That's what *I* say!"

Impenetrability as incommensurability!

"Would you tell me, please," said Alice, "what that means?"

"Now you talk like a reasonable child," said Humpty Dumpty, looking very much pleased. "I meant by 'impenetrability' that we've had enough of that subject, and it would be just as well if you'd mention what you mean to do next, as I suppose you don't mean to stop here all the rest of your life."

"That's a great deal to make one word mean," Alice said in a thoughtful tone.

"When I make a word do a lot of work like that," said Humpty Dumpty, "I always pay it extra."[18]

Carroll does not tell us how Humpty Dumpty feels about reference. (He may have lost interest in the philosophy of language after his great fall from the wall.) But there is a curious passage that could have been influenced by Mill and prefigures some of Kripke's ideas. Alice's rejoinder to Humpty Dumpty. Must a name (or mass term) mean anything at all?

18. *The Annotated Alice*, p. 213. Martin Gardner provides two annotations to this passage: (1) "In his article, 'The Stage and the Spirit of Reverence,' Carroll put it this way: 'no word has a meaning *inseparably* attached to it; a word means what the speaker intends by it, and what the hearer understands by it, and that is all. . . .'" (2) "Lewis Carroll was fully aware of the profundity in Humpty Dumpty's whimsical discourse on semantics. Humpty takes the point of view known in the Middle Ages as nominalism; the view that universal terms do not refer to objective existence but are nothing more than *flatus vocis*, verbal utterances. . . ."

HUMPTY DUMPTY

Lewis Carroll

Illustration by Sir John Tenniel

Humpty Dumpty
 sat on a wall:
Humpty Dumpty
 had a great fall.
All the King's horses
 and all the King's men
Couldn't put Humpty Dumpty
 in his place again.

"Don't stand chattering to yourself like that," Humpty Dumpty said, looking at her for the first time, "but tell me your name and your business."

"My *name* is Alice, but—"

"It's a stupid name enough!" Humpty Dumpty interrupted impatiently. "What does it mean?"

"*Must* a name mean something?" Alice asked doubtfully.[19]

19. *Annotated Alice*, p. 208.

For me, Kuhn is none other than the imperious Humpty Dumpty,
the great (but ultimately, vulnerable) dictator. A perverse dictator.
A dictator regulating the past—turning history into a vast prison—
something like Jeremy Bentham's panopticon, a circular building
with cells along the circumference. "These *cells* are divided from one
another, and the prisoners by that means secluded from all communication with each other, by *partitions* in the form of *radii* issuing
from the circumference towards the centre. . . . The apartment of
the inspector occupies the centre; you may call it if you please the
inspector's lodge."[20] No prisoner can communicate with any other
prisoner, *only* with the inspector.

20. Bentham, *The Panopticon Writings*, p. 35.

Imagine a panopticon in *time* as well as space. A prison of historical paradigms where only Kuhn, installed in his lodge at the center

of the edifice, can compare the meanings of words in one paradigm to the meanings of words in another.

But who gave Kuhn this supreme position—the job of ultimate observer?

———

Furthermore, isn't this a much older story? Doesn't it have biblical origins? What about the Tower of Babel?

Here is Genesis 11, King James Version:

> [1]And the whole earth was of one language, and of one speech.
>
> . . .
>
> [5]And the Lord came down to see the city and the tower, which the children of men builded.
>
> [6]And the Lord said, Behold, the people is one, and they have all one language; and this they begin to do: and now nothing will be restrained from them, which they have imagined to do.
>
> [7]Go to, let us go down, and there confound their language, that they may not understand one another's speech.
>
> [8]So the Lord scattered them abroad from thence upon the face of all the earth: and they left off to build the city.
>
> [9]Therefore is the name of it called Babel; because the Lord did there confound the language of all the earth: and from thence did the Lord scatter them abroad upon the face of all the earth.

Is it hyperbolic (or unreasonable) to compare incommensurability and the Tower of Babel? God appalled by the hubris of men who would feign building a tower to Heaven, and Kuhn, assuming the guise of the Creator, appalled by the hubris of scientists who would feign a *growing* understanding of the universe and an approximation to truth? And then the fire bolt from on high, the devolution of communication into a multiplicity of languages (and meanings) "that they may not understand one another's speech." Had science become the *lingua franca* of mankind? A way toward progress and truth? And Kuhn the maleficent deity who denied that scientists could communicate with each other, even though it was pretty clear that they could?[21]

21. The idea that truth is relative isn't the real bugaboo. The problem is rather with multiple closed systems of relative truths—an anarchy of data, the infernal panopticon of Thomas Kuhn. The story of the Tower of Babel in Genesis doesn't really address this. Augustine takes up the issue in book XVI, chapter 6 of *City of God*: "Therefore there is no need for me to keep explaining the speeches of God in this work. For invariable truth either speaks ineffably by itself to the minds of rational creatures, or speaks through a mutable creature, whether to our minds by means of incorporeal images or to our physical sense by means of corporeal voices" (vol. 5, p. 37). Following Augustine, one would suppose that God's punishment didn't deprive man his access to "invariable truth." God didn't do much more than create a smorgasbord of dialects from the human protolanguage.

Stefan Zweig, an Austrian-Jewish writer in the 1920s and '30s, wrote an essay about the Tower of Babel:

> The bitterest hour of humanity had come. Suddenly, overnight,
> in the midst of their labors, men could no longer understand
> each other. They cried out, but had no concept of each other's

speech, and so they became enraged with each other. They threw down their bricks, picks and trowels, they argued and quarreled until finally they abandoned the communal work, each returning to his own home in his own land. They dispersed into the fields and forests of the earth and there each built his own house which did not reach the clouds, nor God, but merely sheltered his own head and his nightly slumber. The Tower of Babel, that colossal edifice, remained abandoned; the wind and rain gradually tore away the parapets, which were already approaching the sky, and little by little the whole structure crumbled away, subsided and was laid to ruin. Soon it was just a legend that appeared in the canticles and humanity completely forgot the monumental work of its youth.[22]

22. Zweig, *Messages from a Lost World*, pp. 54–55.

The bitterest hour of humanity—but didn't humanity learn to translate one language into another? Don't we understand our locutions? And here comes the ultimate heresy: don't we all communicate?

4. LISTEN, OLD MAN,
WHAT IN HELL'S GONE WRONG HERE?

"And what would you do, . . . if you could rule the world for a day?"
"I suppose I would have no choice but to abolish reality."
—Robert Musil, *The Man without Qualities*

If translation is impossible, how come translators seem to do it every day? The issue surfaced in my discussions with Hilary Putnam, a sometime critic of Kuhn.[1] I asked him—paradigm shifts, incommensurability, reference and belief—could it all come down to issues of translation? Can we translate one language into another? One theory into another? One language (like the Spanish of Cervantes) into itself?

Putnam, who died in 2016, was a fixture around Cambridge, Massachusetts—a former professor at Princeton and MIT, then at Harvard since the 1960s. On Rosh Hashanah and Yom Kippur, Jewish High Holy Days, services are held on the Harvard campus at Sanders Theater, a spectacular Victorian-Gothic pile with an elaborate carved-wood interior. Putnam, along with the cantor, the rabbi, and other officials, would preside over the services. I cannot entirely explain it, but I took enormous comfort in seeing him there. I thought he could help me get written into the Book of Life.

Few philosophers have wrestled with such a range of questions over such an extended period of time. I had lived in Cambridge and attended Putnam's lectures in 1970–1971, the year before I went to Princeton.

HILARY PUTNAM: So how did you come to take my course? You weren't a Harvard graduate student.
ERROL MORRIS: No. I was applying to the History of Science Department. And you were teaching a course on Gödel's proofs

1. I interviewed Putnam at his house in Arlington, Massachusetts, on September 4, 2011, and returned for a second interview in November 2015. We talked for hours, and Putnam made cup after cup of espresso to keep me going. He seemed indefatigable. At the time of our second interview, *The Philosophy of Hilary Putnam* had just come out from the Library of Living Philosophers, and copies of the massive volume were stacked on the dining room table. Sadly, Putnam died soon after. The world is a less intelligent place without him.

2. Progressive Labor was considered a Maoist party. But in 1972, it ended its support
of the Cultural Revolution and split with
the People's Republic of China.

PUTNAM: Well, I never—I taught an upper-level math department course on Gödel and Cohen's proofs.

MORRIS: You were *supposed to be* teaching a course on Gödel, but you were using Mao's *Little Red Book*.

PUTNAM: [*Laughs.*] So it had to be the sixties, because I quit PL [Progressive Labor] in '72.[2]

MORRIS: This was 1971.

PUTNAM: That could be. I was terribly unhappy as a loyal PL'er—conflicted. I quit, and then in the winter of '72, I sat down and typed with great joy on my first electric typewriter, "The Meaning of 'Meaning.'"

MORRIS: A Selectric?

PUTNAM: It had a ball. Before that I always had the classic typewriters, like my father, who was a writer. It was my first Selectric. Oh, I loved it! And because I was so tortured during that period—trying to be a loyal Maoist, but becoming more and more conflicted. As you know, my habit is to reexamine my own ideas—

MORRIS: You're legendary in that regard.[3]

PUTNAM: I was attracted to Maoism, or at least PL's eccentric version, because they didn't claim that there was any actually existing state which lived up to ideal Communism. I was looking for something that would be in the tradition of Marxism-Leninism, but not fascist, not Stalinist. It was a horrible period. And I was under terrific pressure, partly because I didn't know if I would go to jail for a few years for having collected draft cards. I had committed a felony and, until the Carter amnesty, I was liable to have to pay for that felony.[4]

MORRIS: There is the problem of what to do when your government is driving you crazy.

PUTNAM: I still feel like a patriotic American. There's a difference between loving your country and loving its government. But if we elect any member of the Tea Party as president, I don't know that I'll be able to maintain that distinction.

MORRIS: The late '60s and early '70s was a crazy time for many, many reasons. Principally because of Vietnam. I was an undergraduate at the University of Wisconsin–Madison.

PUTNAM: That was a center.

3. Putnam is known for having repeatedly
changed his positions on almost everything. He is a living embodiment of the
adage by Heraclitus—the impossibility of
stepping into the same philosophy twice.

4. Jimmy Carter pardoned Vietnam draft
dodgers on January 21, 1977, the day he
took office. Lance Hickey's essay "Hilary
Putnam" in *American Philosophers, 1950–
2000* (pp. 226–36), details this period
in Putnam's life: "In 1963, while he was
teaching at MIT, he organized one of
the first faculty and student committees
against the war. He was particularly
outraged by David Halberstam's . . .
claim that the U.S. was 'defending' the
peasants of South Vietnam from the
Vietcong by poisoning their rice crop.
As the war continued, Putnam's outrage
intensified, and after moving to Harvard
in 1965, he organized various campus
protests, in conjunction with teaching
courses on Marxism. He was the
official faculty advisor to the Students
for a Democratic Society, which was at
that time the main anti–Vietnam War
organization on campus."

Chapter 4

MORRIS: That *was* a center. I was in several demonstrations in
1967, and I was in Madison during the summer of 1970, when
antiwar radicals blew up the Army Mathematics Research
Center. I was four or five blocks away. And I remember hearing
the explosion—

The demonstrations in 1967 were ferocious. At the time Richard
Cheney, a graduate student in history, and his wife, Lynne, were
safely ensconced on the other side of campus in married student
housing. I was in a demonstration on Bascom Hill. The campus
police as well as the Madison city police were involved. Students
were beaten and teargassed. I came away unharmed.

According to an essay on the website of the Wisconsin Historical Society, "More than 57,000 Wisconsin residents served in
Southeast Asia; 1,239 did not return." Overall, 58,000 Americans
died, and 150,000 were wounded. In 1969 alone more than half
a million US soldiers were stationed in Vietnam, and another

5. Wisconsin Historical Society, "Vietnam and Opposition at Home."
6. Robert S. McNamara, "The Post–Cold War World" (1991), p. 111.
7. Paul L. Sutton, "The History of Agent Orange Use in Vietnam" (2002). See also Michael F. Martin, *Vietnamese Victims of Agent Orange and U.S.-Vietnam Relations* (2008), p. 16.

1.2 million elsewhere in Southeast Asia.[5] Throughout the conflict, over two million Vietnamese were killed.[6] Twelve million gallons of Agent Orange, a chemical defoliant, were dropped.[7] The immiseration of millions of people, the despoliation of their environment.

It's really hard to talk about philosophy in the late 1960s and early 1970s without talking about the war in Vietnam. It was part of what everyone was thinking, whether they were for it or against it. It was the backdrop for everything. Putnam's activism could be contrasted with Kuhn's acceptance of the status quo. Despite the inclusion of the word "revolution" in the title of his magnum opus, Kuhn saw his work as "profoundly conservative." In an autobiographical interview with Vassiliki Kindi, included in his posthumous *Road since Structure*, Kuhn said:

One of [Kindi's] papers talks about how just the things that made me unpopular in the sixties make me popular in the eighties. And that's I think a very revealing and very apt remark, but it's wrong in one respect: the sixties were the years of the student rebellions. And I was told at one point that "Kuhn and Marcuse are the heroes at San Francisco State [University]." Here was the man who had written two books about revolutions. . . . Students used to come to me saying things like "thank you for telling us about paradigms—now that we know what they are we can get along without them." All seen as examples of oppression. That wasn't my point at all. I remember being invited to attend and talk to a seminar at Princeton organized by undergraduates during the times of trouble. And I kept saying, "But I didn't say that! But I didn't say that! But I didn't say that!" And finally, a student of mine, or a student in the program who had sort of helped get me into this, and had come along to listen, said to the students, "You have to realize that in terms of what you are thinking of, this is a profoundly conservative book." And it is; I mean, in the sense that I was trying to explain how it could be that the most rigid of all disciplines, and in certain circumstances the most authoritarian, could also be the most creative of novelty. And to cut my way through that *aporia*, I had to set it up; but of course to set it up as an *aporia* ran into all sorts of resistance. So, it's hard to say how I felt. I thought I was being—I want to say badly treated—badly misunderstood.[8]

Putnam and I continued to talk about his activism and the Gödel course he co-opted.

MORRIS: You never got around to Gödel. But you discussed Herrnstein and IQ tests. [Richard Herrnstein wrote a controversial book on the inheritability of IQ.] You gave an example—I believe it was a multiple-choice question—about the word "angler." Do you remember this?

PUTNAM: No. All these stories about my past—they come back as stories about an interesting fellow I would've liked to know, or the opposite.

8. Kuhn, *Road since Structure*, p. 308. The use of the word "aporia" is suggestive and ironic. I looked it up to make sure I was on solid ground: "An irresolvable internal contradiction or logical disjunction," says *The New Oxford American Dictionary*, 3rd ed. The *OED* offers the somewhat fuzzier definition—"a perplexing difficulty." Kuhn's unwavering complaint is that he is misunderstood and badly treated—but misunderstood precisely because of internal contradictions in his own work. Why is it that I get the feeling Kuhn is running scared most of the time? Like an imposter on the verge of being unmasked?

MORRIS: "Angler." One of the answers was "(A) fisherman." And then, "(B) mountain climber." And kids from Harlem would answer, (B) mountain climber.

PUTNAM: You're going up at an angle. Things that we wouldn't even recognize as culturally biased. Maybe because people don't want to know.

MORRIS: Yes, there is a strong desire *not* to know things.

PUTNAM: There's a term from St. Aquinas. I have to look it up. It's for "*not knowing* something because you don't want to know it."

We were sitting in Putnam's book-lined living room in Arlington, Massachusetts. His wife of more than fifty years, Ruth Anna Putnam, a Wellesley College professor emerita, was writing in the kitchen. A female voice called out, "Willful ignorance." No doubt they had spent countless hours working separately but together. One room apart. I thought this must be what true love is all about.

PUTNAM: Willful ignorance? I'm not sure. I think it's in Latin. I'll have to look it up.[9]

ERROL MORRIS: One of the reasons I wanted to talk with you—part of it is revisiting that period: the late '60s, early '70s. Part of it is reckoning with my experiences as a graduate student with Tom Kuhn. There's a passage in *Reason, Truth and History* where you call Kuhn's use of incommensurability incoherent.

Putnam captures many of my complaints about Kuhn. (I wish he had been in the room to defend me when the ashtray was thrown.) He writes:

> The incommensurability thesis is the thesis that terms used in another culture, say, the term 'temperature' as used by a 17th century scientist, cannot be equated in meaning or reference with any terms or expressions *we* possess. . . . If this [incommensurability] thesis were really true then we could not translate other languages—or even past stages of our own language—at all. . . . To tell us that Galileo had 'incommensurable' notions *and then to go on and describe them at length* is totally incoherent.[10]

9. The reference is to Thomas Aquinas, *Summa Theologica*, part I–II, question 76, articles 1–3.

10. Putnam, *Reason, Truth and History*, pp. 114–15. Essentially he is telling us that we should always be suspicious of those who counsel abstinence and then try to seduce their listeners.

I read the passage back to Putnam.

PUTNAM: Yes. I still stand on that criticism of Kuhn. He was too much of an antirealist for me, even at my most antirealist.

MORRIS: Too antirealist for you?

PUTNAM: Yes. He had various escapes. In the course of our long debates—I knew him well, over the years—my original take was, "Look, we can talk about grass. For the average educated person it is virtually a necessary truth that plants live by photosynthesis."

MORRIS: The Tea Party might not accept that.

PUTNAM: [*Laughter.*] The notion of "grass" is now interconnected with notions like "chlorophyll," "photosynthesis," and so on. So if this is all incommensurable, then "grass" can't be translated—textbooks can't be translated, the word "grass" in an eighteenth-century English novel can't be translated into twentieth-century English. John Austin, whose gift with words I very much admired, once said of philosophers, "There's the bit where you say it and the bit where you take it back."[11] So there's a place where Kuhn says different theories live within different words, then takes it back. From an analytic philosopher's point of view, he loads the cards. According to Kuhn, to say what an ancient text means, you have to have synonyms in the present scientific language for the old concepts—which is not true. Absolutely not true. My father was a translator—the Samuel Putnam *Don Quixote* is my father's translation. The Modern Library version. And every translator knows that you have to explain what people are talking about even though you *don't* have an exact synonym. Excellent examples of this occur in Benjamin Lee Whorf—

11. J. L. Austin, *Sense and Sensibilia* (1964), p. 3.

Benjamin Lee Whorf (1897–1941), an American linguist, spent much of his life working for the Hartford Insurance Company, like the poet Wallace Stevens. Whorf's essays on language, published more than a decade after his death, were incorporated into a volume entitled *Language, Thought, and Reality.* Whorf's central idea—sometimes called "linguistic relativity" or the Sapir-Whorf hypothesis, named for him and his teacher Edward Sapir—argues that how we

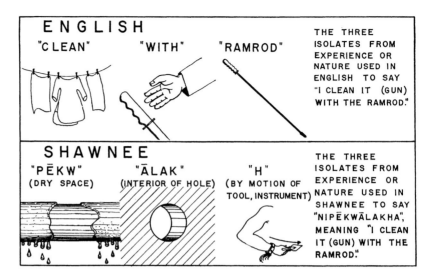

Figure 15.1. Languages dissect nature differently. The different isolates of meaning (thoughts) used by English and Shawnee in reporting the same experience, that of cleaning a gun by running the ramrod through it. The pronouns "I" and "it" are now shown by symbols, as they have the same meaning in each language. In Shawnee ni- equals "I" -a equals "it."

see the world is determined by the language we use. That different cultures—for example, Shawnee and Hopi, which Whorf studied— have different languages means that their members see the world differently. Indeed, Whorf argues that the Hopis have a different conception of time *because* of the construction of their language. The Hopis, the Shawnees, and we exist (to use Kuhnian language) in different linguistic worlds:

> We dissect nature along lines laid down by our native languages. The categories and types that we isolate from the world of phenomena we do not find there because they stare every observer in the face; on the contrary, the world is presented in a kaleidoscopic flux of impressions which has to be organized by our minds— and this means largely by the *linguistic* systems in our minds.[12]

It is Whorf's argument that our linguistic systems constrain what we can and can't think.[13] Reality must be derived from our linguistic systems, not the other way around. Could Whorf be a precursor of Kuhn? Whorf writes:

12. Whorf, *Language, Thought, and Reality* (1956), p. 213 (emphasis mine).
13. Steven Pinker eviscerates Sapir-Whorf in *The Language Instinct* (2000), pp. 48–57. Philosopher Donald Davidson has also ridiculed Whorf's ideas of linguistic relativism, relating them to Kuhn: "Whorf, wanting to demonstrate that Hopi incorporates a metaphysics so alien to ours that Hopi and English cannot, as he puts it, 'be calibrated', uses English to convey the contents of sample Hopi sentences. Kuhn is brilliant at saying what things were like before the revolution using—what else?—our post-revolutionary idiom." *Inquiries into Truth and Interpretation* (1984), p. 184.

We are thus introduced to a new principle of relativity, which holds that all observers are not led by the same physical evidence to the same picture of the universe, unless their linguistic backgrounds are similar, or can in some way be calibrated.[14]

14. Whorf, *Language, Thought, and Reality*, p. 214.

What did Putnam think?

PUTNAM: Kuhn is saying that since you can't translate, synonym by synonym, Newtonian physics into relativistic physics, it follows that—according to Kuhn, anyway—they're incommensurable. Kuhn, in replying to your objection would have taken the other side and said, "Yes, but I'm not saying that I can't say what the world of Newtonian physics was like. *Incommensurable* doesn't mean we can't describe it. It just means we can't translate it."

MORRIS: You can describe it, but you can't translate it?!

PUTNAM: Yes. For Kuhn, it ultimately depends on his antirealism, his rejection of all talk of real objects. Because if you think that there are real things out there to which our present terms refer, then you can say what they were referring to when they talked of distance in Newtonian times.

MORRIS: There's a kind of comfort—that when you're talking about something, you're really talking about *some thing*. Even though our beliefs change—our references do not! As you say, languages are translated, retranslated, and words are added and subtracted. Our beliefs are in flux, but that doesn't mean that reference is in flux. In *Naming and Necessity* there is a realism, a feeling that you are grabbing ahold of—

PUTNAM: Yes. That is what Kripke intends.

MORRIS: When did you first become aware of Kripke's three lectures [*Naming and Necessity*]?

PUTNAM: I got the idea for "Is Semantics Possible?," which is my first sketch of my view that meanings ain't in the head, etc., in a course in philosophy of language—a non-Maoist course in the philosophy of language—that I was teaching at Harvard. Before that, I was at MIT and I set up the philosophy department there. Jerry Fodor was one of the people I hired. And Fodor and I were arguing all the time about how you do semantics. They had this talk of batteries of semantic rules, and that was what

15. Putnam criticized Feyerabend in his 1965 paper "How Not to Talk about Meaning."

16. "David Kaplan, who was present at those lectures, recently wrote me, 'I remember your quickly disabusing me of the idea that the intension of a natural kind word (that which determines the extension in a possible world) is something we "grasp," as Carnap would have put it. It ain't in the head, as you put it. And almost as soon as you said it, it seemed right.'" Putnam, "Intellectual Autobiography," in *The Philosophy of Hilary Putnam* (2015), p. 78.

17. Ian Hacking discusses this in "Putnam's Theory of Natural Kinds and Their Names Is Not the Same as Kripke's" (2007).

18. There are entire books and countless journal articles devoted to an examination of Putnam's ideas in "The Meaning of 'Meaning.'" See, e.g., Andrew Pessin and Sanford Goldberg, *The Twin Earth Chronicles* (1996), p. xi:

   "That psychological state does not determine extension will now be shown with the aid of a little science-fiction." With that humble sentence in 1975 Hilary Putnam changed the face of philosophy forever. Twin Earth burst on the scene like the legendary meteor that did in the dinosaurs; it has been reverberating through philosophy ever since. With implications stretching far beyond its original domain in the philosophy of language and philosophy of psychology, it has left almost no area of contemporary analytic philosophy untouched. Indeed Twin Earth and "The Meaning of 'Meaning,'" the article in which it became famous, comprise perhaps the most influential single philosophical episode in the past half century. Here in 1995, therefore, in celebration of its twentieth anniversary, we have collected in this volume some of the best writings, by some of the best philosophers, on Twin Earth and its implications.

19. My own two cents' worth of opinion is that this approach adds confusion to an already confused issue and allows for a modified description theory. Instead of John Searle's concatenation of descrip-

I was coming from when I debated with Feyerabend.[15] But then I thought, "Wait. What am I talking about with these batteries of semantic rules? How would I capture the meaning of the word 'gold' with a battery of semantic rules?" I started thinking about it. And thought, "No, I depend on examples. I depend on experts. I depend on other people in the world." So that was sketched out in that Harvard class. I didn't know Kripke was thinking about this at all.

I presented my account at the 1968 Summer Institute in Seattle.[16] I then gave a lecture on this at Michigan. We actually camped our way across the country. And when I got involved in the anti–Vietnam War stuff, all that was on the back burner. But I realized I was starved for philosophy. After I told my "comrades" that I was quitting—I didn't tell them I would rather live under Nixon than them—I sat down at my typewriter and typed out "The Meaning of 'Meaning.'" Basically, I made a united front with Kripke. We became allies.[17]

———

"The Meaning of 'Meaning'"—the most famous of Putnam's essays—is a cornucopia of philosophical issues. Identity across possible worlds; an externalist theory of reference; meaning constancy; the nature or essence of natural kind terms—there are many, many thoughts and ideas. It's breathtaking.[18] But if Kripke banishes descriptions from reference, Putnam lets them back in. He creates a quadruple, $<x_1, x_2, x_3, x_4>$, that reflects what we mean by "meaning." Only x_4 is *reference* to something outside of our heads; all of the others are inside our heads. I would call it "the mixed-bag approach."[19] Kripke's approach is completely different. Kripke has created a sort of kosher kitchen—descriptions and beliefs in one sink, reference in the other. Linguistic dietary restrictions forbid the two being amalgamated.

Under the section heading "Are Meanings in the Head?" Putnam suggests a thought experiment—Twin Earth. Its purpose is to show that the "psychological state [of the speaker] does not determine the extension." (Putnam equates *extension* with Frege's *Sinn*, or "sense," distinguishing it from *intension*, which he likens to Frege's *Bedeutung*, or "reference".)

For the purpose of the following science-fiction examples, we shall suppose that somewhere in the galaxy there is a planet we shall call Twin Earth. Twin Earth is very much like Earth; in fact, people on Twin Earth even speak *English*. In fact, apart from the differences we shall specify in our science-fiction examples, the reader may suppose that Twin Earth is *exactly* like Earth.[20]

tions, Putnam provides for a quadruple of descriptions. Both fall to Kripke's skeptical arguments about description theories in general.

20. "The Meaning of 'Meaning,'" p. 223.

When Putnam writes the word "*exactly*," his assumption is that our counterparts on Twin Earth are like us in every way—their brains are in the same state; they use the same language, the same words. Nonetheless, they *mean* different things:

> One of the peculiarities of Twin Earth is that the liquid called "water" is not H_2O but a different liquid whose chemical formula is very long and complicated. I shall abbreviate this chemical formula simply as XYZ. I shall suppose that XYZ is indistinguishable from water at normal temperatures and pressures. . . . If a spaceship from Earth ever visits Twin Earth, then the supposition at first will be that "water" has the same meaning on Earth and on Twin Earth. This supposition will be corrected when it is discovered that "water" on Twin Earth is XYZ, and the Earthian spaceship will report somewhat as follows:
>
> "On Twin Earth the meaning of 'water' is XYZ."[21]

21. Ibid.

Putnam ups the ante by rolling back the time of his science-fiction example to 1750. No one on Earth circa 1750 or on Twin Earth circa 1750 knows that water is H_2O or XYZ. Still, Putnam argues, "water" refers to (and, because for Putnam reference is an element of meaning, means) different things.

If Twin Earth is *exactly* like Earth and, hence, the people on Twin Earth are *exactly* like the people on Earth, we and our Twin Earth counterparts are in the same psychological state. Haven't we stipulated that there is no difference? But then what is in our heads (or brains) cannot determine reference because on Earth when we use the word "water" we are referring to H_2O, but on Twin Earth when our counterparts use the word "water," they are referring to something different, namely, XYZ. The *external* world must be taken into account.

Later in the essay, Putnam shifts the discussion to "possible worlds" rather than "science-fiction examples." He sees this as part of his united front with Kripke. But despite Putnam's best intentions, it creates confusion. Kripke goes to great lengths in *Naming and Necessity* to clarify just what he means by a possible world. And he explicitly warns us: a possible world is an idea, not a place. Significantly, it is not a place you travel to in a spaceship:

> In the present monograph [*Naming and Necessity*] I argued against those misuses of the concept that regard possible worlds as something like distant planets, like our own surroundings but somehow existing in a different dimension. . . . I recommended that 'possible state (or history) of the world', or 'counterfactual situation' might be better. One should even remind oneself that the 'worlds' terminology can often be replaced by modal talk—'It is possible that . . .'

He continues a few pages later:

> Certainly the philosopher of 'possible worlds' must take care that his technical apparatus not push him to ask questions whose meaningfulness is not supported by our original intuitions of possibility that gave the apparatus its point.[22]

Putnam tells us that "meanings ain't in the head," but his underlying idea could be better stated as "meanings ain't *just* in the head."[23] Part of the problem in comparing Kripke and Putnam is that they have different theories of meaning and reference. Putnam has one foot in a mental (or linguistic) world and another foot in the real world. Kripke is a monoped. He has one and only one foot. (Like a snail?) For Kripke, natural kind terms like proper names have reference but *no* meaning. Since meanings (that is, anything *inside* the head) cannot secure reference, he finds it easier to banish meanings from his cosmology. The "meaning" of "gold" is the reference of "gold"—that thing out there in the world that is gold. Nothing more.[24] (Like Alice, in *Through the Looking-Glass*, asking

22. Kripke, *Naming and Necessity*, pp. 15, 18.

23. When Putnam types (on his new IBM Selectric) "meanings ain't in the head," it is a kind of Freudian slip. It's as though he is saying "meaning is reference," in keeping with Kripke's *Naming and Necessity*. But he can't quite go there, and so he falls back on his ordered n-tuples.

24. This doctrine has caused endless confusion. Kripke is *not* saying that we do not have *beliefs* about named objects or even beliefs about *names*—only that these beliefs do not entail reference.

Humpty Dumpty, "*Must* a name mean something?") We are *not* visiting another planet—imaginary or otherwise. We are engaged in an inquiry about *necessity* and *possibility*—about the nature of things in *this* world.

PUTNAM: I tried to justify Kripkean language. All this stuff about possible worlds. I thought: A possible world is just a story.[25] I had said, what we count as being the essence of something—and I still would say this—depends on a tradition of scientific investigation. Kripke disagreed: "No, the science is about discovering the essence. You've got it the wrong way around."

Indeed. For Kripke, science is about discovering *essences* (or necessary properties). It seems that Kuhn was too much of an antirealist, while Kripke was too much of a realist for Putnam.

PUTNAM: From the point of view of a microbiologist the essence of tigers is having a certain DNA. The essence for an evolutionary biologist is belonging to a certain population. They might not always agree. Some organism might be a tiger by one definition and not the other.[26] I see human interests as playing a role, but not in a way that implies that we make up the world. Kripke is more metaphysical. But it seems that Kripke's stuff works pretty well if you limit possible worlds to *physically* possible worlds. Once you start trying to ask about *metaphysically* possible worlds, I'm not sure I understand *that*—

Ironically, Putnam's Twin Earth is not *physically* possible. (But not inconceivable or unimaginable. After all, Putnam conceived it and imagined it.) Is there a world where everything is physically the same as ours except that the word "water" refers to XYZ rather than H_2O? No, I think not. The existence of such a world contravenes all the known laws of nature. Remember, Putnam is asking us to leave all but *one* thing unchanged. (Leibniz, the champion of possible worlds, would disapprove.) You can imagine the impossible, or *think* you can imagine the impossible, without it being physically or metaphysically possible.[27]

In *Naming and Necessity*, Kripke writes:

25. I would qualify this. A possible world is a certain *kind* of story. There are stories that are imaginable but not possible.

26. Linnean ideas of taxonomy, based on interbreeding and surface morphology, are being replaced with new ideas based on genomics and molecular biology. The entire idea of species may come into question. I take up these issues in chapter 8, "Avatars of Progress."

27. Confusions about imaginability versus possibility also infect arguments about mind/brain identity. I can imagine philosophical zombies but does that mean they are possible? Leibniz was aware of this. Nicholas Rescher, an authority on Leibniz, writes, "It is a fundamental tenet of Leibniz's philosophy that even omnipotence cannot accomplish the impossible" (*On Leibniz* [2003], p. 69).

28. Kripke, *Naming and Necessity*, p. 123.

Gold apparently has the atomic number 79. Is it a necessary or a contingent property of gold that it has the atomic number 79? Certainly we could find out that we were mistaken. The whole theory of protons, of atomic numbers, the whole theory of molecular structure and of atomic structure, on which such views are based, could *all* turn out to be false. Certainly we didn't know it from time immemorial. So in that sense, gold could turn out not to have atomic number 79. Given that gold *does* have the atomic number 79, could something be gold without having the atomic number 79?[28]

Kripke's answer is no. Our laws of physics (if true) do not allow it. Now, could there be another planet, Twin Earth, in which everything is the same as on Earth except that "water" refers to XYZ? My answer is no. (I believe Kripke would agree.) Given our understanding of science—any science—there can be no Twin Earth.[29]

29. My reading of Putnam is informed by my understanding of Kripke's arguments about essentialism. Some might argue that Putnam is simply providing an example of how homophones in different languages can refer to distinct kinds, even kinds that are qualitatively identical. For me, the idea of qualitatively identical yet distinct kinds itself causes problems. If water can't be XYZ, I don't see how a qualitatively identical substance indistinguishable from water could be, either. Such a substance would either be water or it wouldn't be qualitatively identical to water. My thanks to Barry Lam for bringing this to my attention.

Why is this important? If possibility is merely imaginability (or conceivability), then everything is possible. Merely imagining a world and then deducing something about the *real* world would be a cheat. If there is *no* possible world in which gold has an atomic number other than 79, then I have asserted something about the nature of gold. And something about our world. (One of the things for which Kripke is justly famous is the idea that there is *a posteriori* necessity—that we can learn from experience that some things are necessary.) If we say (it is true) that gold has an atomic number 78, then it's platinum and *not* gold. If we say (it is true) that gold has an atomic number 80, then it's lead. We can't just redefine the word "gold." We have to revise our entire understanding of the physical universe. I could imagine myriad Twin Earths where everything is the same as it is on Earth except for one salient detail. Take your pick. But imagining something does not make it true or even possible—or else we might all live in a Ptolemaic universe.[30] As in the exchange between Owen Glendower and Hotspur in *Henry IV, Part One*.

30. The Ptolemaic universe is clearly imaginable—Ptolemy, for one, imagined it. But is it possible? Is it possible that *this* universe is a geocentric universe?

GLENDOWER: I can call spirits from the vasty deep.
HOTSPUR: Why, so can I, or so can any man;
    But will they come when you do call for them?

       Chapter 4

GLENDOWER: Why, I can teach you, cousin to command
    The devil.
HOTSPUR: And I can teach thee, coz, to shame the devil
    By telling truth: tell truth and shame the devil.

Our conversation turned back to translation.

MORRIS: These ideas about language and about translation must go
    back to your father—
PUTNAM: My father's translation of *Quixote* is quite different from
    anything that came before, whereas the ones that followed my
    father's are very similar.

31. The discussion, on the journal's blog, lists as an example ways Flaubert's phrase *bouffées d'affadissement* has been translated: "gusts of revulsion / a kind of rancid staleness / stale gusts of dreariness / waves of nausea / fumes of nausea / flavorless, sickening gusts / stagnant dreariness / whiffs of sickliness / waves of nauseous disgust."
Davis, "Why a New *Madame Bovary*?" See also Davis's article on translating Proust, "Loaf or Hot-Water Bottle" (2004), an essay on the extraordinary malleability and ductility of language—how words, in and of themselves, lead us into a labyrinthine world of associations.

MORRIS: I'm friends with—we were in the same class at the Putney School years ago—Lydia Davis, who has become a prominent writer and translator. She recently translated *Madame Bovary*. And there is a discussion in the *Paris Review* about the difficulties of translating various phrases from Flaubert's French into English.[31] There's this belief that even when you can't find a *precise* analogue, you can talk about the imprecision quite precisely. You can explain why a certain phrase is inadequate in certain ways; what you wish you could do with it, why you think you don't quite do justice to it. This also may be true of scientific terms.

PUTNAM: I'd like to go back to Kuhn on that for a minute. This is relevant to what's wrong with Kuhn's argument about incommensurability. Any realist has a move available that Kuhn doesn't allow, because he doesn't allow that there's a real world. In fact, Kuhn *denies* explicitly that there's a real world. Worlds change. He's some kind of an idealist. Once you have the notion of a *real* world, the question isn't in saying what Newton was referring to. It's not necessary to find an expression in the language of our physics which has the *same sense* as Newton's expression. Maybe that's impossible. But we can give an idea of what the sense of a word is in a language other than ours by giving examples of its use.

That's one reason we adopt words from another language, like *flair* from French. Sometimes we evolve, and sometimes we partly change their meanings. Like, in English, someone's *allure* is positive. But that's only one of many uses in French. In French, the way someone walks is their *allure*. We've taken just one use. We didn't have any short way of doing what we do by using the foreign word *allure*, or *flair*, or *sangfroid*. There are words in kindred, Western European languages, like French, which don't have any word with exactly the same sense in English.

When you're talking to physical scientists, the question is whether you have a word with the same reference. Some philosophers have argued that the Newtonian term "mass" is ambiguous, that we should now say in some contexts of classical physics it refers to "*rest* mass," and in other contexts it refers to "*relativistic* mass." Well, even if that were *right*, you could still say in any given context what it refers to, or you can say that it's ambiguous between these two. So the question of whether there's a sense-preserving transfer—

MORRIS: That's not to say that they're incommensurable—

PUTNAM: The word "incommensurable" fudges the question. Is Kuhn saying that there's a term whose *reference* can't be stated in this vocabulary, or is he saying that there's a term in this vocabulary such that no term in a second vocabulary has exactly the same *sense*? The second is more plausible but has no metaphysical consequences. What Kuhn *needs* is the incommensurability of reference, but he can't state an argument for the incommensurability of reference, because he's not willing to accept there is such a thing as reference.

———

Putnam is aware of the differences between conceivability, imaginability, and possibility. And also aware that there is no *possible* world in which water is XYZ. He writes as such in "The Meaning of 'Meaning.'"[32] But he has stated that it makes no difference to his argument whether Twin Earth is possible or not.[33] I disagree. I retain the nagging suspicion that the argument is circular. If you want to assert that meanings are not *just* in the head, construct a counterexample where that is the case. By constructing an imaginary but impossible world in which the word "water" refers to XYZ—even if we don't know it—we have not addressed the fundamental question of how we *refer* to things. What is the relation between words and things? Kripke and Putnam, and Bertrand Russell before them, wrote about knowledge by acquaintance. We are *acquainted* with water. And we have learned that water is H_2O. Kripke is not asking us whether water could be something other than H_2O. He is asking, if "water is H_2O" is *true*, is it then *necessarily* true? He secures reference through essential properties (essences established by science) rather than descriptions. As Kripke writes, "Certainly 'cow' and 'tiger' are *not* short for the conjunction of properties a dictionary would take to define them, as Mill thought. Whether science can discover empirically that certain properties are *necessary* of cows, or of tigers, is another question, which I answer affirmatively."[34]

32. Kuhn criticized the Twin Earth example for this very reason, and in this instance I agree with him. See Kuhn, "Dubbing and Redubbing," pp. 309–10. But Kuhn is under the impression that by criticizing Putnam he has refuted Kripke. He deals with Kripke (if he deals with him at all) by lumping him together with Putnam. He is not alone in this regard, but Putnam and Kripke's views are substantially different. Charles Silver writes about this in *The Futility of Consciousness*: "However interesting it may be to imagine Twin Earth, it can't possibly exist and is therefore unusable as an example of anything." In Kripkean language, there is *no* possible world in which everything is the same as on Earth except that H_2O is XYZ. Just as there is no possible world in which $\sqrt{2}$ can be expressed as the ratio of two whole numbers. If it is true that $\sqrt{2}$ is incommensurable, then it is necessarily true and, hence, true in *all* possible worlds.

33. From Putnam's 2011 Schock Prize essay: "It is irrelevant that there is no such (possible) compound XYZ, because we can imagine that neither Oscar nor Twin Oscar know this esoteric fact. (Indeed, I am not sure I myself *know* such a thing, unless having been told that this is so by a former chemist-turned-philosopher-of-science counts as 'knowing.') The question is what we would say under perfectly imaginable circumstances, not what is chemically or physically possible." "The Development of Externalist Semantics," p. 209.

34. Kripke, *Naming and Necessity*, p. 128.

For me, it is better to criticize Kripke on his own terms than to construct examples (or counterexamples) that do not apply—even when the arguments seemingly support Kripke's views. Kripke's examples are designed to tease out certain intuitions about what reference can accomplish. We want to grab ahold of and, eventually, determine the essence of things. We want to make reference absolutely secure. Kripke, in effect, is telling us that he wants to make reference theory-independent.

The well-informed student of Kuhn's writings may object at this point. I see his hand raised at the back of the class. (Oh, if only he had spoken sooner.) "Putnam is only objecting to the *early* Kuhn," the student says. "In his later writings, Kuhn modified his position." Granted, the multiple worlds of Kuhn's first edition were modified in the postscript to the second edition—"participants in a communications breakdown can . . . recognize each other as members of different language communities and then become translators."[35] And yet, Kuhn never really gave up on multiple worlds or on a socially constructed reality. As recently as 1989, seven years before his death, he wrote:

> Students of literature have long taken for granted that metaphor and its companion devices (those which alter the interrelations among words) provide entree to new worlds and make translation impossible by doing so. . . . But the natural sciences, dealing objectively with the real world (as they do), are generally held to be immune. Their truths (and falsities) are thought to transcend the ravages of temporal, cultural, and linguistic change. I am suggesting, of course, that they cannot do so.[36]

———

I had been surprised to learn that Hilary Putnam's father translated *Don Quixote*. I looked up the name "Putnam, Hilary" in the index. Hilary Putnam is referenced in endnote 2 to book 2, chapter 51—a note that refers also to Bertrand Russell and Alfred North Whitehead. The note concerns Sancho Panza's attempts to resolve the liar paradox.[37] Here is a simple version of the liar paradox: "This statement is false." If it is true, it is false, and if it's false, it is true. And here is Sancho Panza's restatement of the paradox: There is a

35. Kuhn, *Structure* (1970), p. 202.

36. Kuhn, *Road since Structure*, p. 75.
37. Samuel Putnam's note (in Cervantes, *Don Quixote*, pp. 1, 207–8) reads, "This paradox is a very old one going back to the ancient Greek logicians. (Compare the story of the King of the Crocodiles, the Epimenides Paradox, etc.) See the discussion by Bertrand Russell and Alfred North Whitehead, *Principia Mathematica*, Vol. I, p. 61. The Theory of Logical Types invented by Russell represents the first means of circumventing all the known paradoxes within a completely formalized logical system. Other methods have been proposed, and a good deal of investigation of this subject has been made by modern mathematical logicians. (For this note: I am indebted to my son, Hilary Whitehall Putnam.)"

Chapter 4

large river separating two districts. A bridge spans the river. At one end of the bridge there is a gallows and a court of justice where four judges enforce the following law: anyone who crosses the bridge shall swear an oath as to where he is going and why. "If he swears to the truth, he shall be permitted to pass; but if he tells a falsehood, he shall die. . . . And then it happened that one day, when they came to administer the oath to a certain man, he swore and affirmed that his destination was to die upon the gallows . . . and that he had no other purpose in view." The judges have a problem. "This man swore that he was going to die upon the gallows, and if he does, he swore to the truth and the law says he should be freed and permitted to cross the bridge; but if they do not hang him, he swore falsely and according to the same law ought to be hanged."[38]

Sancho provides several bizarre solutions to the conundrum. Let the part of the man that swore to the truth pass unharmed; hang the part of the man that lied. But, he is cautioned, if the man were divided in such a fashion, he would die, and the law still would not be upheld. Sancho then comes up with a powerful solution to the liar paradox. When given a choice, always pick the humane one. Decide on the bases of compassion, kindness, and charity. "This man you speak of deserves to die as much as he deserves to live. . . . [S]ince there is as much reason for acquitting as for condemning him, they ought to let him go free, as it is always more praiseworthy to do good than to do harm."[39] QED.

Hilary Putnam claimed that his father had produced the authoritative translation of the *Quixote*. I wondered whether Andrew Hurley in his translation of Borges's "Menard" had *retranslated* Cervantes's passage into English from the *original* Spanish, or had used an existing translation. I didn't have to look far. I compared the Hurley translation to Samuel Putnam's translation. They were identical—word-for-word.

I called Hurley in May 2013 hoping for some additional insight.

ANDREW HURLEY: I always tried to use the canonical translation—the translation that everybody would have known at the time—a translation at the time of Borges or before. And at that time the Putnam translation was absolutely canonical.

ERROL MORRIS: Why would you call it "canonical"?

38. *Don Quixote*, pp. 996–98.

39. *Don Quixote*, p. 998. Another version of the liar's paradox is presented in Lewis Carroll's example of the Crocodilus. This tragic story runs as follows:

> A Crocodile had stolen a Baby off the banks of the Nile. The Mother implored him to restore her darling. "Well," said the Crocodile, "if you say truly what I shall do, I will restore it: if not, I will devour it."
>
> "You will devour it!" cried the distracted Mother.
>
> "Now," said the wily Crocodile, "I *cannot* restore your Baby: for, if I do, I shall make you speak *falsely*: and I warned you that, if you spoke *falsely*, I would *devour* it."
>
> "On the contrary," said the yet wilier Mother, "you cannot *devour* my Baby: for, if you do, you will make me speak *truly*, and you promised me that, if I spoke *truly*, you would *restore* it!" (We assume, of course, that he was a Crocodile of his word; and that his sense of honour outweighed his love of Babies.)

W. W. Bartley III, "Lewis Carroll's Lost Book on Logic," pp. 42–43.

HURLEY: It was the universal acceptance of the translation that makes it canonical. "Menard" appeared in the late '30s [1939]. Generally speaking, with all the classics, there's going to be a translation that everybody knows. You want to use that. But the translation has to come before the time of the story, because if it comes after the time of the story, then that blows your authenticity. It can't be newer than the time the story is set, or the time the text is set.

MORRIS: There is the additional difficulty with Borges of translating somebody who's so acutely aware of translation. I'll give you an example. In the Borges review of *Citizen Kane*, he quotes Chesterton, and I went back and looked at the Chesterton text. But the Chesterton was different from, at least, the translation of Borges that I was reading. The quote was from a Father Brown mystery, "The Head of Caesar." Chesterton's text (in English) is "What we all dread most . . . is a maze with *no* center," but I prefer the English translation from Borges's review: "There is nothing more frightening than a *labyrinth* that has no center."

HURLEY: That does sound like a translation, unless the translator was trying to say "labyrinth" because Borges is known for his labyrinths. But in my mind, there's absolutely no difference between a "labyrinth" and a "maze."

MORRIS: The words mean different things to me. I have such different associations with them. With "maze" I see a massive hedge, a lot of privet or boxwood. With "labyrinth" I see one of the early tombs—the hypogeum on Malta. In the shadows the Minotaur is waiting for me.

HURLEY: Sure, sure. But Chesterton must have known what he was doing when he wrote "maze" instead of "labyrinth." When he says it has no center— He was a good Catholic boy. He would have wanted something to *fear*.

MORRIS: Probably death. I wanted to ask you about *your* interpretation of "Menard." Do you think that Borges saw himself as Cervantes or Menard?

HURLEY: Borges was always "both/and." He was never "either/or." I feel that in his style, in his sentences, in his themes, in his motifs, in virtually everything you can imagine or think about or grasp in Borges, there is a doubleness, or sometimes a triple-

ness. Borges just won't choose one. It's a world of philosophical conundrums rather than philosophical answers. And on and on and on. He liked to be modern, and he liked to be ancient. He delighted in thwarting expectations of himself. Texts are variable. Even books are infinitely changeable. He had a nightmare when he was a child, that when you close the pages of a book at night, the letters would get all mixed up. That's the way Borges feels about literature, that literature is constantly getting all mixed up.

MORRIS: Borges is writing stories about the mutability of language. But you believe in the possibility of translation, no?

HURLEY: Yes. I don't think that translation ever becomes perfect, because I don't think anybody's a perfect reader and I don't think that two languages are ever congruent at every point. What that means is that even if you were the perfect reader, the language would resist you, or human experience would resist you. There are things in one culture that can't quite be experienced in another culture. I would always give my students the example of body parts. The body is just cut into different parts in Spanish than in English. In Spanish, they talk about *la boca de l'astomaco*, "the mouth of the stomach," as though that were a thing. And we don't talk about that in English—that's not a concept for us.

I had to learn that concept. There's another part of the body called the *batapa*, the "sweet potato." Any idea what that is?

MORRIS: No.

HURLEY: *I* didn't know. It's the muscle on the back of your lower leg. Sometimes human experience itself resists you as a translator. But I believe in translation—of course I do. And I think that the more translations there are of these wonderful texts, the closer you get to maybe what that text is.

My researcher suddenly appeared with the Spanish text of Borges's review. Borges had used the word *laberinto*.[40]

MORRIS: I have the Spanish in front of me. He used *laberinto*.

HURLEY: Borges did?

MORRIS: Yes. So I guess he's the culprit.

HURLEY: No, no. In Spanish *laberinto* is the word for both maze *and* labyrinth.

MORRIS: Ah, so it's my idiocy.

HURLEY: No, it's not your idiocy. It's just the case that if you want to say "maze" in Spanish, you have to say *laberinto*. Spanish doesn't have the same register, or as many currents of influence, as English does. English might have three words that are kind of synonyms, but they've come from different language groups. Spanish will have one.

———

Hilary Putnam's family lived in Paris. His father knew everyone—"The story of those years is told in my father's autobiography *Paris Was Our Mistress* in which I figure mainly as 'the baby': e.g., Ford Maddox Ford pushed my baby carriage, Pirandello came to our house in Fontenay-aux-Roses 'to see the baby' (I am told that I sat on Pirandello's lap), and so on."[41]

It is an extraordinary chronicle of a deracinated past. Samuel Putnam writes,"Perhaps the greatest discovery I have made on this other continent is that I am, when all is said, an American, hopelessly, irretrievably an American and by no means sorry for it." The family returned to America in 1933 in the depths of the Depression. "We had started on our ramblings with a baby and a dozen bags

40. "En uno de los cuentos de Chesterton—*The Head of Caesar*, creo—el héroe observa que nada es tan aterrador como un laberinto sin centro. Este film es exactamente ese laberinto." Borges, "Un Film Abrumador" (1941), p. 88.

41. Putnam, "Intellectual Autobiography," in *Philosophy of Hilary Putnam*, p. 5.

of diapers. We had returned without the diapers but with a very frightened small boy who was bravely terrified by the rush and roar of New York's canyoned streets."[42] Hilary Putnam's first words in America—he was six months old when they left for France and seven years old when they returned—were memorialized by his father—" 'Écoute, mon vieux,' he said to me, 'qu'est-ce qu'il y a de cassé?' " Here is his father's translation—" 'Listen, old man, what the hell's the matter?' I could not tell him precisely what there was that was '*cassé*,' but he was to find out soon enough for himself."[43]

42. Samuel Putnam, *Paris Was Our Mistress* (1947), pp. 247, 251.
43. Ibid., p. 251. A similar account appears in Hilary Putnam's "Intellectual Autobiography": "I was born on July 31, 1926, and about six months later my father, equipped with an advance from the publisher Pat Covici, and a contract to translate 'all the extant works of François Rabelais,' took me and my mother to France. My earliest memories are of my childhood in France, and my first language was French. Originally we lived in Montparnasse, then in Fontenay-aux-Roses, a suburb of Paris, and finally in a beautiful village called Mirmande, near Valence, from which one can see the Rhone Alps, where I went to the one-room schoolhouse for first grade. In 1933 we returned to the United States. I didn't know a word of English when we arrived; according to my father, what I said, as a little boy from the French countryside seeing the New York skyline from the boat, was 'écoute mon vieux, quesque à cassée?' " (p. 5).

Morghen inc.

Ippaso

Illustre Filosofo

Nacque in Metaponto Città della Mag.ª Grecia

Fiorì probabilmente nell'Olimpiade 70

In Napoli presso Nicola Gervasi al Gigante N. 23

5. REVOLUTIONS, REAL AND IMAGINED

When any two things relate like two numbers, they are themselves concealed numbers.
—Hasse and Scholz, "The Foundation
Crisis of Greek Mathematics"

Just what are scientific revolutions? And how are they related to incommensurability? Presumably, a scientific revolution involves things (or the arrangement of things) in our heads. But of course, Kuhn tells us that scientific revolutions involve much more than just a change in ideas, much more than even a radical change in ideas— for Kuhn, many scientific concepts before and after a revolution are incommensurable.

Incommensurable. A strange word. According to the *Oxford English Dictionary*, it means "having no common measure."[1] But like the definition of masturbation as "self-abuse," it doesn't explain much. It just deepens the sense of puzzlement about what the word might mean.

I wondered, *why* did Kuhn choose it? What was the attraction? What did it mean *to him*? By examining it further could I learn something about both revolutions and about incommensurability— and about Kuhn?

Here's one clue. At the end of *Road since Structure*, a compendium of Kuhn's essays published after his death, there is an interview with three philosophers of science, Aristides Baltas, Kostas Gavroglu, and Vassiliki Kindi, in which Kuhn provides a brief account of the historical origins of his idea:

THOMAS KUHN: Look, "incommensurability" is easy.

VASSILIKI KINDI: You mean in mathematics?

KUHN: . . . When I was a bright high school mathematician and beginning to learn Calculus, somebody gave me—or maybe I

1. The *OED* online quotes *A Letter from the Right Honourable Edmund Burke to a Noble Lord, On the Attacks Made upon Him and His Pension, in the House of Lords, by the Duke of Bedford and the Earl of Lauderdale, Early in the Present Sessions of Parliament* (London: J. Owen, 1796), p. 9:

> I challenge the Duke of Bedford as a juror to pass upon the value of my services. Whatever his natural parts may be, I cannot recognize in his few and idle years the competence to judge of my long and laborious life. . . . His Grace thinks I have obtained too much. I answer, that my exertions, whatever they have been, were such as no hopes of pecuniary reward could possibly excite; and no pecuniary compensation can possibly reward them. Between money and such services, if done by abler men than I am, there is no common principle of comparison: they are quantities *incommensurable*.

I find myself entirely sympathetic with Burke's complaint.

asked for it because I'd heard about it—there was sort of a big two-volume Calculus book by, I can't remember whom. And then I never really read it. I read the early parts of it. And early on it gives the proof of the irrationality of √2. And I thought it was beautiful. That was terribly exciting, and I learned what incommensurability was then and there. So, it was all ready for me, I mean, it was a metaphor but it got at nicely what I was after. So, that's where I got it.[2]

"It was all ready for me." I thought, "Wow." The language was suggestive. I imagined √2 provocatively dressed, its lips rouged. But here was an unexpected surprise. The idea didn't come from the physical sciences or philosophy or linguistics, but from *mathematics*— the proof that √2 cannot be expressed as the ratio of two integers. "It was a metaphor but it got at nicely what I was after."

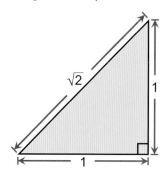

In mathematics, "incommensurability" expresses the fact that not every distance can be measured with whole numbers or fractions of whole numbers.[3] Take an isosceles right triangle, 1 by 1. How long is the hypotenuse? By the Pythagorean theorem, if each side has a length of 1, then the hypotenuse has a length of √2. (The sum of the squares of the sides equals the square of the hypotenuse.) Can that length be expressed as a fraction or as a ratio of two integers, e.g., 99/70 or 577/408? The answer is no.[4]

The proof—along with the proof that there is no largest prime number—is a crowning achievement of Greek mathematics. It established that there are quantities that cannot be expressed as ratios of whole numbers (that is, as rational fractions).[5] As Hamlet says, "There are more things in heaven and earth, Horatio, than are dreamt of in your philosophy."

2. Kuhn, *Road since Structure*, p. 298.

3. John Burgess, a professor of philosophy at Princeton, urges caution—the need to avoid anachronism. "The Greeks don't recognize the ratio of the diagonal to the side as a number," he wrote to me. "Indeed, they don't even recognize it as a ratio. They consider it only in connection with proportionality. So what for us becomes the irrationality of √2 is expressed by saying that there are no (whole) numbers M and N such that the diagonal is to the side as M is to N. Our way of speaking comes in, so far as I know, with Omar Khayyam." Email to author, June 3, 2015.

4. Although √2 cannot be expressed as a fraction or as a ratio of two integers, it easily can be represented geometrically, e.g., as a distance on a line.

5. Those who are familiar with the proof certainly don't want me to explain it here; nor do those who are unfamiliar with it. There are simple proofs in many histories of mathematics—by E. T. Bell, Thomas L. Heath, Morris Kline, et al. My favorite (Brian Clegg, "The Dangerous Ratio"), on the website of the NRICH Project of Cambridge University, includes this narrative:

Imagine a simple square shape, each side 1 unit in length. How long is the square's diagonal?

This seemingly harmless question was the trigger for the Pythagoreans' disturbing discovery. The length of the square's diagonal is easy to work out. It forms the long side of a triangle with a right angle opposite, and two other sides of length 1 unit. Thanks to Pythagoras' theorem we (and the Greeks) know that we can work out the square of the length of the longest side of a right-angled triangle by adding together the squares of the other two sides. So we know the

As mathematics developed through the centuries, the bestiary of numbers (and other mathematical entities) has grown and grown. Today, we have irrational numbers, imaginary numbers, complex numbers, transfinite numbers, and surreal numbers, to name a few. But we are not losing our capacity to understand earlier notions, merely expanding our notion of what is possible.[6]

Kuhn had told Baltas, Gavroglu, and Kindi that incommensurability was a "metaphor." But a metaphor for *what*?[7] I thought, since *mathematical* incommensurability doesn't seem to capture what Kuhn was looking for, namely incommensurable *meanings*, perhaps I should look for an answer in the history of the proof he mentions. Perhaps the history of the term's use in mathematics could shed some light on its use in *Structure*.

There are many modern accounts.[8] Most of them involve a murder. Hippasus, a Pythagorean, comes up with or reveals the proof that √2 cannot be expressed as a fraction of whole numbers. The Pythagoreans kill him. Ostensibly a story of revolution, it fits neatly into the Kuhnian scheme of things. You have *normal* mathematics—the Pythagorean paradigm. In this paradigm, everything can be measured with whole numbers or ratios of whole numbers.

diagonal's length squared is $(1 \times 1) + (1 \times 1) = 2$, making the length of the diagonal itself √2. The number which when multiplied by itself makes 2. But what is that number?

The square root of 2 isn't 1 because 1×1 is 1. And it isn't 2, because 2×2 is 4. It's something in between.

This wasn't a problem for the Pythagoreans. It was obviously a ratio of two whole numbers. They only had to figure out what that ratio was. At least that was the theory.

But after more and more frantic attempts, a horrible discovery was made. There is NO ratio that will produce √2—it simply can't be done. It's what we now call an irrational number, not because it is illogical, but because it can't be represented as a ratio of whole numbers. . . .

As Hippasus discovered to his cost, that inscription over the Pythagorean school *All is number* would have to be extended to cope with more complex ideas than ratios of whole numbers.

6. Gabriel García Márquez remarked upon reading the first line of Kafka's *Metamorphosis*: "I didn't know anyone was *allowed* to write things like that." García Márquez, "The Art of Fiction No. 69," p. 51 (my emphasis).

7. "Most readers of my text have supposed that when I spoke of theories as incommensurable, I meant that they could not be compared. But 'incommensurability' is a term borrowed from mathematics, and there it has no such implication. The hypotenuse of an isosceles right triangle is incommensurable with its side, but the two can be compared to any required degree of precision." Kuhn, *Road since Structure*, p. 189. Kuhn wants it both ways. Either two things can be compared, or they cannot. If they can't be *translated*, then they can't be compared. If they can be *compared,* then they can be translated.

8. See, e.g., Arthur Koestler, *The Sleepwalkers*, (1959), pp. 40f; Charles Seife, *Zero* (2000); David Berlinski, *Infinite Ascent* (2008), pp. 9–10. Alberto A. Martínez, in *The Cult of Pythagoras* (2012), attributes modern versions of the myth primarily to Kurt von Fritz, but also to John Burnet, who writes in the second edition of his *Early Greek Philosophy* (1908), "Our tradition says

that Hippasos of Metapontium was drowned at sea for revealing this skeleton in the cupboard," and, in a footnote, calls Hippasus the *enfant terrible* of Pythagoreanism (p. 117). In Martínez's words, "One free association easily leads to another and guesswork gets sold as history" (p. 81).

An *anomaly* appears—the inability to find a ratio of whole numbers that measures the diagonal of a unit-square. This is followed by a mathematical proof that shows, irrefutably, there is *no* such ratio. Big trouble. The Pythagoreans reject the proof and take an oath to keep it secret because it undermines their philosophy. Hippasus violates the oath, reveals the secret, and as a punishment or an act of vengeance (or an attempt to silence him) is drowned. But it's no use. A *revolution* follows. There is a *paradigm shift* to a new paradigm that allows for irrational numbers.

There is no indication that Kuhn had these events in mind when he adopted the term "incommensurable." The story is so well known that it is hard to believe he wasn't aware of it, but he doesn't mention the legend. Just the mathematical proof. But the history of the proof—or rather the metahistory of the proof, the story of how the history of the proof has been repeatedly revised and rewritten—provides a clue, an insight into what kind of metaphor it might be.

———

The investigation of ancient Greek mathematics is daunting. The historian confronts a constellation of problems—the paucity and sometimes complete absence of evidence; endless exegetical disagreements; biased and unreliable accounts; the general problem of who did what, when, and where. And, of course, the perishability of evidence—crucial documents were often written on papyrus that decayed rapidly and had to be frequently (and not always reliably) copied. Other documents were lost. Many were destroyed—accidentally or on purpose. How much historical evidence disappeared in the burning or burnings of the great library at Alexandria?

A history of irrational numbers is a mathematical detective story. Was Hippasus murdered? If so, why? And if he (or someone else) wasn't murdered for the disclosure of incommensurability, when and where did the legend come from? What is the evidence for the crime and punishment?

Rummaging about for articles on the subject, I came across this from Kurt von Fritz:

> The discovery of incommensurability is one of the most amazing and far-reaching accomplishments of early Greek mathematics. . . .

[T]he tradition concerning the first discovery itself has been preserved only in the works of very late authors, and is frequently connected with stories of obviously legendary character. But the tradition is *unanimous* in attributing the discovery to a Pythagorean philosopher by the name of Hippasus of Metapontum.[9]

9. Von Fritz, "The Discovery of Incommensurability by Hippasus of Metapontum" (1945), pp. 242, 244–45 (emphasis mine).

Unanimous? In a footnote, Von Fritz indicates that the tradition isn't unanimous. Stories of obviously legendary character? Does this mean they never happened? Very late authors? Von Fritz tells us that almost all of what we know about Hippasus derives from Iamblichus of Chalcis (ca. 245–325 CE), an Assyrian neo-Platonist who lived eight hundred years after Hippasus. Late, indeed.

I decided to dig deeper.

It involved a trip to the stacks in Harvard's Widener Library. (The Widener is one good reason to live in Cambridge, Massachusetts—that is, if you can get permission to use it. Fortunately, I have been given faculty borrowing privileges by the Mahindra Humanities Center, Homi Bhabha, and the Harvard History

10. Here are three passages from Iamblichus, as translated in David R. Fideler, ed., *The Pythagorean Sourcebook and Library*:

> As to Hippasus, however, they acknowledge that he was one of the Pythagoreans, but that he met the doom of the impious in the sea in consequence of having divulged and explained the method of forming a sphere from twelve pentagons; but nevertheless he [unjustly] obtained the renown of having made the discovery. (p. 79)

> It is accordingly reported that he who first divulged the theory of commensurable and incommensurable quantities to those unworthy to receive it, was by the Pythagoreans so hated that they not only expelled him from their common association, and from living with him, but also for him constructed a [symbolic] tomb, as for one who had migrated from the human into another life. (p. 116)

> It is also reported that the Divine Power was so indignant with him who divulged the teachings of Pythagoras that he perished at sea, as an impious person who divulged the method of inscribing in a sphere the dodecahedron, one of the so-called solid figures, the composition of the *icostagonus*. But according to others, this is what happened to him who revealed the doctrine of irrational and incommensurable quantities. (p. 116)

11. David Fowler, *The Mathematics of Plato's Academy*, p. 296.

12. Thomas L. Heath writes, "Another argument is based on the passage in the *Laws* where the Athenian stranger speaks of the shameful ignorance of the generality of Greeks, who are not aware that it is not all geometrical magnitudes that are commensurable with one another; the speaker adds that it was only 'late' (ὀψέ ποτε) that he himself learnt the truth. Even if we knew for certain whether 'late' means 'late in the day' or 'late in life,' the expression would not help much towards determining the date of the first discovery of the irrationality of √2; for the language of the passage is that of rhetorical exaggeration (Plato speaks of men who are unacquainted with the existence

Department.) I took the elevator down to floor D, then a tunnel and another elevator down to Pusey 3. Looking for the call number, WID-LC B243.I2613 1986, I stopped. Turned down an aisle to see an older man—possibly in his seventies—walking toward me from the other end of the aisle. The gap closed between us. I bent down to reach for a book—Iamblichus's *Life of Pythagoras*. As he passed me, he muttered, "Be careful. Iamblichus is not to be trusted."

I should have stopped him and gotten his name. I didn't. But it turns out he was right. (Perhaps he had been lingering in the stacks, hoping to warn some naïve writer, such as myself, of the dangers of taking Iamblichus too much to heart.) There are several passages in Iamblichus that deal with Hippasus of Metapontum, and they provide not *one* story but a series of contradictory and overlapping accounts. A roundelay of confusion. The *Rashomon* of incommensurability.[10]

I turned to another account of the discovery of incommensurability—from Pappus of Alexandria, who had produced a series of commentaries (about a century *after* Iamblichus) on the books of Euclid. In this account, there is no Hippasus. An unidentified "soul" has spread the proof "among the common herd" and is condemned by the Pythagoreans and "the Athenian Stranger" to a crepuscular world hovering between existence and non-existence, between past and future:

> The soul which by error or heedlessness discovers or reveals anything of this nature which is in it or in this world, wanders (thereafter) hither and thither on the sea of non-identity (i.e., lacking all similarity of quality or accident), immersed in the stream of the coming-to-be and the passing-away, where there is no standard of measurement. This was the consideration which Pythagoreans and the Athenian Stranger held to be an incentive to particular care and concern for these things and to imply of necessity the grossest foolishness in him who imagined these things to be of no account.[11]

And who is this Athenian Stranger, who also makes an appearance in Plato's dialogue *Laws*?[12] Some commentators liken the Athenian Stranger to Socrates, but no one really knows.[13] And why would Socrates—forthcoming in so many of Plato's dialogues—be disguised here? (The *Laws* and the *Epinomis*—the Extra Laws—are the only dialogues in which Socrates does not appear.)

———

Walter Burkert, who died in 2015, wrote a seminal book on early mathematics, *Lore and Science in Ancient Pythagoreanism.* I called him in 2011 when he was an emeritus professor at the University of Zurich. Perhaps he could set me straight about Hippasus—help me to separate the real from the apocryphal, to find a thread through the labyrinth of Greek mathematics.

ERROL MORRIS: The people you can talk about this with are few and far between.

WALTER BURKERT: [*Laughs.*] Yes. So what is your special idea about Hippasus?

MORRIS: Well, I don't know if it's a special idea, but I was interested in tracking down the source of the legend about the incommensurability of the square root of two, particularly the drowning of Hippasus by the Pythagoreans.

BURKERT: Yeah. This drowning has been taken up by the neo-Platonists, and it fits very well within the neo-Platonist system. But it makes me a little suspicious.

of the irrational as more comparable to swine than to human beings)." *A History of Greek Mathematics,* vol. 1, p. 156. How could two stories be more different? In 500 BCE, Hippasus is drowned because he reveals a secret that no one outside the Pythagorean cult should know. In 350 BCE, Plato is bent out of shape because not every Greek is familiar with the concept of irrational numbers.

13. Leo Strauss, *The Argument and the Action of Plato's Laws* (1983), p. 2; W. H. F. Altman, "A Tale of Two Drinking Parties: Plato's *Laws* in Context," (2010).

MORRIS: A little suspicious?

BURKERT: Yes. It fits a little *too* well. They have a kind of dualistic system. There is the One, there is God, there is number. And then there is indistinctness. The discovery that you cannot express the square root of two with numbers—you have indistinctness against number. It can be seen as the epitome of this neo-Platonic system.

MORRIS: The first question is about when and where the myth originated: whether it emerged much later than Hippasus, and if so, who originated it?

BURKERT: It's difficult, first of all, to make people understand what irrationality in numbers means. Who cares if you have a decimal system? Who cares whether a third is an *indefinite* number—.3333333333 . . .? Or whether this is a sequence in which the next number can never be uncertain? So this basic difference between 0.333 . . . and the square root of two is difficult to make understood to a modern public. Usually people do not like mathematics so very much.

MORRIS: That may well be true.

BURKERT: I remember when I first realized this problem of a square root versus normal division.

MORRIS: How old were you?

BURKERT: Well, I would say about thirteen or fourteen.

MORRIS: And what did you make of it at the time?

BURKERT: I simply realized that this was different. It seems to have been truly a discovery of *Greek* mathematics. There is no evidence of this in Babylonian mathematics—in contrast to the theory of Pythagoras, which was well known in cuneiform mathematics. But then we have this story which *may* go back to Aristotle. And if this really is a historical tradition, then how does Hippasus fit in? That's never been clear.

MORRIS: But if the Pythagoreans killed Hippasus—assuming that they did—*why* did they kill him? Did they kill him because they didn't understand the proof, but felt threatened by it? Did they kill him because they understood the proof *and* felt threatened by it? Did they kill him because Hippasus had divulged a secret? Betrayed an oath?

BURKERT: Then there is always another possibility—that he was drowned, and that it was an accident rather than an execution.

MORRIS: An accident? But doesn't that miss the point? Don't we *need* to kill Hippasus? Isn't that part of the legend? If he dies inadvertently, where's the storyline?

BURKERT: But we know so desperately little about the Pythagoreans. And about Hippasus. Even since I wrote that book [*Lore and Science in Ancient Pythagoreanism*, first published in German in 1962], I don't think any new evidence has come up. No inscription which brings us to safe ground. There is a similar problem with Socrates, but with Socrates we have the texts of his immediate pupils—Plato and Xenophon. But we have no writing of any immediate pupil of Pythagoras. It is a desperate historical situation.

MORRIS: Desperate?

BURKERT: Oh, yes. We have so very little historical information.

MORRIS: And yet this legend of Hippasus has become popular over the years. People tell it, retell it, again and again. Why?

BURKERT: Because legends *are* nice. Instead of thinking, what is irrationality, we can think about the legend. But we should remember legends are absolutely independent from fact.

Here are Burkert's thoughts in a nutshell. Very little is known about either Hippasus or Pythagoras. The historical record is not just incomplete; it is virtually nonexistent. There are no surviving documents. Nothing that Pythagoras or Hippasus wrote is extant. They are known only through the writings of others. The details are sketchy. Hippasus may or may not have been drowned. Pythagoras may or may not have been a mathematician. Perhaps he was only a nutcase. A forerunner of Jim Jones, drinking Kool-Aid with his numerological cohort. The contrast is nicely captured in two Renaissance interpretations of Pythagoras—a fresco by Raphael, *The School of Athens* (ca. 1509–1510), and a painting by Rubens, *Pythagoras Advocating Vegetarianism* (ca. 1618–1619). In the Raphael, Pythagoras is a scholar, a teacher, a sober, thoughtful mathematician; in the Rubens, he is a rather dissolute and louche figure, every inch the raving cult-leader. Two thousand years after he lived, people are still confused about Pythagoras. Who was the *real* Pythagoras—scholar or crank?

For Burkert, Pythagoras is not "a sharply outlined figure, standing in the bright light of history. . . . From the very beginning, his

influence was mainly felt in an atmosphere of miracle, secrecy, and revelation. . . . Pythagoras represents not the origin of the new, but the survival or revival of ancient, pre-scientific lore, based on superhuman authority and expressed in ritual obligation."[14] He is the Pythagoras of Rubens, not the Pythagoras of Raphael.

And Hippasus? What really happened to him? Is his drowning at the hands of angry Pythagoreans a Whiggish reading of the past? An exaggerated, heightened, melodramatic event that never happened? Did the fourth-century geometer Pappus, along with neo-Platonists like Iamblichus and Proclus, invent the story and then publicize it? If so, why? Did nineteenth- and twentieth-century historians imagine a crisis, and then invent a figure and a story to embody it? Could this "paradigmatic" example of incommensurability be a Whiggish phantasm, the product of an overactive *modern* imagination?

14. Burkert, *Lore and Science in Ancient Pythagoreanism*, "Preface to the German Edition."

Burkert says, yes.

> The discovery of the problem of the irrational in geometry, and the development of the ability to cope with it, is a fundamental accomplishment of Greek mathematics which holds a lasting fascination for modern historians of science. The tradition of secrecy, betrayal, and divine punishment provided the occasion for the reconstruction of a veritable melodrama in intellectual history. . . . Thus one comes to speak of a *Grundlagenkrisis* [a foundational crisis]—a crossroads or dilemma as to the very foundations of Greek and Pythagorean mathematics in the fifth century [BCE]—and to see in the tradition about the death of the "traitor" a reflection of the shock and despair that this discovery must have brought: "O that the irrational had never been discovered!" But had the painful fact of its existence really been held as a carefully guarded *arcanum imperii* [state secret]?

His conclusion is uncompromising. "The thesis of the Pythagorean foundation of Greek geometry cannot stand, any more than the legend of a great mathematics held secret."[15] According to Burkert there is insufficient evidence to support the neo-Platonist accounts of Hippasus's demise. I would go further: it probably never happened. It is narrative fiction.

One of the oddities of history is that legends often supersede facts. Particularly with ancient history where there is little or no evidence. (Paucity or absence of evidence is different from incommensurability. Incommensurability, as Kuhn originally imagined it, could occur in situations where there is considerable evidence.) Monographs are written, and popular retellings of *apocryphal* stories proliferate. Otto Neugebauer has written:

> In the "Cloisters" of the Metropolitan Museum in New York hangs a magnificent tapestry which tells the tale of the Unicorn. At the end we see the miraculous animal captured, gracefully resigned to his fate, standing in an enclosure surrounded by a neat little fence. This picture may serve as a simile for [the reconstruction of ancient science]. . . . [W]e hope to have enclosed what may appear as a possible, living creature. Reality,

15. Burkert, *Lore and Science* pp. 455–56, 465.

16. Neugebauer, *The Exact Sciences in Antiquity*, p. 177.

however, may be vastly different from the product of our imagination; perhaps it is vain to hope for anything more than a picture which is pleasing to the constructive mind when we try to restore the past.[16]

In John Ford's movie *The Man Who Shot Liberty Valance* (1962), Ransom Stoddard (James Stewart), fresh out of law school, follows Horace Greeley's injunction, "Go West, young man." He ends up in a lawless frontier town, Shinbone, and in a life-or-death struggle with Liberty Valance (Lee Marvin), a gunslinger and the paid stooge of the cattle barons.

In the final shootout, Stoddard seemingly kills Valance, but Tom Doniphon (John Wayne)—hidden in the shadows, unbeknownst to Stoddard—is really the man who kills Valance. Only Doniphon and Stoddard (and the motion picture audience) know the *truth*. Stoddard marries Doniphon's girl and goes on to a spectacular political career—governor, senator, ambassador, and possible vice-president.

We are back in the world of Goldie and Greenie. Remember Goldie and Greenie? Goldie remains Goldie no matter what color Goldie becomes. And Greenie remains Greenie. Just as Stoddard remains Stoddard. And Doniphon remains Doniphon. I hope the reader is not discomfited by the fact that Doniphon and Stoddard are characters in a movie. For the sake of this discussion, we can assume that Doniphon, Stoddard, and Liberty Valance are flesh-and-blood people like you and me. And "the man who shot Liberty Valance"? The phrase is a definite description, but who does it describe? Bertrand Russell wrote about proper names as disguised definite descriptions. What about definite descriptions as disguised proper names? According to Russell's description theory, the reference of a proper name is the reference of a definite description ("the so-and-so") associated with that name. The definite description "the man who shot Liberty Valance" picks out *that man, that one unique man*, who shot Liberty Valance, namely Tom Doniphon.

But what if most people believe *that man* is Ransom Stoddard? *Contra* Kripke, don't our beliefs sometimes matter in reference?

This ambiguity is crucial to the final irony in the film. Stoddard is returning by train to Washington following Doniphon's funeral. The conductor tells him that the railroad is holding the express train for him—for *Stoddard*—saying, "Nothing's too good for the man who shot Liberty Valance." The conductor thinks he is referring to Stoddard, who is seated right in front of him. If you asked the conductor, he would point to Stoddard and say, "That's the man who shot Liberty Valance." But Stoddard *knows* the conductor is referring to Doniphon. Or is he? Here's the paradox. Who is right? To whom is the conductor *really* referring?[17]

John Ford's masterpiece was released in 1962, the same year Kuhn's *Structure of Scientific Revolutions* was published. Mercifully they do *not* share a postmodern rejection of truth—or an antirealist philosophy. In *The Man Who Shot Liberty Valance*, we, the audience

17. This is similar to Kripke's arguments about Gödel and his friend Schmidt. In Kripke's Kafkaesque parable, a man named "Schmidt" is found dead in Vienna under mysterious circumstances. Kripke asks us to imagine that it is Schmidt (and not Gödel) who is responsible for Gödel's proof of the incompleteness of arithmetic: "On the view in question, then, when our ordinary man uses the name 'Gödel', he really means to refer to Schmidt, because Schmidt is the unique person satisfying the description 'the man who discovered the incompleteness of arithmetic.' . . . So, since the man who discovered the incompleteness of arithmetic is in fact Schmidt, we, when we talk about 'Gödel', are in fact always referring to Schmidt. But it seems to me that we are not. We simply are not." *Naming and Necessity*, p. 84.

(along with Stoddard) know *the truth*. We know that even if a hundred million people believe that Stoddard killed Liberty Valance, in fact, he did not.

We see the shooting in two different ways. Once with Stoddard and Valance and then again with Stoddard, Valance, *and* Doniphon. Stoddard believes he has killed Liberty Valance. But he is mistaken.

DONIPHON: You talk too much. Think too much. Besides you didn't kill Liberty Valance.

STODDARD: What?!

DONIPHON: Think back, Pilgrim. Valance came out of the saloon. You were walking toward him when he fired his first shot, remember?

A flashback follows. Here is a clear elucidation of the difference between the social construction of reality and *reality*—between the social construction of truth and real truth. Stoddard is walking toward Liberty Valance. Valance wounds Stoddard. Stoddard is clearly outclassed—he really doesn't know how to use a gun. Valance is going to shoot again, but this time he is going to aim "between the eyes." Doniphon intervenes. Hidden in the shadows, Doniphon shoots and kills Valance before he can kill Stoddard—an act of murder that Doniphon says he can live with.

A legend that is not true can never *become fact*, but often it gets printed *as fact*. (I could even imagine a movie, *The Man Who Drowned Hippasus of Metapontum*.) With Hippasus, it is easy to imagine *why* the legend of his drowning got "printed" as fact even before printing had been invented. Someone imagined it. Someone in the years between Hippasus and the neo-Platonists believed there *should* have been a crisis even if there wasn't one. They believed the Pythagoreans *should* have been upset about the discovery of incommensurable magnitudes. But it was a *retrospective* belief, a belief formed hundreds, if not thousands, of years after the crisis was supposed to have occurred. And it most likely describes an event that never happened. I find it mildly amusing—even ironic—that Kuhn's metaphor for "incommensurability" could be derived from a Whiggish interpretation of an apocryphal story.[18]

18. A variant on this theme comes from G. K. Chesterton: "It is quite easy to see why a legend is treated, and ought to be treated, more respectfully than a book of history. The legend is generally made by the majority of the people in the village, who are sane. The book is generally written by the one man in the village who is mad" (*Orthodoxy*, p. 84). Needless to say, I do not agree with Chesterton, at least in this instance. A legend made by a majority of people in the village can be apocryphal, while a book written by a madman can be true.

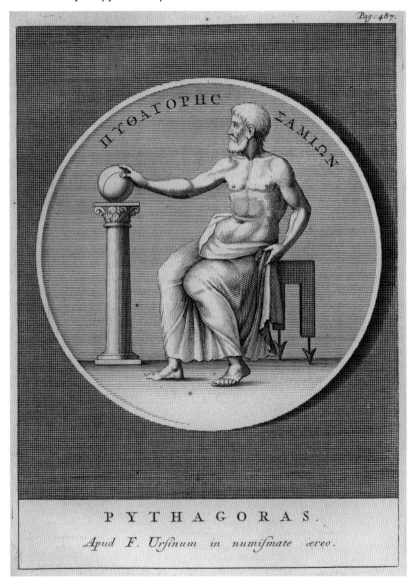

PYTHAGORAS.

Apud F. Ursinum in numismate æreo.

There's a further problem. Take the legend of Hippasus at face value: the Pythagoreans killed him because he couldn't keep a secret. But taken at face value, the legend is *not* about the inability of one group to understand another. Hippasus was *not* killed (if he was killed) because the Pythagoreans couldn't understand his proof. They *could* understand it. His murder was not born out of some deep *incomprehension*. It was an act of *intolerance*—like the throwing of an ashtray.

6. THE LEAP INTO THE DARK

To divide humanity into irreconcilable groups with irreconcilable attitudes, having no common language of truth and morality, is, ultimately, to rob both groups of their humanity.
—Stephen Spender, *World within World*

Kuhn was a tortured human being. I believe that the ashtray incident was motivated not only by his annoyance with me, but also by doubts about his own work. My belief is reinforced by a 2010 memoir, *Little Did I Know*, by Stanley Cavell, who had been a junior fellow at Harvard with Kuhn in the 1950s. Subsequently, they both joined the faculty at the University of California, Berkeley—Cavell as a member of the Philosophy Department; Kuhn with a joint appointment in philosophy and in history.

Cavell recounts a conversation with Kuhn that took place in Berkeley around 1957.[1] Kuhn was in the process of writing *The Structure of Scientific Revolutions*. Following a Philosophy Department meeting, Kuhn had accompanied Cavell home for a drink. And had Hitler on his mind. Was Kuhn—like any good Jewish boy of the postwar period, including myself—struggling with the meaning of the Third Reich? If there are no absolute value judgments to be made about one historical period (read: paradigm), what about the Nazis? Cavell writes:

> Talking past midnight Tom was becoming agitated in a way I had not seen. He suddenly lurched forward in his chair with a somewhat tortured look that I had begun to be familiar with. "I know Wittgenstein uses the idea of 'paradigm.' But I do not see its implications in his work. How do I answer the objection that this destroys the truth of science? I deplore the idea. Yet if instruction and agreement are the essence of the matter, then Hitler could instruct me that a theory is true and get me to agree."[2]

1. I date this conversation to 1957. It is early in their relationship at Berkeley. Kuhn arrived in 1956 and started his teaching duties in 1957. Cavell refers to it as an "early formative conversation between us." *Little Did I Know* (2010), p. 354.

2. *Little Did I Know*, pp. 354–55.

3. "Kuhn himself acknowledges his debt to Wittgenstein. As reported by Cedarbaum (1983, p. 188), Kuhn had read a pre-publication typescript of Wittgenstein's *Blue and Brown Books* (1958) before 1959. At that time, having formulated the basic themes of *The Structure of Scientific Revolutions*, he came upon Wittgenstein's *Philosophical Investigations* (1968 [citation is to 3rd ed.]), a book that helped him capture basic features of normal science. The concepts of paradigm, the function of rules, the importance of tradition, training and education, all, implicitly or explicitly, drew upon such Wittgensteinian concepts as language games, family resemblance, forms of life. In *The Structure* itself Kuhn refers explicitly to Wittgenstein's analysis of family likeness terms, as well as his account of naming in language (p. 45)." Vasso P. Kindi, "Kuhn's *The Structure of Scientific Revolutions* Revisited" (1995), p. 80.

4. Wittgenstein, *Philosophical Investigations*, paragraph 43.

5. *Little Did I Know*, p. 355. There Cavell also writes, "Once, lingering over too much coffee and many too many cigarettes, after a particularly resonant blast of disagreement from him, I replied: 'Tom, please do not address me. I am not a convention.' He was shocked, put his forehead to the table, and banging it gently several times, he said, in rhythm, and softly: 'I know. I know I do that.'"

This is Kuhn's debt to Wittgenstein.[3] Wittgenstein uses the idea of a "paradigm" based on his concepts of language games and family resemblance. And on his belief that "for a *large* class of cases of the employment of the word 'meaning' . . . the meaning of a word is its use in the language."[4] Kuhn, early on and before the publication of *Structure*, is asking what happens when instruction and agreement lead to falsehood? (Unless there is no such thing.) Ultimately, the problem becomes a question about rule-following. What does it mean to follow a rule? Cavell resumes the story:

> My reply I cast as follows, using the words I remember using then. "No, he could not; he could not *educate* you in, *convince* you of, *show* you, its truth. Hitler could declare a theory to be true, as an edict. He could effectively threaten to kill you if you refuse to, or fail to, believe it. But all that means is that he is going to kill you; or perhaps kill you if you do not convince him, show him, that you accept and will follow the edict. I don't say this is clear. But it is something I cannot doubt is worth doing whatever work it will take to make it clear." Tom's response was startling. He arose almost violent from his chair, began pacing in front of the fireplace, saying something like, "Yah. Yah." What causes conviction? What, perhaps rather, may undo an unnoticed conviction? After that night we arranged to meet for lunch regularly once a week, whatever other times we might be together, and discuss mostly the material he would develop the following year as *The Structure of Scientific Revolutions*.[5]

An extraordinary passage. Hitler "could declare a theory to be true, as an edict. He could effectively threaten to kill you . . . or perhaps kill you if you do not convince him, show him, that you accept and follow the edict." Agreement, conviction, truth. Threats and the application of force. A hint of Kuhn's violent nature. But what is Cavell really saying? He writes, "I don't say this is clear." My rejoinder: What isn't clear about it? To declare a theory to be true doesn't make it true. No more than declaring that $\pi = 3$.

Cavell stops with the difference between declaring something to be true and convincing someone of the truth of something. But I am bothered by a further consideration. *Is* the theory true? *Contra* Cavell and Wittgenstein, the central issue isn't about agreement or conviction. It's about truth. As Cavell quotes Kuhn, "How do I answer the objection that this destroys *the truth* of science?" Indeed. Not just the truth of science but the truth of anything and everything. I believe ✓ that Kuhn understood from the 1950s on—even before the first edition of *Structure*—that there were fundamental problems with his philosophy. And they concerned not just agreement and conviction, but also truth. (Of course, he had to deny truth; truth gets in the way.)

What's the difference between being convinced by Einstein that special relativity is true and $E = mc^2$ and being convinced by Hitler that the *Protocols of the Elders of Zion* is true and Jews should be eradicated from the face of the earth? George Orwell wrote about similar themes in his novel *Nineteen Eighty-Four*:

> In the end the Party would announce that two and two made five, and you would have to believe it. It was inevitable that they should make that claim sooner or later: the logic of their position demanded it. Not merely the validity of experience, but the very existence of external reality, was tacitly denied by their philosophy. The heresy of heresies was common sense. And what was terrifying was not that they would kill you for thinking otherwise, but that they might be right. For, after all, how do we know that two and two make four? Or that the force of gravity works? Or that the past is unchangeable? If both the past and the external world exist only in the mind, and if the mind itself is controllable—what then?[6]

6. *Nineteen Eighty-Four*, pp. 83–84.

The difference between forcing someone to state an untruth and getting them to believe it is at the heart of Orwell's novel. "You must love Big Brother. It is not enough to obey him, you must love him."[7] Winston Smith, Orwell's protagonist, finally succumbs to threats from the State. His love for Big Brother emerges from fear—fear of rats, the threat of a cage filled with starving rats being strapped to his face. It is not a perfect metaphor for being Kuhn's graduate student, but it comes close.

7. *Nineteen Eighty-Four*, p. 295.

Cavell lives in Brookline, Massachusetts; I live in nearby Cambridge. So I called him and set up a meeting at his house. I was particularly interested in the passage I've quoted from his memoir. To me, it seemed like he had revealed the underlying problem with *Structure* and with Kuhn's work in general.

STANLEY CAVELL: Kuhn was really alarmed that Wittgenstein was denying the rationality of truth. That, somehow, everything was going to come down to agreement. It would be circling around that. . . . Which I don't think is a non-issue. I think it's quite real.

ERROL MORRIS: And what were your feelings about it?

CAVELL: That it was a genuine issue, that Wittgenstein was opening that up. Part of it was a matter of getting down in the mud and figuring out what "agreement" meant.

MORRIS: This would be in *Philosophical Investigations*?

CAVELL: Yes. *Philosophical Investigations*. That's what we talked about. The early Wittgenstein, as far as we were concerned, was frozen history. Nobody was really interested in trying to make *that* work; it was *Investigations* that was really *hot*. The issue about what human agreement could establish, and how deep that agreement was. Wittgenstein's quote: "We don't agree in judgement, we agree in form of life." Whether that meant that knowledge of the universe was relative to human forms of life. We went around the track with that a lot, and, why not?

Alas, in order to make sense of this discussion, one must descend into the foul rag-and-bone shop of Wittgenstein exegesis. Wittgenstein's quote is from paragraph 241 of *Philosophical Investigations*:

241. "So you are saying that human agreement decides what is true and what is false?"—What is true or false is what human beings *say*; and it is in their *language* that human beings agree. This is agreement not in opinions, but rather in form of life.

This passage, like many others in *Philosophical Investigations*, has produced seemingly endless commentary. Part of the difficulty is that so many diverse concepts are introduced—agreement, truth, form of life. A grab bag of murky, possibly related, possibly unrelated ideas. The problems are compounded by how the argument is presented: Wittgenstein is arguing with himself.[8] Paragraph 241 opens with his reply to an imagined interlocutor. "So, you are saying that human agreement decides what is true and what is false?" Is he interviewing himself? Then corrects *himself*. No, it's not agreement in *opinions*, but in form of life (*Lebensform*).

The paragraph is puzzling. At least to me. Just what is *form of life*? Is it cultural? Biological—in our DNA? And agreement (*Übereinstimmung*)? A group of people shaking hands and agreeing on something? Shriners agreeing on a tassel design for a fez? Theoretical physicists agreeing on the mass of the Higgs boson? And what about truth? Does mere agreement make something true?[9] And if so, isn't Wittgenstein flirting with relativism?

The surrounding paragraphs in *Investigations* don't help all that much. They just deepen the mystery. Look at paragraph 241 in context.

240. Disputes do not break out (among mathematicians, say) over the question of whether or not a rule has been followed. People don't come to blows over it, for example. This belongs to the scaffolding from which our language operates (for example, yields descriptions).

241. "So you are saying that human agreement decides what is true and what is false?"—What is true or false is what human beings *say*; and it is in their *language* that human beings agree. This is agreement not in opinions, but rather in form of life [*Lebensform*].

242. It is not only agreement in definitions, but also (odd as it may sound) agreement in judgements that is required for communication by means of language. This seems to abolish logic, but does not do so . . .

8. Saul Kripke addresses this in his book on Wittgenstein. "It should be bourn in mind that *Philosophical Investigations* is not a systematic philosophical work where conclusions, once definitely established, need not be re-argued. Rather the *Investigations* is written as a perpetual dialectic, where persisting worries, expressed by the voice of the imaginary interlocutor, are never definitely silenced." *Wittgenstein on Rules and Private Language* (1982), p. 3.

9. What about the attempt in Indiana—a law that didn't pass—to change the value of π?

> The bill establishing a new mathematical truth in squaring the circle was about to be passed by the Senate when the point was raised that the Legislature had no power to declare a truth, and it was indefinitely postponed. The State Superintendent has accepted the demonstration, and it is understood will introduce the same in Indiana text books. The demonstration shows that the time-honored multiple of 3.1416 plus, by which the diameter of a circle is multiplied to find the circumference, should be 3.2. Dr. Goodwin of Solitude, Posey County, the author of the rule, has his formula copyrighted not only in this country but also in seven countries of Europe. ("Senators Afraid to Change Pi," *Chicago Daily Tribune*, February 13, 1897)

Dr. Goodwin's promise to donate the proceeds of his copyright to the state of Indiana no doubt helped the bill advance as far as it did. See Underwood Dudley, "Legislating Pi" (1999).

10. My Wittgenstein-as-relativist claim antagonizes many Wittgenstein commentators. See Dave Maier, "Errol Morris on Wittgenstein, or Someone Like Him in Certain Respects" (2001).

11. Anat Biletzki and Anat Matar, "Ludwig Wittgenstein" (emphasis mine).

12. Similar to the Wittgenstein-Didn't-Really-Say-That game. Relatively easy to play. Someone claims, "Wittgenstein said such-and-such." You reply, "Wittgenstein didn't *really* say that." Fun for the whole family! Nobody wins.

13. Kripke writes that he was working on these issues in the late 1960s and early '70s—around the same time as *Naming and Necessity*. "I did give lectures on both topics before anything appeared," he told me. "*Naming and Necessity* is a transcription of a series of three invited lectures, but *Wittgenstein on Rules and Private Language* was written because I was dissatisfied in various ways with the transcript I got from a talk I gave in London, Ontario. (An earlier version of the book appeared in the proceedings of the conference in question.)" Email to author, May 14, 2017.

14. This has produced extensive argument. A cacophony of competing, angry voices. And finger-pointing. Kripke is wrong. Wrong, wrong, wrong. Wittgenstein didn't say *this*; he said *that*. The private language argument starts after Kripke says it ends, in paragraph 243. Kripke didn't quote the relevant parts of paragraph 201; he only pays lip service to Wittgenstein's argument. Kripke misunderstands private language altogether or construes it as he does just so he can undermine it. See, e.g., John McDowell, "Wittgenstein on Following a Rule" (1984).

My own opinion: Philosophers do not like locating the private language argument in the earlier paragraphs because it becomes clear when one does so that Wittgenstein's argument is infirm, *or* rather—to use Kripke's phrase—"self-defeating."

"This *seems* to abolish logic, but *does not do so*"? Had I gotten myself into trouble (with an assortment of Wittgenstein enthusiasts) by suggesting that Kuhn and Cavell had worried that paragraph 241 implied relativism?[10] In Cavell's words, "that knowledge of the universe was *relative* to human forms of life"? Hadn't Cavell told me that he and Kuhn worried about just such an interpretation? Yes, he did. But this is not just *my* possible interpretation of Wittgenstein, or Kuhn's and Cavell's possible interpretation of Wittgenstein. The entry on Wittgenstein in *The Stanford Encyclopedia of Philosophy* also states this view: "Forms of life can be understood as changing and contingent, dependent on culture, context, history, etc.; this appeal to forms of life grounds a *relativistic* reading of Wittgenstein."[11] But not so surprisingly—given the elusiveness of Wittgenstein's ultimate meanings—the *Encyclopedia* writers hedge their bets. They write, "On the other hand, it is the form of life common to humankind, 'shared human behavior' which is 'the system of reference by means of which we interpret an unknown language.' This might be seen as a universalistic turn, recognizing that the use of language is made possible by the human form of life." "Changing and contingent," yet "universalistic"?! It reminds me of Whac-A-Mole.[12] You think you've knocked it down, but it pops up somewhere else.

Forget for a moment what Wittgenstein *really* meant. (A fool's errand in my opinion—akin to Bible exegesis. Useful to deepen our understanding of things, but unlikely to result in a definitive interpretation of anything.) The question is, What did Kuhn and Cavell think he meant?

———

Saul Kripke has addressed, in *Wittgenstein on Rules and Private Language*, many of the issues raised by Wittgenstein's *Philosophical Investigations*.[13] Kripke is ostensibly wrestling with Wittgenstein's argument about private language—Wittgenstein's claim that there can be no such thing—but broadens the inquiry to include all of language. In fact, *all of knowledge*. Kripke (unlike most commentators on Wittgenstein) locates the private language argument in paragraphs 201–242 of *Philosophical Investigations*—Wittgenstein's discussion of what it means to follow a rule.[14] Wittgenstein states a paradox: if language is about following rules, how do we know whether we are following a rule?[15]

> 201. This was our paradox: no course of action could be determined by a rule, because every course of action can be brought into accord with that rule. The answer was: if every course of action can be brought into accord with the rule, then it can also be brought into conflict with it. And so there would be neither accord nor conflict here.

Kripke argues that Wittgenstein's skeptical argument for private language holds for public language as well.[16] (I believe this is Kripke's single most important contribution to the discussion.) Wittgenstein (or at least Wittgenstein according to Kripke) tells us—there can be no private language because a private language user cannot be wrong. A single person has only his own memory to check his "rules." When I first heard this argument I was convinced I had heard it wrong. Or didn't understand it. It seemed too simplistic. A variation on "Two heads are better than one." As my friend Charles Silver argues:

> "Community memory" seems more solid. But just because many people are involved doesn't mean that they can't be mistaken. . . . Suppose a bunch of persons, let them be experts of some sort, make up a rule, then they write it down on a piece of paper and bury it. . . . We'll suppose each of the people who agreed on that rule really felt as strongly as possible that they *knew* the rule without having to unearth it. Time passes. . . . For some reason or other, the piece of paper with the rule on it is unearthed. It turns out—Heavens to Betsy—that they were not following that rule at all. They were mistaken.[17]

Public rule-checking may mitigate the problem but does not solve it. Kripke summarizes: if Wittgenstein's skeptical paradox is taken seriously, "there can be no such thing as meaning anything by any word. Each new application we make is a leap in the dark; any present intention could be interpreted so as to accord with anything we may choose to do." He continues, some pages later, "Wittgenstein

15. The following discussion, once again, is a simplification of complex and often tortuous arguments. I do not claim to have captured Wittgenstein's or Kripke's every idea, but I believe that *in essence* the arguments come down to the private individual versus the community.

16. "If I were really in doubt as to whether I could identify any sensations correctly, how would a connection of my sensations with external behavior, or confirmation by others, be any help?" Kripke, *Wittgenstein on Rules*, pp. 60–61.

17. Charles Silver, emails to author, April 17 and 29, 2013.

18. Kripke, *Wittgenstein on Rules*, pp. 55, 60.

19. See, e.g., Warren Goldfarb, "Kripke on Wittgenstein on Rules" (1985); Paul Horwich, "Kripke's Wittgenstein" (2015).

20. Burgess, *Saul Kripke* (2013), pp. 109–10. In his lecture on Kripke, "The Origin of Necessity and the Necessity of Origin" (2012), Burgess compares the reading of Wittgenstein to the interpretation of a Rorschach inkblot:

> Many people don't seem to rank the discovery of the skeptical paradox right up there with the discovery of *a posteriori* knowledge among Saul's contributions to philosophy. I would rank it right up there. . . . One reason people don't give Saul as much credit is because he, as it were, disclaims originality for this and says that he only saw this when he was looking at Ludwig Wittgenstein's *Philosophical Investigations*.
>
> I would say that the relation of Saul to the *Philosophical Investigations* is just like the relation of the patient to the Rorschach blots in the old joke. If you remember . . . the old joke is that the patient gives an X-rated description of each of the Rorschach blots and the

has invented a new form of skepticism. Personally, I am inclined to regard it as the most radical and skeptical problem that philosophy has seen to date."[18]

Some commentators have complained that Kripke does not address the *real* Wittgenstein (whoever he might be) but rather some monstrous creature of Kripke's own devising.[19] John Burgess, the Princeton philosopher and logician, even cites "Pierre Menard":

> Others have adopted the fiction that Kripke is writing, not about the famous *Philosophical Investigations* of the famous Ludwig Wittgenstein, but about another work of the same title by another philosopher of the same name. . . . The texts of the one *Philosophical Investigations* and the other are word-for-word identical, at any rate in the passages Kripke quotes, though the meanings may be very different, as in the case of . . . Pierre Menard in the the well-known Borges story.[20]

Call Kripke's creature what you will—Kripke's Wittgenstein; Kripkenstein; Frankenkripke; the Ghosts of Wittgensteins Past,

Present, and Yet-to-come—the name makes little difference.[21] It is in Kripke's analysis of *Philosophical Investigations* that essential problems with Wittgenstein (and with Kuhn) come into focus.

For example, Kripke restates Wittgenstein's paradox in the form of an arithmetical rule—

68 plus 57 = 125

Who would argue? He then provides a slightly different rule. It involves quus not plus, quaddition not addition—*x* quus *y* is the same as *x* plus *y* if either *x* or *y* is less than 57; otherwise *x* quus *y* = 5.

Silly? But say all of your addition problems have involved numbers less than 57. You have *no experience* adding larger numbers. So for all intents and purposes, you have *no knowledge* of which rule you're following—the rule of addition or quaddition. Remember, the rule is learned by example. Let's follow along with Kripke:

$$
y \text{ quus } x = \begin{cases} y + x & \text{if } x, y < 57 \\ 5 & \text{otherwise} \end{cases}
$$

Who is to say that [quus] is not the function I previously meant by '+'? The sceptic claims (or feigns to claim) that I am now misinterpreting my own previous usage. By 'plus', he says, I *always meant* quus; now, under the influence of some insane frenzy, or a bout of LSD, I have come to misinterpret my own previous usage. Ridiculous and fantastic though it is, the sceptic's hypothesis is not logically impossible.[22]

Kripke's question—when you are performing an arithmetic operation how do you know that "+" means "plus," not "quus"?[23]— goes back to Wittgenstein and Kuhn's belief that meaning comes from community agreement. We could think we are following a rule, but what is the rule? We have followed the rule up to 57, and we think we understand it. We think we *know* what "plus" means. But our knowledge of what "plus" means depends on our belief that we know the rule. On our experience of individual

doctor says, "You're obsessed." And the patient says, "What do you mean I'm obsessed, doctor? You're the one that has all the dirty pictures!" So Saul is seeing the dirty picture of a skeptical paradox in this text where none of the author's immediate personal disciples saw it and where I myself must confess I see nothing but blobs of ink. So I am prepared to give the credit for the skeptical paradox to Saul Kripke rather than Ludwig Rorschach.

21. Kripke's *Wittgenstein on Rules and Private Language* is accompanied by a disclaimer (like the endless warnings that accompany pharmaceutical ads) that Kripke does not purport to replicate exactly Wittgenstein's arguments, only how they "struck" him: "I suspect . . . that to attempt to present Wittgenstein's argument is to some extent to falsify it. Probably many of my formulations and recastings of the argument are done in a way Wittgenstein would not himself approve. So the present paper should be thought of as expounding neither 'Wittgenstein's' argument nor 'Kripke's': rather Wittgenstein's argument as it struck Kripke, as it presented a problem for him" (p. 5).

22. *Wittgenstein on Rules*, p. 9.
23. Kripke's use of a mathematical example merely follows Wittgenstein, who explicitly references mathematical rules in *Philosophical Investigations*, e.g., paragraph 226: "Suppose someone continues the sequence 1, 3, 5, 7 . . ." Series present their own difficulties. They can be completed in different ways. When I was a teenager, I struggled for days with the series 4, 14, 34, 42, 59 . . . When I was told the text term was 125, I still couldn't figure it out. It turns out to be a series of express stops for the "A" train on the Eighth Avenue Line of the New York City Subway: W. 4th St. (Washington Square); 14th St.; 34th St. (Pennsylvania Station); 42nd Street (Port Authority Bus Terminal); 59th Street (Columbus Circle), 125th Street . . .

24. The problem of rule-following also appears in Bertrand Russell's *Nightmares of Eminent Persons*. In "The Metaphysician's Nightmare," the metaphysician is trapped in Hell, "a place full of those happenings that are improbable but not impossible": "There is a peculiarly painful chamber inhabited solely by philosophers who have refuted Hume. These philosophers, though in Hell, have not learned wisdom. They continue to be governed by their animal propensity toward induction. But every time that they have made an induction, the next instance falsifies it. This, however, happens only during the first hundred years of their damnation. After that, they learn to expect that an induction will be falsified, and therefore it is not falsified until another century of logical torment has altered their expectation" (pp. 30–31).
25. Carroll, *Annotated Alice*, p. 253.
26. Of course, Cavell would demur. The White Queen could declare something as true but not get you to agree.

27. *Wittgenstein on Rules*, p. 58.

applications of the rule. On how the rule has played out up to a certain point in time.[24]

Let's go back to Lewis Carroll. The White Queen presents a problem to Alice (in *Through the Looking-Glass*): "'Can you do Addition?' the White Queen asked. 'What's one and one and one and one and one and one and one and one and one and one?' 'I don't know,' said Alice. 'I lost count.'"[25] Does someone have to tell Alice, "The answer is 10"? And what if the community agrees the answer is 11? In Kuhn's parlance (as expressed to Cavell), the White Queen could instruct Alice that the answer is 11 and get her to agree.[26] (Or recall Winston Smith in *Nineteen Eighty-Four*, who wonders whether the State could effectively declare that two plus two equals five. Clearly, after the application of hungry rats they would be successful in the endeavor.)

Does Kripke's skepticism about rules apply to non-mathematical rules? To rules in general? There can be little doubt. Kripke is clear on this issue. As far as he is concerned, it applies to everything: "Although our paradigm of Wittgenstein's problem was formulated for a mathematical problem, it was emphasized that it is completely general and can be applied to any rule or word."[27]

But what is Kripke's *attitude* to Wittgenstein? Does he take the skeptical thesis (as outlined by himself) seriously? Is he attacking Wittgenstein? Is he being coy? Ironic? Does he admire Wittgenstein's writing, if not his philosophy? All of the above?[28] And if he believes that Wittgenstein has essentially argued that language *and* knowledge are impossible, does he have a remedy? A positive program?

One important clue as to how Kripke feels can be found (characteristically) in a footnote, footnote 76.[29] Kripke writes about a device called the "*inversion* of a conditional," quoting what he characterizes as William James's summary of "his famous theory of emotions," then extending it (with various qualifications) to much of philosophy. Here is the footnote in its entirety:

> As will be seen immediately, inversion in this sense is a device for reversing priorities. William James summarized his famous theory of the emotions (*The Principles of Psychology*, Henry Holt & Co., New York, 1913, in 2 volumes; chapter 25 [vol. 2, 442–85], "The Emotions") by the assertion, ". . . the . . . rational statement is that we feel sorry because we cry . . . not that we cry . . . because we are sorry . . ." (p. 450). Many philosophies can be summed up crudely (no doubt, not really accurately) by slogans in a similar form.: "We do not condemn certain acts because they are immoral; they are immoral because we condemn them." "We do not accept the law of contradiction because it is a necessary truth; it is a necessary truth because we accept it (by convention)." "Fire and heat are not constantly conjoined because fire causes heat; fire causes heat because they are constantly conjoined" (Hume). "We do not say $12 + 7 = 19$ and the like because we all grasp the concept of addition; we say we all grasp the concept of addition because we all say $12 + 7 = 19$ and the like" (Wittgenstein).
>
> The device of inversion of a conditional in the text achieves the effect of reversing priorities in a way congenial to such slogans. Speaking for myself, I am suspicious of philosophical problems of the types illustrated by the slogans, whether or not they are so crudely put.[30]

I have read and reread that last line: *Speaking for myself, I am suspicious of philosophical problems of the types illustrated by the slogans.* Kripke's words. There is no doubt that he would *not* invert the conditional. He would say, "Yes. $12 + 7 = 19$ because we all grasp the *concept* of addition." As Kripke puts it, "The addition function is not in

28. In an early footnote (p. 5), Kripke writes, "The role of stylistic considerations here cannot be denied. . . . His own stylistic preference obviously contributes to the difficulty of his work as well as to its beauty." I would agree.

29. Kripke's best work, like the best work of David Foster Wallace, can often be found in the footnotes. I could argue that footnote 76 is the best footnote in Kripke's *Wittgenstein*, but there are many superlative examples. Take footnote 87—a curious note added just before the manuscript went to press. It concludes, "I feel some uneasiness may remain regarding these questions. Considerations of time and space, as well as the fact that I might have to abandon the role of advocate and expositor in favor of that of critic, have led me not to carry out a more extensive discussion" (p. 146).

30. *Wittgenstein on Rules*, pp. 93–94.

31. *Wittgenstein on Rules*, p. 53.

any particular mind, nor is it the common property of all minds."[31] Indeed, mathematical realists or Platonists have little trouble with the idea that we all grasp the concept of addition.

Arithmetical operations have an objective existence. As such, the concept of addition stands apart from us (and our minds), much as does the Andromeda galaxy. Ask yourself, What was the concept of addition in Cambrian times—600 million years ago? I'm not asking, What would a trilobite think about addition? Or about the

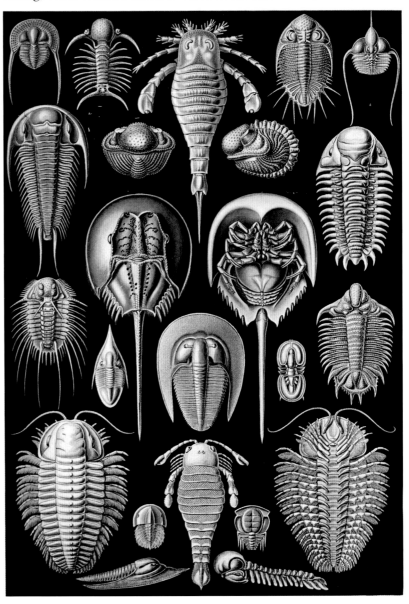

Lebensform of trilobites "scuttling across silent seas." The question has nothing to do with their biology or ours. Doesn't the concept of addition precede *us*? And *them*? Is *life* needed for addition? Or does addition stand apart from all living things?

I hate to oversimplify the complex. But what if the complex deserves simplification? To me, the later Wittgenstein—the Wittgenstein of *Philosophical Investigations* and *Remarks on the Foundations of Mathematics*—describes a false picture of the world. It is a world in which we *create* truth rather than a world in which we *discover* it.[32] In paragraph 194 of *Investigations*, Wittgenstein tells us, "When we do philosophy, we are like savages, primitive people, who hear the way in which civilized people talk, put a false interpretation on it, and then draw the oddest conclusions from this." Kripke replies, "Personally I can only report that . . . the 'primitive' interpretation often sounds rather good to me."[33]

32. Juliet Floyd writes, "Wittgenstein's overarching philosophical spirit was anti-rationalist, in sharpest contrast, among twentieth-century philosophers, to that of Gödel. For Wittgenstein, as earlier for Kant, philosophy and logic are quests for self-understanding and self-knowledge, activities of self-criticism, self-definition, and reconciliation with the imperfections of life, rather than special branches of knowledge aiming directly at the discovery of impersonal truth." "Wittgenstein on Philosophy of Logic and Mathematics," p. 77.
33. *Wittgenstein on Rules*, p. 66.

Let's take a step back. Kripke's arguments in *Naming and Necessity* and in *Wittgenstein on Rules and Private Language* (in part) show how certain assumptions lead to absurdities.[34] In *Naming and Necessity*, it's the assumption that the reference of a proper name is associated with a set of descriptions. Kripke shows us that if description theorists are correct—any one of them: Russell, Wittgenstein, Searle, et al.—then reference is on shaky ground. Sally, with one set of descriptions (or cluster of descriptions or subset of a family of descriptions) of a proper name, could be referring to one thing, and Susie, with another set, to something else

34. In the latter, Kripke describes various practitioners of *quaddition*, including himself—"now, under the influence of some insane frenzy, or a bout of LSD, I have come to misinterpret my own previous usage" (*Wittgenstein on Rules*, p. 9). Or "Someone—a child, an individual muddled by a drug—may think he is following a rule even though he is actually acting at random, in accordance with no rule at all" (p. 88). Or "If someone . . .

suddenly gives answers according to procedures that differ bizarrely from my own . . . I will judge him probably to have gone insane" (p. 90). Or "he may even be judged a madman, following no coherent rule at all" (p. 93). And on and on. My favorite examples involve Smith and Jones, two individuals in conversation. "Sometimes Smith, by substituting some alternative interpretation for Jones's word 'plus', will be able to bring Jones's responses in line with his own. More often, he will be unable able to do so and will be inclined to judge that Jones is not really following any rule at all" (p. 91). But what if they "were reduced to a babble of disagreement, with Smith and Jones asserting of each other that they are following the rule wrongly . . ." (p. 91)? What if . . . ?

35. Kripke provides a *direct* refutation of Searle's cluster theory of descriptions in *Naming and Necessity*, pp. 71–80.

36. "I do not in this piece of writing attempt to speak for myself, or, except in occasional or minor asides, to say anything about my own views on substantive issues. . . . If the work has a main thesis of its own, it is that Wittgenstein's sceptical problem and argument are important, deserving of serious consideration." *Wittgenstein on Rules*, p. ix.

altogether. (And what if the descriptions are theory-dependent, as in Kuhn?)

Kripke's intuition, stated with devastating effect in *Naming and Necessity*, is that no cluster or concatenation of descriptions can ever capture our deep intuitions about what it is to refer to something.[35] I would take it a step further. If reference is relative (to our beliefs), what good is it? Relative reference—just like relative truth—is no reference at all.

Kripke can be thought of as a one-man demolition crew, his wrecking ball swinging in a wide arc. Despite his supposed admiration for Wittgenstein—announced in the preface to his book—he provides devastating criticisms.[36] Kripke tells us that Wittgenstein's "sceptical thesis" should be taken seriously. But he also tells us that if Wittgenstein's arguments about rule-following are taken to their conclusion then all language, all mathematics, all knowledge, is impossible. If all knowledge is based on community acceptance, as Kuhn said to Cavell, "How do I answer the objection that this destroys the truth of science? . . . [I]f instruction and agreement are the essence of the matter, then Hitler could instruct me that a theory is true and get me to agree." The answer, of course, is that instruction and agreement are *not* the essence of the matter.

———

The very concept of private language suggests a man marooned on a desert island, and indeed, Robinson Crusoe makes an appearance in Wittgenstein's lectures in 1936:

> Robinson Crusoe may have held soliloquies. And then he talks to himself alone. But he talks the language he has talked with people before.
>
> But imagine him *inventing* a *private* language. Imagine that he gives a name to a sensation of his. What then does he do with it?—Suppose he kept a diary, and that in this diary he put x against each day when he had a toothache. We must assume that what he wants to say no one understands anyway, and he can't explain it. How are we to describe what he does?
>
> "He had a toothache, and he remembers and puts a cross." How does he know he remembers? In the end we have to say just "He puts crosses"—we must not use the word "toothache," for it is not used as we generally use "toothache," and he is not using 'x' for this.[37]

What does it come down to? That we can't have a language—a *real* language—without other people? If Crusoe is communicating only with himself, how do we know he's communicating at all? This was the subject of a debate between A. J. Ayer and Rush Rhees, a student of Wittgenstein's. Ayer, arguing *for* the possibility of private language, writes:

> The development of language . . . is a social phenomenon. But surely it is not self-contradictory to suppose that someone, uninstructed in the use of any existing language, makes up a language for himself. . . . The hypothesis of G. K. Chesterton's dancing professor about the origin of language, that it came "from the formulated language of some individual creature" is very probably false, but it is certainly not unintelligible.[38]

37. "The Language of Sense Data and Private Experience (Notes taken by Rush Rhees of Wittgenstein's Lectures, 1936)," in Wittgenstein, *Philosophical Occasions: 1912–1951*, p. 320.

38. Ayer and Rhees, "Symposium: Can There Be a Private Language?" (1954), p. 70.

Chesterton's dancing professor appears in the novel *The Club of Queer Trades*, chapter 5, "The Noticeable Conduct of Professor Chadd."[39] First published in 1904, long before the publication of the *Philosophical Investigations*, the two main characters are Basil Grant, a retired judge, and Professor James Chadd, "known to the ethnological world . . . as the second greatest, if not the greatest, authority on the relations of savages to language . . . an unaccountable Nonconformist who had forgotten how to be angry. He went to and fro between the British Museum and a selection of blameless tea-shops, with an armful of books and a poor but honest umbrella."[40]

A discussion ensues—Who knows more about the Zulus? Those, like Professor Chadd, who live within the arid, antiseptic confines of the British Museum, or those, like Basil Grant, who are engaged with life? Grant claims:

> I know more about [the Zulus] in the sense that I am a savage. For instance, your theory of the origin of language, something about its having come from the formulated secret language of some individual creature, though you knocked me silly with facts and scholarship in its favor, still does not convince me, because I have a feeling that that is not the way that things happen. If you ask me why I think so, I can only answer that I am a Zulu; and if you ask me (as you most certainly will) what is my definition of a Zulu, I can answer that also. He is one who has climbed a Sussex apple-tree at seven and been afraid of a ghost in an English lane.

Professor Chadd responds,

> The real objection to your argument . . . is that it does not merely presuppose a Zulu truth apart from the facts, but infers that the discovery of it is absolutely impeded by the facts.[41]

And then, as if to emphasize the futility of the discussion, Professor Chadd begins dancing. It is a private language of his own devising, composed entirely of dance steps. And he will *not stop* until people understand him. Grant admits defeat:

39. The story may have been an inspiration for the Monty Python sketch "The Ministry of Silly Walks." A further discussion of Basil Grant and Professor Chadd can be found in Ruth Hoberman, *Museum Trouble* (Charlottesville: University of Virginia Press, 2011), pp. 152–54.

40. Chesterton, *The Club of Queer Trades*, p. 181.

41. *Club of Queer Trades*, pp. 187–88, 190–91.

Have you seen the man? Have you looked at James Chadd going dismally to and fro from his dingy house to your miserable library, with his futile books and his confounded umbrella, and never seen that he has the eyes of a fanatic? Have you never noticed, stuck casually behind his spectacles and above his seedy old collar, the face of a man who might have burned heretics, or died for the philosopher's stone? It is all my fault, in a way; I lit the dynamite of his deadly faith. I argued against him on the score of his famous theory about language—the theory that language was complete in certain individuals and was picked up by others simply by watching them. I also chaffed him about not understanding things in rough and ready practice. What has this glorious bigot done? He has answered me. He has worked out a system of language of his own (it would take too long to explain); he has made up, I say, a language of his own. And he has sworn that till people understand it, till he can speak to us in this language, he will not speak in any other.[42]

42. *Club of Queer Trades*, pp. 214–15.

Of course, there is always the possibility that he is dancing nonsense.

43. In the postscript to the second edition of *Structure* (1970), Kuhn tells us that paradigms are really disciplinary matrices. Replace one ill-defined concept with another, see if anyone notices? "All or most of the objects of group commitment that my original text makes paradigms, parts of paradigms, or paradigmatic are constituents of the disciplinary matrix, and as such they form a whole and function together" (p. 182).

44. *Wittgenstein on Rules*, pp. 62, 71.

45. There are many passages in *On Certainty* that suggest a relativistic reading of Wittgenstein, e.g.: "Supposing we met people who did not regard [an appeal to science] as a telling reason. Now, how do we imagine this? Instead of the physicist, they consult an oracle. (And for that we consider them primitive.) Is it wrong for them to consult an oracle and be guided by it?—If we call this 'wrong' aren't we using our language-game as a base from which to *combat* theirs?" Paragraph 609.

Imagine a variant of Wittgenstein's private language argument. A scientist is practicing his trade in one paradigm. If I'm part of a scientific community; if I'm using the same "disciplinary matrix," whatever that means;[43] if I'm solving the same problems, the same puzzle sets; if I'm playing the same language game—then everything is OK. But oopsies, a revolution occurs. Scientists in separate paradigms are like Robinson Crusoe and us. How are we (or they) to know whether they are referring to toothaches or to aardvarks? As Kripke tastefully puts it, "The main problem is *not*, 'How can we show private language—or some other special form of language—to be *impossible*?'; rather it is, 'How can we show *any language* at all (public, private or what-have-you) to be *possible?*'" Kripke then administers the *coup de théâtre*: "What *can* be said on behalf of our ordinary attributions of meaningful language to ourselves and others? Has not the incredible self-defeating conclusion, that all language is meaningless, already been drawn?"[44]

I asked Kripke—

ERROL MORRIS: Were you ridiculing Wittgenstein? Taking him seriously—maybe more seriously than he takes himself?

SAUL KRIPKE: Yes—well, I expressed some doubts about whether this whole thing can really work. And worried whether this view makes sense. Or if it's highly cultural-relativistic—

MORRIS: That it leads to relativism?

KRIPKE: Wittgenstein certainly worried about it. There is a conversation he had with one of his leading disciples—reported by her—Elizabeth Anscombe. There's actually a passage in his book *On Certainty* about it—people who would, instead of consulting physicians, consult a witch doctor.[45] And then she said, "Well, how would you feel if a friend of yours got interested in following witch doctors? How would you feel?" You have to look this up in her papers. It's called "The Question of Linguistic Idealism." Wittgenstein replied, well, he wouldn't like it, but he doesn't know why. Or something like that.

The passage in Anscombe is indeed suggestive:

Wittgenstein rejected the idea that 'our science' shows that magical practices and beliefs are errors. Above all, he thought it stupid to take magic for mistaken science. Science can correct only scientific error, can detect error only in its own domain; in thoughts belonging to its own system of proceedings. About the merits of other proceedings it has nothing to say except perhaps for making predictions.

But could witch doctors be considered on par with medical doctors? Anscombe continues:

> I once asked Wittgenstein whether, if he had a friend who went in for witch-doctoring, he would want to stop him. He thought about this for a little and said "Yes, but I don't know why." I believe that the objection is a religious one. A scientist cannot condemn superstitious practices on the basis of his science. He may do so on the basis of a 'scientistic' philosophy. But there is no need for him to hold such a philosophy in order to pursue his science. . . . In his work up to *On Certainty* we might think we could discern a straightforward thesis: there can be no such things as 'rational grounds' for our criticizing practices and beliefs that are so different from our own. These alien practices and language games are simply there. They are not ours, we cannot move in them.[46]

46. Anscombe, "The Question of Linguistic Idealism," p. 125.

The passage not only underlines Wittgenstein's relativism but shows it's just a hop, skip, and a jump from Wittgenstein to Kuhn. "There can be no such things as 'rational grounds' for our criticizing practices and beliefs that are so different from our own."

I returned to plus and quus.

MORRIS: Isn't the plus/quus thing a way of saying, if you adopt Wittgenstein's position, it leads to nonsense?

KRIPKE: Yes. I think it is plausibly viewed that way, I will say—cautiously. Someone has written a whole book defending the view I portray as not only coherent but as the truth.[47] I don't know whether I agree with him completely, but I thought a lot of what the book says is right. I say in the preface [to *Wittgenstein on*

47. Martin Kusch, *A Sceptical Guide to Meaning and Rules* (2006).

48. Kripke, in an email to me dated February 6, 2012, expressed his reluctance to go further but defended his interpretation of Wittgenstein: "I am, as you see, rather cautious as to how accurate my book is as exegesis of Wittgenstein. As I say, W probably wouldn't like any attempt to state his views more precisely. And I liked David Lewis's comment that if W didn't say that (what I attribute to him), so much the worse for him! However, I have been unimpressed with the attempts to refute my interpretation as exegesis. It stands against any criticism I know."

Rules]—I'm not saying that this is the truth, but I'm arguing like a lawyer for my position. But I express some sort of doubt-fear in there.[48]

It may not be that Kripke is right and Wittgenstein is wrong. Or the other way around. It may come down to completely antithetical views about the world. Looking from the inside out (from inside our brains out at the universe) versus looking from the outside in (from the universe back at ourselves). You, the critical reader, might say, "But how is that possible? How is it possible to look from the outside in? We are *trapped* inside of ourselves." Indeed. Moored inside our biological frame—like a mummy in a sarcophagus. There is no escape. A similar argument could be made for historical knowledge. If we are trapped inside the bubble of the present, how is it possible for us to have any knowledge of past events? Isn't all history hopelessly distorted by the predilections and biases of the present? Indeed. But allow me to propose an alternative—investigative realism. I am saying that there is a *real* world out there—a world of science and of history—and that we can come to know it. How? It's not given to us on a platter. A luncheon counter offering next to the potato salad or the macaroni and cheese. We learn about it through reason, through observation, through investigation, through thought, through science. If the moon and the stars are out there, if the universe is real, our task is to show how we are part of it. And have *knowledge* of it. Not to undermine that fact.

7. THE FURNITURE OF THE WORLD

Oh, East is East, and West is West, and never the twain shall meet,
Till Earth and Sky stand presently at God's great Judgment Seat;
But there is neither East nor West, Border, nor Breed, nor Birth,
When two strong men stand face to face, tho' they come from the ends of the earth!
—Rudyard Kipling, "The Ballad of East and West"

In fifth grade I got into an argument. I was ten years old. I bet this
kid a dollar that Reno, Nevada, is west of Los Angeles, California.
He refused to believe me, so I got out an atlas and showed him that
it was. But he wouldn't pay up.

39° 31' 38" N, 119° 49' 19" W Reno, Nevada

34° 03' 00" N, 118° 15' 00" W Los Angeles, California

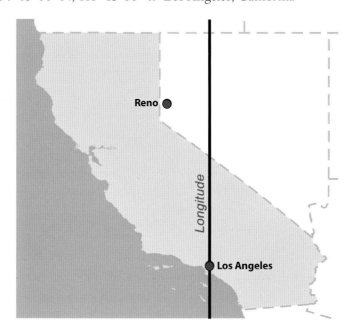

Instead, he argued that lines of longitude don't cross the ocean. That's right—that's what he said. Well, the longitude of Reno (119° 49' 19" W) intersects the California coastline somewhere around Santa Barbara, and the longitude of Los Angeles (118° 15' 00" W) passes somewhere around Lovelock, Nevada, a hundred miles (more or less) *east* of Reno. There doesn't seem to be much room for argument, but as we all know, that never stopped anyone. But what is his argument? Is he arguing that it depends on what "west" means? Perhaps "west" means "anything on the western *coast* of the United States." That anything on the west coast is farther west than anything that isn't on the west coast. In that sense, Los Angeles would be farther west than Reno. But what sense is that? It's like *quus*. Except this time it's *qwest*. (One of the directions on a *qwompass*?) We are reduced to the "babble of disagreement" Kripke found in Wittgenstein. You say this, I say that. Let's call the whole thing off. The insane, the pugilistic, and the dumb will resist all entreaties. If the kid is allowed to redefine "west," all bets are off, literally. Haven't we all heard that argument—It depends what you mean by "west"?

OK. We can't communicate if we do not have a common understanding of what "west" means. The *Oxford English Dictionary* tells us, somewhat circumspectly, that west "is 90 degrees clockwise from the south point." But the answer to the question, Which is farther west? hinges on something more than mere agreement. It hinges on the world—the crust of the earth and the location of cities on it. It hinges on the truth or falsity of the claim. As Philip K. Dick expressed it, "Reality is that which, when you stop believing in it, doesn't go away."[1]

1. Dick, "How to Build a Universe that Doesn't Fall Apart Two Days Later," p. 261.

———

Noam Chomsky hardly needs an introduction. He is one of the world's leading public intellectuals, a renowned linguist, cognitive scientist, philosopher, and also historian. I studied his *Syntactic Structures* and *Cartesian Linguistics* while still an undergraduate at the University of Wisconsin. The first included his now famous sentence "Colorless green ideas sleep furiously"; the second was an exploration of the Port-Royal School as a precursor to Chomsky's ideas about universal grammar. And then in the 1970s—I had graduated from college and was on to one graduate school or

another—two essays gripped me with their remarkable intellectual power: Chomsky's criticism of the behaviorist theory of language in "A Review of B. F. Skinner's *Verbal Behavior*" and Kripke's *Naming and Necessity*. The essays were devastating. B. F. Skinner's theories of language acquisition and description theories of reference were essentially put to rest. Although many have tried to resuscitate them, they absorbed devastating body punches.[2]

I felt Chomsky would be an ideal person to consult about scientific change, and Kuhn, as well as reference and truth. (Both had taught at MIT after Kuhn left Princeton.) Chomsky's ideas are often—at least for me—difficult to understand. And I hoped by talking with him, I could come to a deeper understanding of some of his philosophical positions and his thoughts about Kuhn and history of science. For example, on scientific revolutions. For Chomsky, it's "revolution" in the singular. There is only one. *The*

2. I have often wondered about the political right and the left. Whether metaphysical theories are in any way related to politics. While this is hardly the place to weigh in on these themes—wouldn't it take a book in and of itself?—the belief in a *real* world, in truth and in reference, does seem to speak to the left; the denial of the real world, of truth and reference, to the right.

Scientific Revolution—the revolution from pre-Galilean narratives to a post-Galilean mathematical world picture. Chomsky has gone on record saying that even his own "revolution" in linguistics (his rejection of Skinner and the behaviorist school) was no revolution at all.[3] He wrote to me, "There's no criterion to determine whether some change is a scientific revolution. It's a matter of judgment."[4] (Hear, hear. I myself would argue that many scientific revolutions never occurred but were *imagined* long after the fact, just as the neo-Platonists in the fourth and fifth centuries CE *imagined* the murder of Hippasus over his supposed proof of the irrationality of $\sqrt{2}$.)

So no scientific revolutions. What about reference? Chomsky sent me a chapter, "Notes on Denotation and Denoting," in which he argues that there are "acts of referring" but no reference per se. But if Kuhn argues that there is no reference in science, Chomsky believes that there may be no reference *except* in science: possible reference in scientific language; none in ordinary language. For example, Chomsky's determination of whether the sentence "Water is H_2O" is true hinges on the language system in use:

> It is not the "language of chemistry," which does not have the term *water* (though it is used informally). It is not the natural language English, which does not have the term H_2O. . . . If we consider the mixed system in which the expression appears, its status will depend on whether *water* is used in the sense of normal English (in which case the expression is false) or in the sense of of chemistry (in which case it is true by definition . . .).[5]

I would call Chomsky a reluctant realist, a realist about scientific terms but not about terms in ordinary language. "In the sciences, one goal is to adhere as closely as possible to the referentialist doctrine. Thus in devising technical notions like *electron* or *phoneme*, researchers *hope* to be identifying entities that exist in the world, and seek to adhere to the referentialist doctrine in using these notions."[6]

The phrase "referentialist doctrine" is a fancy way of describing the idea that there are things (entities) in the world to which we can unambiguously refer. In ordinary language, Chomsky argues, the doctrine fails. If reference is a mind-world relation—a relation between some specific thing in the mind (or brain) and some

3. Chomsky, Gary A. Olson, and Lester Faigley, "Language, Politics, and Composition" (1991), p. 2.
4. Email to author, August 4, 2014.

5. Chomsky, "Notes on Denotation and Denoting," pp. 42–43.

6. "Notes on Denotation," p. 42. The italics on "hope" are mine. It is a peculiar word here. Hence, it is given a quasi-religious significance. (Like transubstantiation.)

specific thing in the world—our attempts fall short. We are archers hoping to hit targets when, properly speaking, we can't even say the targets exist, let alone, whether we hit them.

> In the elementary case, a name like *Pavarotti* "refers to or denotes its bearer (the popular singer)"; and generally, "from a denotational point of view, symbols stand for objects." This core notion—the *referentialist doctrine*—is standard, as indicated even in the titles of some of the founding works on these topics in the early days of contemporary linguistic semantics over half a century ago: *Words and Things* (Brown 1958) and *Word and Object* (Quine 1960). And of course the referentialist doctrine has much deeper roots. . . . [Some] argue that it should serve a dual function, leading to explanation of the two fundamental questions of semantics: the link between symbols and their information content, the "aboutness of language," its connection to the external world; and "language as a social activity."[7]

7. "Notes on Denotation," p. 38.

Chomsky believes we are making some kind of leap when we imagine that we have referred to anything outside of our conceptual schemes. But still, for Chomsky there is no incommensurability. (That is, there can be an absence of metaphysical certainty without the gobbledegook of Kuhnian paradigms.) There is our common human conceptual scheme and no other. He dismisses the issue with a rhetorical question: "Can you think of cases where apparent incommensurability has remained as a barrier to scientific progress?"

NOAM CHOMSKY: As far as I can see, there's too much commonality of cognitive capacities for there to be anything like incommensurability. We should always be able to find some level of agreement from which a discussion can begin. And then we'll either find insistence on doctrine independent of fact, at which point, of course, you can't debate anymore, or else we'll find a rational resolution. So, for example, if you're debating evolution with a confirmed evangelical Christian who's committed to a belief in the literal truth of the Bible, you reach a point where you can't carry out a discussion anymore. But there's nothing profound about that. That's just insistence on doctrine independent of evidence.

ERROL MORRIS: Dogmatism.

CHOMSKY: Yes. But if you don't have that kind of irrational factor, it's hard for me to believe that there's no way to move from some shared set of assumptions to a serious interaction—It's *not* that you can't understand one another.

MORRIS: Indeed, it happens all the time.

CHOMSKY: Yes, of course.

MORRIS: Even in the case of the Bible-thumping evangelist and, say, Richard Dawkins, there still is a discussion.

CHOMSKY: Exactly. They understand one another, and they have their beliefs that are unshakable no matter what the facts are.

MORRIS: It's inflexibility and intractability—not incommensurability.

CHOMSKY: I've never been convinced by the various historical arguments about incommensurability. It seems to me the arguments were always on grounds that began with a common basis but different interpretations of the evidence.

I returned to history. Chomsky told me that if given a second life, he would devote himself to intellectual history. But is history, as my wife often describes it, just mythology with numbers?

MORRIS: Don't we, not unreasonably, believe that we are referring to things in history?

CHOMSKY: We *are*. I agree with that. But referring—

MORRIS: For you, referring without reference—

CHOMSKY: Yes. Referring is an action. And it certainly takes place. The two of us could be referring to Robert S. McNamara [secretary of defense for Presidents Kennedy and Johnson]. But the question—the serious philosophical, linguistic, psychological question—is, Is there a relation of reference or denotation in the technical sense between the symbol "McNamara" that you and I are using when we refer, and some extra-mental entity that a physicist could identify? And I think there is not.

MORRIS: Don't you think that's a little perverse?

CHOMSKY: It sounds perverse, but I think it's true. There is a kind of dogma. It seems intuitively clear that I say the Charles River happens to flow outside the apartment where I live. [The Charles River separates Cambridge, Massachusetts, from

Boston.] It's there; I see it. But do I identify it as a river in terms of extra-mental characteristics that a physicist could identify? The evidence is that I don't. And, in fact, this goes back to the Greeks. It's nothing new.

MORRIS: But what if you are talking about entities where it's really hard to pinpoint reference?

CHOMSKY: Person is an easy case. Locke wrote about it. Hume wrote about it. They all recognized that we individuate persons on the basis of properties that cannot be physically detected. Like for example, psychic continuity. Infants understand this. Take the fairy tale where the wicked witch turns the handsome prince into a frog, and he has all the physical characteristics of a frog, until the beautiful princess kisses the frog and he turns back into the handsome prince. Every child understands this. But that means he was the prince all along. It didn't matter what his physical characteristics were.[8]

8. I understand psychic continuity, but is this not conflating imaginability and possibility? Can a prince be a frog? No. Can a child *imagine* a frog is a prince, and vice versa? Yes. When we talk about something being possible, we're saying something very specific in the Kripkean sense.

But take rivers—for example, the Charles River. Thomas Hobbes argued that a river is individuated by its point of origin.[9] So what makes it the same river is that its origin is in the same place. But that can't be true. Take the Amazon or the Nile. They have many different points of origin. Furthermore, if the flow of the river was reversed, it would still be the same river. You can think of innumerable radical changes that would still keep it the same river. On the other hand, there are trivial changes which will change it so that it isn't a river at all. If you put walls along the side and start using it for moving freight, it's a canal, it's not a river. If you harden the surface somehow and paint a line

9. Hobbes, *Elements of Philosophy The First Section, Concerning Body* (1656), p. 101: "Also if the Name be given for such Form as is the beginning of Motion, then as long as that Motion remains it will be the same Individual thing; as that Man will be always the same, whose Actions and Thoughts proceed all from the same beginning of Motion, namely, that which was in his generation; and that will be the same River, which flows from one and the same Fountain, whether the same Water, or other Water, or something else than Water flow from thence."

through the middle of it, then people start using it to commute to Boston. It's a highway, not a river. It might have been a minuscule phase change that hardened the surface to something glasslike. And if you continue with this, you see that what determines that it's a river is a set of mental operations which are well beyond anything that's detectable in the physical world.

For me, there *is* a difference between entities like the Charles River, which are vague, and the frog that the beautiful princess kisses. I can believe that the frog is a prince, but that doesn't mean that he (or she) is one.

MORRIS: But does this mean there are *no* entities out there?

CHOMSKY: Oh, there are. But I'm talking about ordinary language and ordinary thought here. In the sciences, you depart from that and you start trying to develop systems in which there really *is* reference. Take the question—is water H_2O? Scientists will say water is H_2O. But they're not using the word "water" with its meaning in natural language. So, for example, let's take water. Suppose that I have a cup of pure H_2O in front of me and somebody puts a teabag into it. Then it's not water anymore, it's tea. Suppose that there's a tannic acid filter in the water supply upstream. When I turn on the sink it's chemically identical to the substance that was created by putting a teabag into water. Then it's water. But it's chemically identical to what isn't water, namely tea. That's the way language and thought work. Scientists, of course, don't want that. They want their terms to really pick out some mentally independent entity in the outside world. That's naïve realism, which we all intuitively accept even if there are arguments about it. We say water is H_2O, but it's true by science.

MORRIS: If there are things in our world—the furniture of our world, so to speak—wouldn't our cognitive abilities evolve in such a way as to recognize that fact: the need to know that there's a caveman with a spear that's going to kill us or a carnivore with extremely large teeth that's going to eat us?

CHOMSKY: Oh, sure. But that doesn't mean that we need to introduce the notion of reference. For example, there's pretty strong evidence that apes can't even develop the concept of a name. If you take a look at the books about Nim Chimpsky, supposedly it was all a fantastic success. Until finally, when they got to the point where they had to terminate the experiment—one of the graduate students was doing a frame-by-frame analysis of the whole process. They were very careful experimenters. They knew what they were doing, and they kept very good records; the protocols were excellent. He went through the frames and he found out that nothing was happening. They were deceiving themselves. It was like Clever Hans.[10] They were hinting unconsciously in ways that the ape could pick up on and then react to. The other part was they were deluding themselves in their interpretations of the signs that he was producing. Nim, with all the training, was never able to grasp the concept that there's a word, say "banana," that picks out the fruit. He would use the symbol that the experimenters called "banana," but nothing ever like our concept of a name. So evolution didn't do it for them and there's no reason to think it should do it for us.

MORRIS: We can easily become delusional about the world. Self-deception is ubiquitous. Clever Hans's trainer really believed that Hans was computing arithmetic sums. And Nim Chimpsky's trainer really believed that Nim was referring to

10. One of the ultimate stories of self-deception. Clever Hans's trainer believed he had taught his horse to count. But the horse was reacting to unconscious cues from his trainer.

a banana. You're telling me that there is a fact of the matter—Clever Hans doesn't know arithmetic, and Nim Chimpsky doesn't and can't refer. But does that mean we can't either?

CHOMSKY: What evolution did for apes you can investigate, but what it did for humans is create a symbolic system which has no counterpart in the animal world. We don't produce the word "apple" every time we see something associated with an apple. A lot of people who believe in tiny steps and who believe in evolution caused by natural selection don't like to believe this, but that's just what seems to be the case. There's a famous paragraph in *The Origin of Species* which everyone quotes all the time where Darwin says that unless what's evolved has evolved by very small, almost imperceptible steps—unless by natural selection, unless that's true—my whole theory collapses.[11] Now it's known not to be true. There are very small mutations or even changes in the way regulatory mechanisms work that lead to very large phenotypical differences. That's been known for thirty years. Modern biology doesn't find that surprising any longer. In the case of humans, it's a total mystery. We have no idea how human symbolic systems evolved with their special characteristics.

MORRIS: Do you find it, after all of these years, even more mysterious than you did initially?

CHOMSKY: Yes. The more we learn, the more mysterious it gets. But, that's true of the sciences generally. Take physics—the star science. The more they learn, the more they discover that they can't even find 90 percent of the mass-energy in the universe. That's pretty mysterious.

MORRIS: But they find they can understand many things that they didn't understand before—

CHOMSKY: They can understand a lot of things, but more mysteries keep showing up—and deeper ones. Physicists are playing around with the idea of multiverses where other universes have different physical laws and so on and so forth. All of this is sheer mystery.

MORRIS: I was surprised to read that you are in sympathy with the mysterians—

CHOMSKY: Not only in sympathy, I'm the original one.

11. "As natural selection acts solely by accumulating slight, successive, favourable variations, it can produce no great or sudden modification; it can act only by very short and slow steps." Darwin, *On the Origin of Species*, p. 492.

MORRIS: The original mysterian? From your article about problems and mysteries?

CHOMSKY: That was the first one, but that's forty years ago. This is in the December issue [2013] of the *Journal of Philosophy*—the Dewey lectures at Columbia.[12] And the second of these lectures reviews the history of so-called mysterianism, where I'm regarded as the main culprit, and traces it back to its origin, which is Isaac Newton. Newton concluded that the truth about the world is incomprehensible. It's known to historians of science. I don't think philosophers of science have assimilated it. But you have to recall that modern science, the Galilean Revolution, was based on a principle. The principle was what they called "the mechanical philosophy"—that the world is a machine. For Galileo and Leibniz, Huygens, Newton, and so on, unless you could produce a *mechanical* explanation of something, you had *no* explanation. It was just a mystery. And mechanical meant what we intuitively mean by "mechanical": gears and levers and so on. No interaction without contact. That was crucial. Newton showed it's just not true. He described this conclusion as an absurdity that no person with any scientific understanding could possibly accept. Actually, Locke and Hume and the classical philosophers understood this very well. David Hume wrote a history of England, and there's a chapter on Newton, in which he praises Newton as the greatest genius who ever existed. And he said one of his great achievements was not to unveil some of the mysteries of nature, but to demonstrate that there are other mysteries of nature which we will never comprehend. He was referring to action at a distance.[13]

The sciences just lowered their sights. From Galileo through Newton, they were really trying to explain things in terms that are coherent to us. By the time Newton's discoveries just became assimilated into scientific common sense, what science sought was something much more limited. The world is indeed incomprehensible, it's a mystery, but we can at least construct intelligible theories. That's a much weaker goal, and people like Bertrand Russell understood this. Alexandre Koyré and others understood it, but philosophers of science don't. So that's mysterianism, really deep mysterianism. And I have a different take on it

12. Chomsky, "The Dewey Lectures 2013: What Kind of Creatures Are We?"

13. "While Newton seemed to draw off the veil from some of the mysteries of nature, he showed at the same time the imperfections of the mechanical philosophy, and thereby restored her ultimate secrets to that obscurity in which they ever did and ever will remain." Hume, *The History of England*, p. 381.

because it reduces to the fact that we're organisms and not angels. If we're organisms, our cognitive capacities are like all biological capacities. They have scope and limits. There are some things that are simply beyond our limits—like the nature of the world.

And yet science is endlessly conjuring with the nature of the world. And attempts to penetrate to the nature of things. When we ask, What is water? or What is gold?, we are asking about the essence of a thing, about necessary properties, about things that could not be otherwise. Science often deals with such properties. Indeed, the very idea of a scientific *law* suggests that there are necessary (or essential) properties. But necessary properties are anathema to Chomsky (and many philosophers), at least in ordinary language—the language we use in everyday life.[14]

Chomsky disputed Kripke's essentialist picture of reference early on. He writes in his landmark 1975 book *Reflections on Language*:

> Kripke (1972) suggests that there could be no situation in which Queen Elizabeth II of England, this very woman, might have had different parents; it is a necessary truth that she had the particular parents she had (though again, we do not know it *a priori*). His conclusion is that "anything coming from a different origin would not be this object."
>
> My own intuitions differ about the example. Thus, it does not seem that a logical[15] problem would arise if Queen Elizabeth II were to write a fictionalized autobiography in which she, this very person, had different parents; we might, I think, take this as a description of this person in a different "possible world," a description of a possible state of this world with the very objects that appear in it.[16]

But Kripke is not asking whether we could *imagine* that Elizabeth II could have different parents. Or if we could write a fictionalized biography in which Elizabeth II has different parents. My intuition is, yes, we could *imagine* such things. There are imaginable worlds and imaginary worlds. (An imaginable world could turn out to be a

14. Kripke writes, "Something about the periodic table gave a description of elements as metals in terms of their valency properties. This may make some people think right away that there are really two concepts of metal operating here, a phenomenological one and a scientific one which then replaces it. This I reject" (*Naming and Necessity*, pp. 117–18). For Chomsky, on the other hand, there *are at least* two concepts of metal (or of water)—the phenomenological and the scientific.

15. The word "logical" muddies the waters. At least, it confuses me. Do I agree with Chomsky that "it does not seem that a logical problem would arise." Yes. But what is Chomsky saying? Does a logical problem arise in a fictionalized autobiography of Queen Elizabeth II in which $\pi = 3$. No. The fictionalized autobiography has expressed something that is not possible, not illogical. (After all, it *is* fiction.)

16. Chomsky, "The Object of Inquiry," in *Reflections on Language* (1975), pp. 48–49.

real world, where an imaginary world could not.) Kripke is asking a different question—is it *possible* that Elizabeth II, *that person*, could have different parents or a different set of chromosomes or different DNA and still be Elizabeth II?[17] (Or could Elizabeth II have a different genetic provenance?) Ask yourself, Could I be an aardvark and still be me?[18] Remember, you're *not* asking yourself the question, Could I imagine myself to be an aardvark? You're asking yourself the question, Could I still be me *and* be an aardvark? The answer, for me, is, No.[19]

17. The problem is exacerbated by the name "Elizabeth II." It creates confusion. Couldn't some other person be Elizabeth II? For example, if Edward VIII had not abdicated the throne and had had a daughter named "Elizabeth," mightn't *she* be Elizabeth II? But Elizabeth II, *that woman*, sitting on the throne of England, could not have had different parents (nor could she be an aardvark). Kripke writes, "One can imagine, *given* the woman, that various things in her life could have changed: that she should have become a pauper; that her royal blood should have been unknown, and so on. One is given, let's say, a previous history of the world up to a certain time, and from that time it diverges from the actual course. This seems to be possible. And so it's possible that even though she was born of these parents she never became queen. Even though she was born of these parents, like Mark Twain's character, she was switched off with another girl. . . . It seems to me that anything coming from a different origin would not be this object." *Naming and Necessity*, p. 113.

18. Kafka, of course, asks, Could I be a dung-beetle and still be me? Kafka notwithstanding, the answer is still no. Gregor Samsa could be a fictive dung-beetle who believes that he is a dung-beetle. He could believe that he is a dung-beetle. He just can't be a dung-beetle and be a human being in *our* world.

19. Imagining myself to be an aardvark, mercifully, doesn't require me to construct a world in which I must provide an aardvark-like version of myself.

20. Hilary Putnam pointed out to me that we could imagine the sperm and egg coming from different *physically* possible individuals. Hopefully, making this about chromosomes resolves this difficulty.

21. Chomsky, *Of Minds and Language*, pp. 381–82.

22. "The ship on which Theseus sailed with the youths and returned in safety, the thirty-oared galley, was preserved by the Athenians down to the time of Demetrius Phalereus. They took away the old timbers from time to time, and put new and sound ones in their places, so that the vessel became a standing illustration for the philosophers in the mooted question of growth, some declaring that it remained the same, others that it was not the same vessel." Plutarch, *Lives*, vol. 1, p. 49.

Clearly, the Ship of Theseus also involves museum science. In the effort by the Athenians to preserve the ship, boards were replaced. Possible worlds and provenance are hopelessly confused here. Let me explain. Are there possible worlds in which various boards are replaced and it still remains the Ship of Theseus? Maybe. But are we talking about the *essence* of the Ship of Theseus or its *provenance*? To my way of thinking the ship may have *no* essence. No *essential* properties. But it does have a *provenance*. As long the ship is causally or historically linked to the original, it is the Ship of Theseus.

23. Hobbes, *Elements of Philosophy The First Section, Concerning Body*, p. 100.

Questions of identity and individuality are bound up now with biological science—in this instance, genetics: the twenty-three chromosomes a child gets from her mother and the twenty-three chromosomes she gets from her father. (For Kripke in 1972, this takes a slightly different form. The structure of DNA had been announced only twenty years earlier.) Could Queen Elizabeth have a different set of chromosomes and still be Queen Elizabeth?[20]

Clearly, for Chomsky the very act of referring is filled with ambiguities. How do we refer to a thing when we don't really know what a "thing" is? Or even whether there *are* things? Chomsky invokes the Ship of Theseus—the ship Theseus took to Crete to slay the Minotaur.[21] In an account given by Plutarch, the Ship of Theseus is dismantled and then reconstructed with different materials.[22] Is it still the Ship of Theseus? Thomas Hobbes provides a further wrinkle.[23] The Ship of Theseus is dismantled, reconstructed with different materials, and the original boards, nails and other fittings are used to construct another ship. Which of the two is the *real* Ship of Theseus?

Questions of this kind come down to "It depends on what you mean by 'x'." Neither? Both? And to questions of provenance rather than identity. The cells in my body are replaced every seven years—or so they say. Does this mean I'm the Ship of Theseus in human form? Actually, the seven years is an old wives' tale; the cells of the human body are replaced at different rates. Among the fastest are the lungs. Cells on the surface of the lung are replaced every couple of weeks.[24] Should I refer to my lungs as the Lungs of Theseus?

Should the conclusion be that there is no reference? No Ship of Theseus? I don't think so.

———

In 1953, as the Sapir-Whorf hypothesis—that our conception of the world is determined by the languages we use—started attracting a lot of attention in the academic world, an unusual article appeared in *Astounding Science Fiction*: G. R. Shipman's "How to Talk to a Martian." Clearly influenced by Benjamin Lee Whorf, it provides a blueprint for the possible limitations of communication with aliens. Shipman's crisp explanation captures the essence of the problem. It is another example of the inversion of the conditional discussed by Kripke (We do not accept the law of contradiction because it is a necessary truth; it is a necessary truth because we accept it—by convention, and so on and so forth):

> The Seventeenth Century philosophers used to speculate about "general grammar." All languages—so they reasoned—are attempts to *translate* the "reality" of the universe; a single logic underlies all of them. Our increased knowledge makes it seem more likely that the opposite is true. Languages do not depend on universal logic; logic depends on the structure of languages.[25]

Language does not depend on logic; logic depends on the structure of language. Shipman goes on to debunk the very possibility of universal translation, advocating some sort of literary cosmophagic justice—in this instance, eating alive science-fiction characters.[26] He writes, "Of all the stock characters in science fiction that I wish the BEM's would eat alive, number one on my list is the Telepathic Martian. You know the one I mean." (BEM's? I had to look it up. It's an acronym for *bug-eyed monster*.)

> His spaceship lands in an Iowa cornfield one hot July day. The nation panics; a frantic Defense Department throws a cordon around the farm; the yokels take to the woods; reporters and TV cameramen trample on inquisitive scientists; the *Chicago Tribune*

24. "The cells in the lungs constantly renew themselves, explains Dr. Keith Prowse, vice-president of the British Lung Foundation. However, the lungs contain different cells that renew at different rates. The alveoli or air sac cells—needed for the exchange of oxygen and gases—deep in the lungs have a steady progress of regeneration that takes about a year. Meanwhile, the cells on the lung's surface have to renew every two or three weeks. 'These are the lungs' first line of defense, so have to be able to renew quickly,' says Dr. Prowse." Angela Epstein, "Believe It or Not, Your Lungs Are Six Weeks Old," *Daily Mail*, October 13, 2009.

25. Shipman, "How to Talk to a Martian," p. 119.

26. Hmm. If I eat Gregor Samsa, should I be labeled a cannibal or an insectivore? Neither? It happens all the time in fiction, e.g., Morlocks eating the Eloi. Fictional characters eating other fictional characters, fictional characters eating real people. Clearly, we can imagine a fictional character eating a real person, and vice versa, but such a thing is not *physically* possible.

gets out an extra to warn us that the whole thing is probably a Fair Deal plot. Then, as the world and his wife sit with their ears glued to the radio, the hatches of the spaceship open and the Martian emerges to tell us he wishes us well and only wants to save our civilization from self-destruction.

In American English, no less. By some miracle the authors never explain, this visitor from outer space cannot only project his thoughts into human brains, but can force them to rearrange his extraterrestrial ideas into the patterns of American speech. . . . But I have yet to see a science-fiction opus that meets this problem of communication across cultural boundaries head-on and tries to solve it by extrapolating from our present techniques.[27]

27. "How to Talk to a Martian," pp. 112–13.

"For any human being," Shipman tells us, " 'reality' is the sum total of the abstracts his *language* can make from observed events." In other words, reality is an artifact of language and not the other way around. It is pure Sapir-Whorf:

Now Hopi has no imaginary plurals. For a Hopi Indian, the idea "ten days is longer than nine days" becomes "the tenth day is later than the ninth." He does not conceive of "ten days" as a length of time. . . . No Hopi Einstein, uninfluenced by European ideas, would ever evolve the notion of a four-dimensional space-time continuum. His mathematical picture of the universe would have no more in common with ours than a Greek painting has with a canvas by Picasso.

Now, perhaps, you begin to understand why I want to feed the Telepathic Martian and his universal translating machine to the BEM's. [A rather uncharitable thought.] If human languages can be so different as English and Nootka, the grammatical categories of Martian must be something completely outside our experience. The Telepathic Martian's thought-waves would have to be so powerful that they could make our brain cells aware of logical and grammatical relationships that have no equivalent whatever in our language.

Imagine, for the sake of the argument, that a telepathic English-speaking American and a telepathic Nootka-speaking

American sit down for a chat. . . . But how does the white man translate into pictures: "I paid off the mortgage on my house last year"? How do you visualize a mortgage to an Indian who barely understands money? Is the mortgage "on" the house the same way the shingles are on it? How do you picture the past-tense notion in "paid" and the concept "last year"?

See what I mean? When the Martians land, we'll have to learn their language in the same laborious way we have learned Nootka and Salish and all the rest. Though there won't be any informants on their spaceship, we can teach them a limited amount of English by the time-honored process of ostensive definition. This means pointing at a chair and saying "chair," or dropping a brick and remarking "I have just dropped a brick." Simple verbs can be acted out, like eat, wash, shave, die, scratch, draw, write. For more complicated ideas, we might begin by verbalizing arithmetical or mathematical statements, like "two and two make four" or "The square of the hypotenuse of a right triangle is equal to the sum of the squares of the other two sides." Presumably the Martians could teach us some of their language in the same way. It would be slow, but not impossible.[28]

28. "How to Talk to a Martian," pp. 119–20.

We could introduce the Martians to our language games. "Although there won't be any informants on their spaceship, we can teach them a limited amount of English. . . ."

But I am confused. Shipman tells us, "[The Martians'] mathematical picture of the universe would have no more in common with ours than a Greek painting has with a canvas by Picasso." Of course, much of Picasso's work is heavily influenced by Greek mythology and painting (Minotaurs, etc.). Still, I think I understand. Or do I? Is Shipman telling me that *their mathematics* is completely different from ours. Different in what way? Is their logic different? No negation, no law of the excluded middle, no *modus tollens*, no *modus ponens* (basic logical operations)? How could we hope to communicate? How could they hope to communicate even with themselves?

If the Martians have a conceptual scheme, how different is it from our own? How different is their mathematics, their logic? Shipman tells us that their mathematics and ours are as different as

29. Someone I know says, "It's like comparing apples and refrigerators," rather than apples and oranges. Apples and oranges? Aren't they both fruit?

30. Though it is only explicitly mentioned in passing (IAN: Look, I did some research and there's this idea that immersing yourself in a foreign language can rewire your brain— LOUISE: The Sapir-Whorf hypothesis, yes. The theory that the language you speak determines how you think), the eventual revelation of what the alien visitors are offering humanity confirms the centrality of Sapir-Whorf (LOUISE: Wait—I figured out the gift! . . . It's their language. They gave it all to us. . . . When you learn it, truly learn it, you perceive time the way they do).

the painting on a Greek vase and a Picasso. But we should remember: *both* are paintings.[29] More recently, the film *Arrival* (2016) used the Sapir-Whorf hypothesis, and its famous example of different perceptions of time, as a pivotal plot point.[30] But do differences in perception mean that time itself is different? Imagine the world in the Cambrian Period, 600 million years ago. Trilobites are scuttling about. There is no language, but *time* still progresses. There is still a *before* and an *after*, even though there is no language to express that fact. And yet, the fantasy of hidden realities still has a powerful appeal. It's wonderful to imagine that if we could comprehend the voice of God (or aliens), the universe would open itself up to us that we might see it more clearly or truly. Fans of the Old Testament would surely concur. (Isn't this part of the romance of the Tower of Babel—the magical promise of a unitary worldview uniting us in a common project?) But the leading theories of language do not and cannot support such a fantasy. It could be argued that our notions of time, say, the notions of *before* and *after*, need to be modified. Fine. Time could be different from what we imagine it to be, but that doesn't mean time is dependent on the structure of our brains or the structure of language.

———

Chomsky's universal grammar—the idea that the syntax of language is hard-wired into our brains—is thought to be the antithesis of the Sapir-Whorf hypothesis (linguistic relativity). But to me, it could be just a variant. Whorf tell us that there are insuperable *mental* constraints imposed by language. In Whorf's—false, as it turns out—analysis of the Hopi language, there are no tenses that differentiate between past, present, and future. Language constrains how we see the world. Our metaphysics is *relative* to language. Chomsky, on the other hand, tells us that there are mental constraints imposed by our biology. That our metaphysics is *relative* to our biology:

> Either we're angels or we're organic creatures. If we're organic creatures, every capacity is going to have its scope and limits. . . . [Charles] Peirce, for example, thought that truth is just the limit science reaches. That's not a good definition of truth. If our cognitive capacities are organic entities, which I take for granted

they are, there is some limit they'll reach; but we have no confidence that that's the truth about the world. It may be part of the truth; but maybe some Martian with different cognitive capacities is laughing at us and asking why we're going off in this false direction all the time. And the Martian might be right.[31]

31. Chomsky, *The Science of Language*, p. 133.

There is some *limit*. Some *cognitive* limit. But what is that limit? For Chomsky, there are problems and there are mysteries. As he claims, "problems are things that we can solve." We can work hard and find solutions—the missing word in an acrostic, the proof of Fermat's Last Theorem, the unknown ingredients in KFC's formula for fried chicken. (The CEO of KFC told me that even he isn't allowed to know the ingredients.) In principle, problems are epistemic. We *can* know the answer to a problem, even though we (currently) don't. Mysteries are different. Solutions will never be forthcoming. We are barred, because of how we are constituted (call it the hard-wiring of our brains or our DNA), from ever knowing these things—possibly the origins of consciousness or the solution to the P-NP problem.

Again the analogy—an analogy I don't much care for: dogs (and rats) are to humans as humans are to some superior being. A rat, supposedly, with good maze-solving abilities, is stopped in its tracks by a maze based on prime numbers—2, 3, 5, 7, 11, 13, 17, 19, 23—numbers that can only be divided by themselves and one. (Would this also hold true for a rat designed by a human, e.g., Theseus, the electronic mouse designed by Claude Shannon, the father of information theory?) Presumably their brain capacity is too small—they can never understand the concept of "prime number," no matter how hard or how long they might try. They can never understand the concept "turn left at 3, 5, 7 and 11." They have reached *the fur ceiling.*

Imagine two worlds. Creton, the planet of the super-dumb, and Smarton, the planet of the super-gifted. The small-brained inhabitants of Creton are unable to escape from a prime-number maze—and as a result, get eaten by the Minotaur. (They are like the Athenian hero Theseus in the labyrinth without the benefit of Ariadne's thread.) The large-brained inhabitants of Smarton run the maze with ease and the Minotaur goes hungry (save for the small bird trapped under its paw). But will even the Smartonians be able to prove all of the true statements in arithmetic? And will they be able to prove that Gödel's First Incompleteness Theorem is false? Unlikely.

Some people may be more capable than a run-of-the-mill Cretonian—but they are essentially no better or worse than Smartonians. Once we have access to mathematical truth, to necessary truth, there may be mysteries. But they are the same for all of us—for Smartonians, Super-Smartonians, Super-Duper Smartonians, and so on.

Newton wrote, *"Hypotheses non fingo"* (I do not feign hypotheses), and agonized over his abandonment of a mechanical worldview. He could never make sense of action at a distance. How does the gravity of the sun reach out across millions of miles of empty space and commandeer the earth into orbit? It created in him a profound unease.

This unease is echoed a century and a half later in Darwin's famous letter to Asa Gray:

There seems to me too much misery in the world. I cannot persuade myself that a beneficent and omnipotent God would have designedly created the [parasitic wasps] with the express intention of their feeding within the living bodies of Caterpillars, or that a cat should play with mice. Not believing this, I see no necessity in the belief that the eye was expressly designed. On the other hand, I cannot anyhow be contented to view this wonderful universe, and especially the nature of man, and to conclude that everything is the result of brute force. I am inclined to look at everything as resulting from designed laws, with the details, whether good or bad, left to the working out of what we may call chance. Not that this notion *at all* satisfies me. I feel most deeply that the whole subject is too profound for the human intellect. A dog might as well speculate on the mind of Newton. Let each man hope and believe what he can.[32]

Both Darwin *and* Newton expressed this view.[33] For me, what is striking is their sense of awe. A dog might as well speculate on the mind of Newton? That hardly seems out of the question. At least one eighteenth-century dog *did* just that. Newton's beloved dog Diamond was supposedly credited by his master with the discovery of a number of mathematical theorems. And accused of having started a fire that destroyed much of Newton's work, plunging his

32. Darwin, "Letter to Asa Gray" (1860).

33. As did others. John Locke: "He that will not set himself proudly at the top of all things, but will consider the immensity of this fabric [the world], and the great variety that is to be found in this little and inconsiderable part of it, which he has to do with, may be apt to think, that in other mansions of it, there may be other and different intelligent beings, of whose faculties he has as little knowledge or apprehension, as a worm shut up in one drawer of a cabinet hath of the senses or understanding of a man; such variety and excellency being suitable to the wisdom and power of the Maker." *An Essay Concerning Human Understanding* (1836), p. 64.

(Dog, worm . . . I have always been fascinated by the possibility of mentally challenged creatures from outer space. Replace the insufferable *Close Encounters* line, "Einstein was right," with "My God, they're stupider than we are." When extraterrestrials are involved, why are *we* always the cognitively impaired?)

And James Clerk Maxwell: "Man has indeed but little knowledge of the *simplest* of God's creatures, the nature of a drop of water has in it mysteries within mysteries utterly unknown to us at present, but what we do know we know *distinctly*; and we see before us distinct physical truths to be discovered and we are confident that these mysteries are an inheritance of knowledge, not revealed at once, lest we should become proud in knowledge, and despite patient inquiry, but so arranged that, as each new truth is unravelled it becomes a clear, well-established addition to science, quite free from the mystery which must still remain, to show that every atom of creation is *unfathomable* in its perfection." "Inaugural Lecture at Marischal College" (1856)," in *Scientific Letters and Papers*, vol. 1, p. 427.

34. " 'My dog Diamond knows some mathematics. Today he proved two theorems before lunch,' said Newton. 'Your dog must be a genius,' replied [mathetician John] Wallis. 'Oh I wouldn't go that far,' said Newton. 'The first theorem had an error and the second had a pathological exception.' " Bibek Debroy, *Sarama and Her Children: The Dog in Indian Myth*, p. 50. See also J. Edleston, ed., *Correspondence of Sir Isaac Newton and Professor Cotes*, p. lxiii.

35. A limit is quite different from an impossibility proof. To say that it is impossible to express $\sqrt{2}$ as a rational fraction is not to say that it represents a limit to human intelligence.

master into years of severe depression.[34] We do not know whether Diamond's actions were the result of inadvertence, carelessness, or even malice—jealous that his master had come up with a theory of universal gravitation.

Why imagine limits when there is little proof there are any?[35] Untranslatable languages, incommensurabilities, innate cognitive impediments—epistemological constraints of one kind or another. Isn't bare bones epistemology enough? The almost certain knowledge that we can be (and often are) wrong about everything? But being wrong doesn't mean we are barred from being right.

Darwin and Newton were *not* writing about the unknowable. They were trying to express the ineffable. (Unsuccessfully. After all is said and done, the ineffable is inexpressible.) Newton knew that his inverse-square law accounts for planetary motion; Darwin, that natural selection accounts for the diversity and complexity of life on earth. But there remains a mystery—the mystery of *why* it should be so.

8. AVATARS OF PROGRESS

Progress in our world will be progress towards more pain.
—George Orwell, *Nineteen Eighty-Four*

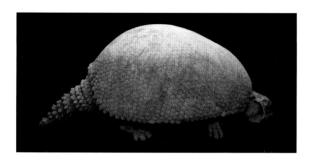

Kuhn in the final chapter of *The Structure of Scientific Revolutions* addresses the concept of progress. Is there such a thing? Scientific progress? Any kind of progress? Since Kuhn does not believe in truth, and therefore, does not believe in progress toward truth, he wonders where the widespread association of science with progress comes from. Much to my surprise, he invokes George Orwell's novel *Nineteen Eighty-Four*:

> More than the practitioners of other creative fields, [the scientist] comes to see [history] as leading in a straight line to the discipline's present vantage. In short, he comes to see it as progress. No alternative is available to him while he remains in the field.
>
> Inevitably those remarks will suggest that the member of a mature scientific community is, like the typical character of Orwell's *1984*, the victim of a history rewritten by the powers that be.[1]

1. Kuhn, *Structure* (1962), p. 166.

Is a scientist really like a "typical character" in Orwell's dystopian novel? Could it be that a belief in progress is a form of groupthink imposed on a scientific community with no egress? If scientists are *all* Winston Smith, Orwell's doomed protagonist, who is Big Brother? Who does the rewriting of history? Kuhn continues:

> If authority alone, and particularly if nonprofessional authority, were the arbiter of paradigm debates, the outcome of those debates might still be revolution, but it would not be *scientific* revolution. The very existence of science depends upon vesting the power to choose between paradigms in the members of a special kind of community. Just how special that community must be if science is to survive and grow may be indicated by the very tenuousness of humanity's hold on the scientific enterprise.[2]

In the first quote, Kuhn suggests that scientists are trapped and impotent. In the second, that they constitute "a special kind of community" with the power to chose between paradigms. They are Winston Smith *and* Big Brother. What should we remember here? In *Nineteen Eighty-Four* truth is not absent, it is just denied. Orwell introduces a cornucopia of concepts—thought crime, double-speak, double-think, the memory hole. He constructs a bizarro world where traditional concepts and understandings are endlessly undermined by the state. In the end, Winston Smith capitulates. It is a horrible, sad capitulation. But it could never have such dramatic force if the reader didn't see it as tragic and understand what has been lost.

There is none of this irony in *Structure*. We are left with just the herky-jerky succession of incommensurable paradigms. And the absence of truth.

At the very end of *Structure*—in a flourish to cap his arguments—Kuhn compares the evolution of species and the evolution of scientific ideas:

> The developmental process described in this essay has been a process of evolution *from* primitive beginnings—a process whose successive stages are characterized by an increasingly detailed and refined understanding of nature. But nothing that has been or will be said makes it a process of evolution *toward* anything. Inevitably that lacuna will have disturbed many readers. We are all deeply accustomed to seeing science as the one enterprise that draws constantly nearer to some goal set by nature in advance.[3]

2. *Structure* (1962), p. 166.

3. *Structure* (1962), pp. 169–70. Kuhn remained impressed with his analogy between scientific change and Darwinian evolution. He says, years later, in his interview with Baltas, Gavroglu, and Kindi, "I tried in the end of *Structure* to say in what sense I thought there is progress. I largely squeezed out the answer to that, talked about the accumulation of puzzles, and I think I would now argue very strongly that the Darwinian metaphor at the end of the book is right, and should have been taken more seriously than it was; and *nobody* took it seriously. People passed it right by. This question of stopping to see us, i.e., ceasing to see us, as getting *closer to* something, but see us instead as moving *away from* where we were—that was beyond anything I'd really quite grasped until the point at which I had to really wrestle with that problem. But saying that was important to me and it led to things that have happened since. And I think it might have been picked up and recognized more." *Road since Structure*, pp. 307–8.

"Nothing . . . makes it a process of evolution *toward* anything." This seems like an impressive idea. Allow me to employ a possible-worlds argument. Evolutionary change is indeed contingent. (Like many possible-worlds arguments this is based on our intuitions. If I lost an arm, would I still be me? My intuitions tell me, yes. Hence, having two arms is a *contingent* property of being me. I would still be me with one arm.) Whether an animal lives or dies at any given time (or place) is not a necessary property of that animal. Let's imagine one possible scenario. Ten thousand years ago, a giant armadillo (*Glyptodon*) is killed by a saber-toothed tiger (*Smilodon*), and hence does not get to pass its genes on to future giant armadillo generations. But it is entirely possible that that same saber-toothed tiger could have died at an earlier age. It could have fallen into a tar pit. Hence, no saber-toothed tiger to kill Mr. Giant Armadillo. Mr. Giant Armadillo is free to mate with Mrs. Giant Armadillo, and together they produce a giant armadillo family.

This is just another way of saying that evolutionary change could have happened otherwise. No animal (or plant) is the *necessary* outcome of evolution. On the other hand, new species are defined by *necessary properties*. It is an example of what Kripke calls the necessary *a posteriori*.[4]

4. This argument, like Kuhn and Cavell's discussion of Wittgenstein, hinges on how Kuhn interpreted natural selection. Ultimately, we may decide that Darwin was right or Darwin was wrong. We may imagine variations in post-Darwinian accounts of evolution. But at issue here is how Kuhn interprets it. And it is pretty clear Kuhn is trying to argue that outcomes in science are possible but never necessary.

5. Glyptodonts, in a somewhat different context, appear in Ian Hacking, *Representing and Intervening* (1983), pp. 75–77.

Let's continue with glyptodonts.[5] Doesn't everybody like glyptodonts? But what are they? Here's one descriptive answer—a glyptodont is a two-ton herbivore with a carapace of fused bony plates (the osteoderm) that became extinct roughly ten thousand years ago. The carapace was so large that it could have been used for primitive housing, although I know of no empirical evidence that it was.

Riesengürteltier.

I should pause to distinguish between glyptodons and glyptodonts: glyptodont is a subfamily; glyptodon, a genus. All glyptodons are glyptodonts, but not all glyptodonts are glyptodons. For example, *Doedicurus* is a non-glyptodon glyptodont with a spiky tail.

Chapter 8

Fine, you might say, but what *really* is a glyptodont? Not just a description or cluster of descriptions, but what is it—*really*? (We might ask, along with Kripke, If a definite description like "the so-and-so" or a cluster of descriptions can never determine reference, what can?) And how can we distinguish it from other armadillos and armadillo-like creatures? Are there necessary properties that define a glyptodont and distinguish glyptodonts from all other living things? A good question, with historical antecedents that go back several hundred years.

In the early nineteenth century, explorers and scientists started pulling fossils of gigantic creatures from the pampas of Argentina. They later became known as the megafauna of the last ice age. At first, the excavated bones were an undifferentiated muddle—one animal or many? Later, they were identified as the megatherium, the glyptodont, and the toxodon—all hopelessly mixed together. Fledgling paleontologists couldn't figure out what they were dealing with—armadillos, sloths, or giant rats? The glyptodont was thought to be just another megatherium, a gigantic ground sloth.[6]

One might wonder—what were they thinking? Size seems to be the determining factor. You see one big thing and you think it's like another big thing? Clearly, we are dealing with a lot of *something*. We now know that a glyptodont weighs two tons—four thousand pounds of armadillo—while a megatherium is four tons—eight thousand pounds of sloth. But this turned out to be a poor basis for classification.

And then, very recently, in 2015, glyptodont DNA was recovered and analyzed.[7] What did we learn? I asked Ross MacPhee, a curator at the American Museum of Natural History and coauthor of the recent paper analyzing glyptodont DNA, about the role of DNA in the study of glyptodonts. Has it changed things? If so, what has it changed? Has there been progress in our understanding? And more to the point, what did he think about Kuhn's use of evolution to justify his beliefs?

ROSS MACPHEE: These kinds of identification can be done only through molecular biology. It would have been impossible to do this morphologically. There's something of a similar nature that's going on with bison. We know that as well. But these

6. "It fell to Richard Owen to set matters straight. Owen (1839) founded the genus *Glyptodon* on material collected near Buenos Aires and shipped to London by the English secretary, Woodbine Parish. A year later, Owen reviewed all references to armored megatheres and established that the big armored animals were actually glyptodonts, a group related to armadillos, and that megatheres did not have a carapace." Richard A. Fariña, Sergio F. Vizcaíno and Gerry de Iuliis, *Megafauna*, p. 39.

7. "Among the fossils of hitherto unknown mammals that Darwin collected in South America between 1832 and 1833 during the Beagle expedition were examples of the large, heavily armored herbivores later known as glyptodonts. Ever since, glyptodonts have fascinated evolutionary biologists because of their remarkable skeletal adaptations and seemingly isolated phylogenetic position even within their natural group, the cingulate xenarthrans (armadillos and their allies). In possessing a carapace comprised of fused osteoderms, the glyptodonts were clearly related to other cingulates, but their precise phylogenetic position as suggested by morphology

remains unresolved. To provide a molecular perspective on this issue, we designed sequence-capture baits using *in silico* reconstructed ancestral sequences and successfully assembled the complete mitochondrial genome of *doedicurus sp.,* one of the largest glyptodonts. Our phylogenetic reconstructions establish that glyptodonts are in fact deeply nested within the armadillo crown-group, representing a distinct subfamily (*Glyptodontinae*) within family *Chlamyphoridae*. Molecular dating suggests that glyptodonts diverged no earlier than around 35 million years ago, in good agreement with their fossil record. Our results highlight the derived nature of the glyptodont morphotype, one aspect of which is a spectacular increase in body size until their extinction at the end of the last ice age." Frédéric Delsuc et al., "The Phylogenetic Affinities of the Extinct Glyptodonts," pp. R155–56.

happen to be two of the megafauna that are best represented in the fossil record. There are lots and lots of fossils of them. For other groups, it's going to be a lot harder to do because they don't have as good or as dense a fossil record. But my point here is that genetically, at some point, we will be able to distinguish populations among or within species and be able to trace them as what they are. Those are the real evolutionary actors. This is where things happen, like natural selection. A species is a generality. Things that look so much like one another that they get grouped together. But you don't really know what's going on inside the species—except via morphology in a very general way. If you have lineages that you can actually detect by molecular evidence, then you can do very much more. So it's a totally new world, all of this stuff.

ERROL MORRIS: A detail that fascinated me in that article on extinct glyptodonts was a conjecture: Take *Doedicurus*. What existing species is it most closely related to? The claim was—it was the pink fairy armadillo.

MACPHEE: Not *just* the pink fairy armadillo. That family is somewhat larger than that. It also includes the largest living armadillo, *Priodontes maximus*. But the largest living armadillo comes in at about twenty kilograms. And glyptodonts are fifty, sixty times that. The family has the whole spectrum of largest and smallest. But there's no argument that the family as a whole is quite tiny, of which the fairy is a good example. These are very small armadillos. All of these branching diagrams go back to a root, and then they splay out from there, usually bifurcate, in some cases trifurcate. The way to read this diagram is that *Doedicurus* is not most closely related to fairies, even though the image of the fairy is there, but it's related to that group as a whole. The branching sequence is such that the glyptodonts separated at some point from all other members of this group, which we now know today as the *Tolypeutids*.

MORRIS: So from this diagram, it's not really possible to say what it is most closely related to—

MACPHEE: In terms of living species, no. It's corporately related to all of them because the split occurred before these modern species had appeared.

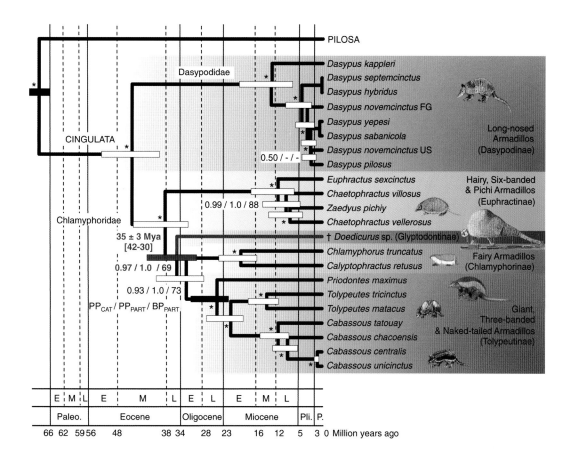

PILOSA

Dasypus kappleri
Dasypus septemcinctus
Dasypus hybridus
Dasypus novemcinctus FG
Dasypus yepesi
Dasypus sabanicola
Dasypus novemcinctus US
Dasypus pilosus

Long-nosed
Armadillos
(Dasypodinae)

Euphractus sexcinctus
Chaetophractus villosus
Zaedyus pichiy
Chaetophractus vellerosus

Hairy, Six-banded
& Pichi Armadillos
(Euphractinae)

† Doedicurus sp. (Glyptodontinae)

Chlamyphorus truncatus
Calyptophractus retusus

Fairy Armadillos
(Chlamyphorinae)

Priodontes maximus
Tolypeutes tricinctus
Tolypeutes matacus
Cabassous tatouay
Cabassous chacoensis
Cabassous centralis
Cabassous unicinctus

Giant,
Three-banded
& Naked-tailed Armadillos
(Tolypeutinae)

Dasypodidae

CINGULATA

Chlamyphoridae

35 ± 3 Mya
[42-30]

0.50 / - / -

0.99 / 1.0 / 88

0.97 / 1.0 / 69

0.93 / 1.0 / 73

PP_{CAT} / PP_{PART} / BP_{PART}

E ¦ M ¦ L	E ¦ M ¦ L	E ¦ L	E ¦ M ¦ L		
Paleo.	Eocene	Oligocene	Miocene	Pli.	P.

66 62 59 56   48   38 34   28   23   16   12   5   3 0 Million years ago

MORRIS: I'm glad I talked to you, because you have saved me from making a terrible error.

MACPHEE: It's not a terrible error; it's just another way of thinking about this. All of these trees are based on statistical probabilities. If the genetic compositions had been somewhat different, then we would have gotten somewhat different results. This happens to be the best of the resolutions that we got. But it doesn't mean that there aren't others, and it doesn't mean that under other circumstances with other genes—in other words, other kinds of information—we wouldn't have gotten a slightly different result. If you see the scores here, you see 0.97 and 0.99, 0.50? Those are probability estimates that the branching sequence you see is the correct one. So 0.50. That means it's a tossup. We're showing one of them, but it's a tossup. As you get up to 99 percent, of course, you don't expect flops of that sort, though there's still a probability attached to it. But what we've got with glyptodonts, with *Doedicurus*, is that it's in the 97th percentile, which is very high.

MORRIS: Do these figures give us confidence that we are defining one animal as opposed to another? Independent of epistemic problems, that is? We might not be able to ever *know* with certainty what that is. Don't you have a belief, in terms of molecular biology, that there is one set of properties that says, I am *Doedicurus*, I am *Chlamyphorus*?

MACPHEE: In relation to other species, certainly. Obviously we can do it. We can do it inductively. We can separate these things out from one another without having any notion of evolution or anything else. They look different—it's enough in most cases.

MORRIS: Let me explain what I mean. By essential properties, I mean that you could come up with a set of DNA characteristics of a pink fairy armadillo or *Doedicurus* that says, this is what I am. I am this. A glyptodont is *this*. And if it didn't have these characteristics, it wouldn't be a glyptodont.

MACPHEE: I have to say yes and no. First of all, you have to permit variation. It's not like there's a single defining sequence. A second thing: we don't know what a lot of the interactions are that end up making a living thing look the way that it does. There are epigenetic factors. There are gene interactions that are either closed off or opened up by very subtle changes in the genetic code. Perhaps this is what a lot of what we call junk DNA is for. It doesn't make any sense to us because it just repeats, repeats, repeats. It doesn't make anything. So what is it? Is it excelsior and filler? Or is it desperately important? There are a lot of questions connected with that. But I see where you're going. If we had the capacity to resolve such issues so that we got in some future point the complete sense of the whole coding, what makes the organism, would that uniquely identify it?

MORRIS: Would it be an essential property of *Doedicurus*? Could you say that if it were different, it wouldn't be *Doedicurus* anymore, it would be something else?

MACPHEE: Yes. It would be something else.

MORRIS: I'll give you an example. You could say it's contingent on our current understanding of the physical world, but I believe that gold has an atomic number of 79. And if it didn't have an atomic number of 79—

MACPHEE: It would be something else, clearly.

MORRIS: Yes, it would be something else. If it had an atomic number of 78 it would be platinum; if it had an atomic number of 80 it would be lead. I feel justified on that basis of saying that the atomic number 79 is an essential property of gold.

MACPHEE: OK, but the essential property of all elements is that from the Big Bang forward their properties are determined by what's involved in making up their nuclei. And there's more than one way of doing that; there's fission and there's fusion. So we're going all the way from helium at the outset to iron metals at the other end. But they all have an ultimate history that goes back to an event twenty billion or more years ago. Of course, gold is gold. But is there anything essential about that? I don't know the answer to that. But I'm going to give you a conundrum in return. Do you know the term "de-extinction"?

MORRIS: No.

MACPHEE: This is the notion—that is actually realistic, to a degree— that with genetic engineering nowadays we could reinvent the mammoth. But is a reinvented mammoth a mammoth?

MORRIS: I would say yes.

MACPHEE: Why would you say yes? Because it's something that's patched together in the laboratory. We're using genetic scaffolding based on the genome of the Asian elephant. The similarity is huge; they're 98, 99 percent similar. So there's only a few functional genes that are different. Using something like CRISPR [gene splicing] technology, we could get all of those Asian elephant genes to look like they did in the mammoth genome. And we would get something—not in the first generation, but as a result of crosses made again and again—we would get something that, sure, had long hair, a particular form of trunk, and a big dome on top, and maybe spiral tusks. But is it a mammoth, or is it a creation, an invention made by us to look like a mammoth? And at what point do the two blend together? Phylogenetically it's not a mammoth, because it's not part of the phylogenetic series that resulted in mammoths in the last several million years until they all died out ten thousand years ago.

That branch is broken. Instead we're going further back into the history of elephants, to a relative, and using that in order to make something that looks like a mammoth. To all intents and purposes it's a mammoth. My question to you is, is it *essentially* a mammoth?

MORRIS: Probably not. This is a question about provenance and lineage. What defines a thing. For example, in *Macbeth*, Shakespeare tells us that Macduff is a man not born of woman—he was "untimely ripped" from his mother's womb, born by Caesarian section.[8] And here is a mammoth not born of woman. Or at least not born of a woman mammoth. Maybe it's a woman elephant, but—

8. "Despair thy charm; / And let the angel whom thou still hast served / Tell thee, Macduff was from his mother's womb / Untimely ripp'd." *Macbeth*, act 5, scene 8.

MACPHEE: It would have to be.

MORRIS: Philosophers are endlessly absorbed by this kind of question. I have a painting that is, molecule by molecule, identical to Vermeer's *The Music Lesson*. Is it a Vermeer? I would think, no, it's not a Vermeer, because it had to have come from the hand of Vermeer. It has to be traced back to that hand that held the brush. Part of the essential property of being a Vermeer is—it's not looking like a Vermeer—it has to be painted *by* Vermeer and not by anyone else. It has provenance, a history.

MACPHEE: So transferring that to the mammoth example, don't you have to be *of a* mammoth to *be* a mammoth?

MORRIS: I'm not sure I have an immediate answer.

MACPHEE: That's good.

MORRIS: What is it that makes a thing a thing? Is it just that it has a certain molecular structure? You would say, no, it goes beyond that.

MACPHEE: Or you could take a completely reductionist point of view and say, if it is a mammoth genetically, if it is identical to the mammoth genome, then by definition it is a mammoth. I see that. But you only get so far in life by being a reductionist. You can't put everything into a bucket and not think in terms of how one bucket is related to another. After a point it becomes pointless. You understand less, not more. Just because you've got data doesn't mean you understand anything at all.

———

Molecular biology affords us an opportunity to identify necessary properties, but it does something more. It helps us discover not just the idea of what a glyptodont is, but also how it has evolved, what it has evolved from, and how it is related to current species. Call it *progress* in scientific understanding. (Even though Kuhn would argue there is no such thing.[9]) And what have we learned? The startling revelation that one of the glyptodont's closest relatives, extant, is the pink fairy armadillo—*Chlamyphorus truncatus*. The smallest armadillo known. A five-inch long, quarter-pound armadillo feasting on grubs and ants in central Argentina.[10] Proof that size doesn't matter. On visual inspection (although I am admittedly not an armadillo expert), *Doedicurus* and *Chlamyphorus* look different. Very, very different. But they come from the same branch on an evolutionary tree.

What's more, we see that the frontiers of cladistics are expanding, that our present knowledge of molecular biology allows us a more granular picture of evolution in action. MacPhee told me, "A species is a generality. Things that look so much like one another that they get grouped together. But you don't really know what's going on inside the species—except via morphology in a very general way. If you have lineages that you can actually detect by molecular evidence, then you can do very much more. So it's a totally new world." If there is such a thing as DNA, if our biology is correct, then we're coming closer and closer to understanding what it means to be a glyptodont: what a glyptodont is and what it is not, what it came from, and what it became.

9. I asked Andrew Berry, who teaches evolutionary biology at Harvard, to read this chapter. I worried, and still worry, that my attack on Kuhn might be untimely, that academics have moved on from his ideas. Particularly, Kuhn's criticism of the idea of progress. Here is part of his reply: "I teach a little History of Science (stemming from my interest in evolutionary biology—perhaps it's inevitable that a science dedicated to an exploration of how the past has shaped the present should attract practitioners interested in the history of their own discipline), with courses on the development of evolutionary thinking—where did Darwin, Wallace, et al. come from? As part of these courses, I often have students read Kuhn. Generally, I'm dealing with science undergraduates who are naïvely invested in the idea that science is essentially a tabulation of absolute truths. The hope is that reading Kuhn will shake that certainty. I'm not asking students to buy the whole relativistic paradigm-as-arbitrary-construct argument; rather, I want them to appreciate that science is not done in some kind of objective vacuum, but, instead, is a socially influenced exercise. In short, I want them to get elements of Kuhn without swallowing the whole argument.

"Normally this exercise goes OK, but once I ran into trouble on this section of the course. Unusually, my grad student teaching assistant was a card-carrying historian of science, raised on a diet of postmodernism and Kuhn in particular. My contention that we understand the natural world today better than we did in the past—that our current model of foetal development is more accurate, if you like, than preformationism—was greeted with disdain: No, the new paradigm is *not* necessarily an improvement [in terms of explanatory power, or whatever your preferred go-to is] on the old one—it's just different. Bullshit. Anyway, this is my explanation of why I'm particularly sympathetic to your crusade."

10. *C. truncatus* is nocturnal and sluggish except when burrowing. One of the reasons I strongly identify with the animal.

We might not be able to agree about all the essential properties in biology or physics, but what matters is not that a group of experts can offer *descriptions* of elms and beeches or molybdenum and aluminum, but that we have come closer to identifying essential or necessary properties of these things.[11]

11. We have come a long way. The article to which MacPhee contributed on glyptodont phylogeny explains how molecular biology and various statistical methods have deepened our understanding of what it means to be a glyptodon. See Delsuc et al.,"Phylogenetic Affinities," p. R155.

Glyptodont fossils were first recorded in the seventeenth century. The following passage comes from the English Jesuit Thomas Falkner:

On the banks of the River Carcarania, or Tercero, about three or four leagues before it enters into the Parana, are found great numbers of bones, of an extraordinary bigness, which seem human. There are some greater and some less, as if they were of persons of different ages. I have seen thigh-bones, ribs, breast-bones, and pieces of skulls. I have also seen teeth, and particularly some grinders which were three inches in diameter at the base. These bones (as I have been informed) are likewise found on the banks of the Rivers Parana and Paraguay, as likewise in Peru. The Indian historian, Garcilasso de la Vega Inga, makes mention of these bones in Peru, and tells us that the Indians have a tradition, that giants formerly inhabited those countries, and were destroyed by God for the crime of sodomy. I myself found the shell of an animal, composed of little hexagonal bones, each bone an inch in diameter at least; and the shell was near three yards over. It seemed in all respects, except its size, to be the upper part of the shell of the armadillo; which, in these times, is not above a span in breadth.[12]

The "little hexagonal bones" and the shell "near three yards over." What else could it be but the remains of a glyptodont? Sixty years later Darwin arrives in South America. A stopping point on his circumnavigation of the world aboard the HMS *Beagle*. He is only twenty-two years old. He writes in 1834, "This wonderful relationship in the same continent between the dead and the living, will, I do not doubt, hereafter throw more light on the appearance of organic beings on our earth, and their disappearance from it, than any other class of facts."[13]

The collected specimens, sent to Darwin's mentor John Stevens Henslow in Cambridge, were subsequently deposited at the Royal College of Surgeons in London. Richard Owen, perhaps the premier naturalist of his times, and later an outspoken critic of Darwin's theory of evolution, analyzed and catalogued the collections. Owen described eleven species, including *Toxodon platensis*, *Macrauchenia patachonica*, *Equus curvidens*, *Scelidotherium leptocephalum*, *Mylodon darwinii*, and *Glossotherium sp.*[14] Darwin supplied

12. Falkner, *A Description of Patagonia, and the Adjoining Parts of South America* (1774), pp. 54–55.

13. Darwin, *The Voyage of the Beagle: The Illustrated Edition*, p. 146.

14. Juan Carlos Fernicola, Sergio F. Vizcaíno and Gerardo de Iuliis, "The Fossil Mammals Collected by Charles Darwin," p. 147.

bones and a theory; Owen supplied equivocation and occasional enmity. In response to an 1860 "anonymous" review of *Origin*, Darwin wrote in a letter to geologist Charles Lyell, "I have just read the *Edinburg* [*Review*] which is without doubt by Owen. It is extremely malignant, clever and I fear will be very damaging. . . . It is painful to be hated in the intense degree with which Owen hates me."[15]

A hundred years later, the peaceful repose of those bones was disturbed by the Blitz. The intense bombardment by the Nazis during May 10 and 11, 1941, destroyed a large part of the collections both in the Royal College and in the associated Hunterian Museum. (Like the library at Alexandria, the concentration of evidence in a single place made it vulnerable to the depredations of history.) A. J. E. Cave's 1942 catalogue of the surviving specimens showed that 95 percent of the collections had been destroyed—of

15. John Bowlby, *Charles Darwin: A New Life*, p. 352.

5,000 specimens, only 175 remained.[16] Among these, fortunately, were some of the specimens collected by Darwin.

The irony of it all. Fossils that had survived for over a hundred thousand years—through climate change, continental drift, the impact of meteors, the migration of the poles, corrasion, corrosion, and a host of other geological and meteorological processes—succumbed to two days of heavy bombardment by the Nazis.[17] A reminder that evidence—historical evidence, for fossils are a form of historical evidence—is supremely perishable.

The original accounts of the megafauna of the Argentinian pampas suggested that the bones were the residue of the Nephilim, a race of giants, supposedly destroyed by God because of their sexual deviance. Hence, the glyptodont, the toxodon, the megatherium—the megafauna of the late Pleistocene—were thought to be the remains of a benighted humanity. We now have different views.

16. Fernicola, Vizcaíno, and de Iuliis, "Fossil Mammals Collected by Charles Darwin in South America," p. 148.

17. "The attack on London between 1939 and 1945 is one of the most significant events in the city's modern history, the impact of which can still be seen it its urban and social landscapes. As a key record of the attack, the maps represent destruction on a huge scale, recording buildings and streets reduced to smoke and rubble." See Laurence Ward, *The London County Council Bomb Damage Maps, 1939–1945*, p. 6.

Trace the evolution of thought about the nature of these fossils, and it provides a history of a deeper and deeper understanding of evolving life. We know many of the milestones—particularly, Darwin's *Origin of the Species* and Watson and Crick's discovery of the structure of DNA, about one hundred years later, which ushered in the era of molecular biology.

———

Here is our story. Biological evolution is *not* teleological. There was no guarantee that *Chlamyphorus* would follow *Doedicurus*. None. It could have happened differently. (Could it have happened the other way around?) It could have happened such that *Chlamyphorus* or *Doedicurus* would never come into existence at all. In evolution nothing is *discovered*. We can *discover* the structure of glyptodont DNA, but new species are *created* through the happenstance of natural selection.

And the evolution of science? There was also no guarantee that Watson and Crick would discover the structure of DNA in 1953. Other scientists might have discovered it in a different year. There is also a possible world where the structure of DNA is *never* discovered. (But *no* possible world in which the structure of DNA is other than what it is.) Imagine a possible world in which no creature has an IQ greater than a nematode, an unsegmented worm. In such a world, DNA would probably not be discovered. But in a world inhabited by somewhat sentient creatures, like ourselves, it is likely that someone (or something) would eventually discover it. Why? Because it exists. It is a discovery, *not an invention*. A discovery, *not a social construction*. The sharp distinction between *created* and *discovered* is crucial to an understanding of science, a distinction that Kuhn muddies.[18] Discovering something in the physical world is like discovering a previously unknown continent or island.[19] It can be discovered—to echo George Mallory's supposed reason for climbing Everest—because it is *there*.[20]

And once DNA is discovered, it is more or less inevitable that the discovery will lead to progress, if you will—to a deeper understanding of all living things, including what it means to be a glyptodont. As David Deutsch writes:

18. As Norwood Russell Hanson wrote, "Discovery is what science is all about" ("An Anatomy of Discovery," p. 352). The role of discovery in science is extensively examined in Wootton, *The Invention of Science*, particularly pp. 57f.

19. Judith Schalansky writes about Tromelin, an island so small and so remote that there is no reason to visit it. And yet it was discovered (in a shipwreck) and even briefly inhabited. If you have enough people crisscrossing the globe, the discovery of the remote and inaccessible is close to inevitable. See Schalansky, *Pocket Atlas of Remote Islands*. An extended account of the shipwreck can be found in a December 19, 2015, article in the *Economist*, "Lèse Humanité: What Happened When Slaves and Free Men Were Shipwrecked Together."

20. Matthew Lund, a philosopher and biographer of Norwood Russell Hanson, pointed out to me that Hanson's article "An Anatomy of Discovery" begins with a reference to Mallory's famous quote: "In 1924—that was the year I was born, so I remember it well—a distinguished mountain climber named Mallory was often asked: 'Why climb Everest?' His resonant and memorable response was always 'Because it is there!' Some people ask me: 'Why agonize about discovery?' My timid response is usually 'Mallorian'; I say 'Because it's there!'" Lund adds, "Ironic that Hanson mailed this article to the *Journal of Philosophy* on the very day he died on a mountainside, as did Mallory on his famed climb to the top of Everest (he never made it back down)." Email to author, January 10, 2017.

Kuhn's theory suffers from a fatal flaw. It explains the *succession* from one paradigm to another in sociological or psychological terms, rather than as having primarily to do with the objective merit of the rival explanations. Yet unless one understands science as a quest for explanations, the fact that it does find successive explanations, each objectively better than the last, is inexplicable.[21]

21. Deutsch, *The Fabric of Reality*, p. 323.

Years ago I was challenged by a graduate student in history of science: What do Kripke's theories have to do with Kuhn's? The question seemed naïve, even silly. Of course, they are related. They both focus on the relation between language and the world. Kripke establishes something that undermines the entire basis of Kuhn's work—the necessary *a posteriori*. It may well be the ultimate goal of scientific inquiry. When we argue that the atomic number of gold is known through scientific investigation and cannot be other than what it is, we are saying that the atomic number of gold is an example of the necessary *a posteriori*. The same goes for the structure of glyptodont DNA.

We may not know what these properties are, exactly, but we're closing in on them; we're *progressing* toward that understanding. The external world is applying pressure on us to reach the *only* conclusion possible. There is no room for this in Kuhn's system. Natural selection as we conceive of it includes no provision for a necessary *a posteriori*. Quite the opposite. But if you accept that an essential property of gold is that its atomic number is 79, or that an essential property of the glyptodont is its DNA, then you are accepting that some things cannot be otherwise.

Matthew Meselson—a molecular biologist famous for his discovery of messenger RNA and for the Meselson-Stahl experiment demonstrating the semi-conservative replication of DNA—not only sees the double helix as real, he actually gives it a voice. DNA says, "Here I am":

The application of molecular biology to the problem of heredity got going with the proposal of the double helical structure of DNA by Watson and Crick in 1953.

Knowing the molecular structure of a protein or a lipid or a carbohydrate molecule doesn't tell you what to do. But the structure of DNA set the research agenda for the next quarter century. The structure itself literally dictated what needed to be done.

It says here I am, a long sequence of four different kinds of subunits: A, T, G, C. Knowing that genes specify proteins, go figure out how my four-letter language is decoded into the 20 amino acid language of proteins.

Or here I am, confined to the cell nucleus. But proteins are made out in the cytoplasm. So there must be an intermediate copy of my information that goes from the nucleus to the cytoplasm. Go find it—the messenger. This is DNA telling you what to do. . . .

Or here I am, the substance of genes. Genes recombine in meiosis. Go figure out how that happens.

Or here I am, I mutate, damage in me is repaired, I am folded into chromosomes—go find out how these things are done!

This is a very big agenda. It is dictated, like the Wizard of Oz, except this was no fraud—by a molecule.

And of course from the start the double helix said, here I am with two complementary chains. Go figure out how this complementarity is used to make copies of myself.[22]

22. Meselson, "McGill 2013 Honorary Doctorate Address." May 27, 2013.

23. For an overview, see Frederic Lawrence Holmes, *Meselson, Stahl, and the Replication of DNA*.

Meselson and Frank Stahl, in one of the great experiments of the twentieth century, proceeded to do just that.[23] Here I am, go figure out how knowledge of the structure of DNA leads to further scientific progress. And truth.

9. THIS CONTEST OF INTERPRETATION

Of knowledge naught remained I did not know,
Of secrets, scarcely any, high or low;
All day and night for three score and twelve years,
I pondered, just to learn that naught I know.
　　　　　　　　　—*Ruba'iyat of Omar Khayyam*

Steven Weinberg, a Nobel Prize–winning physicist and well-known polymath, summarized his uneasiness with Kuhn and *The Structure of Scientific Revolutions* in a series of articles for the *New York Review of Books*.[1] He argues that Kuhn was describing "Kuhnian science" (that is, science as Kuhn *imagined* it) and not *actual* science:

> What does bother me on rereading *Structure* and some of Kuhn's later writings is his radically skeptical conclusions about what is accomplished in the work of science. And it is just these

1. Weinberg does such a good job analyzing Kuhn that I can scarcely avoid repeating some arguments he has made already. If I were to contrast our approaches, Weinberg's criticisms emphasize Kuhn's rejection of scientific *progress*, while mine emphasize Kuhn's rejection of reference and truth. It may amount to the same thing. See Weinberg, "The Revolution That Didn't Happen" (1998), and Alex Levine and Weinberg, "T. S. Kuhn's 'Non-Revolution': An Exchange" (1999).

conclusions that have made Kuhn a hero to the philosophers, historians, sociologists, and cultural critics who question the objective character of scientific knowledge, and who prefer to describe scientific theories as social constructions, not so different from democracy or baseball. Kuhn made the shift from one paradigm to another seem *more like a religious conversion than an exercise of reason.*[2]

2. "Revolution That Didn't Happen," p. 48 (emphasis mine).

Then, later in the essay:

> Kuhn's view of scientific progress would leave us with a mystery: Why does anyone bother? If one scientific theory is only better than another in its ability to solve the problems that happen to be on our minds today, then why not save ourselves a lot of trouble by putting these problems out of our minds? We don't study elementary particles because they are intrinsically interesting, like people. They are not—if you have seen one electron, you've seen them all. What drives us onward in the work of science is precisely the sense that there are truths out there to be discovered, truths that once discovered will form a permanent part of human knowledge.

And more about truth and paradigm shifts:

> [Kuhn] went on to reason that since a paradigm shift means complete abandonment of an earlier paradigm, and there is no common standard to judge scientific theories developed under different paradigms, there can be no sense in which theories developed after a scientific revolution can be said to add cumulatively to what was known before the revolution. Only within the context of a paradigm can we speak of one theory being true or false.[3]

3. "Revolution That Didn't Happen," pp. 50, 48.

The wholesale abandonment of truth and of progress. I recently called Weinberg to ask him about Kuhn.

STEVEN WEINBERG: Well, a historian might argue that the history of science is possible only in the sense that you have to submerge yourself in the paradigms of any past epoch that you're writing about. Just trying to understand, as Kuhn did, for example, what Aristotle was up to without trying to refer it in any way to a cumulative advance of scientific knowledge. And some historians would say that's what you have to do with everything. If you want to understand feudalism you have to immerse yourself in feudalism and not think at all about what it led to later, what its relation might be with the democratic revolutions of the nineteenth and twentieth centuries.

ERROL MORRIS: History with blinders.

WEINBERG: The claim is—you have to look at things as they actually were at the time and not relate them to the present. That I think is the guiding spirit of a lot of professional historians, and it may make sense when you're writing about something like, say, the history of fashion or even the history of art, where you can't really say that there is—the word "progress" doesn't mean much. But I reject this point of view when it comes to the history of science, which is cumulative, in which we do learn more and more, where we can say some things in the past would turn out to lead to progress and other things would not. Progress has an absolute meaning, something that brings us closer to truth about the world. But that's just what Kuhn would deny.

MORRIS: Progress.

WEINBERG: Not only Kuhn, but a lot of modern historians of science reject any idea of historians writing about the *progress* of science. They want just to drown you in the goals and criteria of ancient ages without worrying about whether it was helpful or unhelpful, correct or incorrect.

MORRIS: Yes, but it has to be about something more than a contrarian attitude to science.

WEINBERG: In one of my earlier books, *Dreams of a Final Theory*, I referred to this kind of skepticism about scientific truth as giving the philosopher or historian a sense of superiority over his subject matter—the working scientist—in the same way that an anthropologist studying the cargo cults of Pacific Islanders would feel a delicious sense of superiority because he can look at their cargo cults as having no value in terms of truth but just as expressing their culture, whereas he can stand back and study their culture the way he would study bacteria under a microscope. The general reader doesn't have to be so impressed with scientific discoveries if what the scientist says is merely a cultural artifact. So there may be something of that in it. But I think it is decreasing. It hasn't gone away, and the argument I'm having with historians now is an example of it.

In his preface to the fiftieth anniversary edition of *Structure*, Ian Hacking suggests a "simplistic parody" of Kuhn's linguistic turn. It may be a simplistic parody, but it captures Kuhn's way of thinking—an unappetizing admixture of history of science and late Wittgenstein:

> It was thought that the names of things you can observe can be learned by pointing. But what about theoretical entities, such as electrons, at which one cannot point? They get their meaning, it was taught, only from the context of the theory in which they occur. Hence a change in theory must entail a change in meaning. Hence a statement about electrons in the context of one theory means something different from the same string of words in the context of another theory. If one theory says the sentence is true and another says it is false, there is no contradiction, for the statement expresses different statements in the two theories, and they cannot be compared.[4]

If two scientists have two different versions of the truth, how is truth different from mere belief? What good is it?

At the heart of Weinberg's complaints is a story Kuhn was fond of telling about how he learned about Aristotle's theory of motion when he was a young teacher working for James B. Conant, then president of Harvard University.[5] It does not appear in *Structure*, but in a number of essays written about how he became a historian of science:

> My own enlightenment began in 1947, when I was asked to interrupt my current physics project for a time in order to prepare a set of lectures on the origins of seventeenth-century mechanics. For that purpose, I needed first to discover what the

4. Hacking, "Introductory Essay," in Kuhn, *Structure* (2012), p. xxx.

5. Kuhn's accounts neglect to tell us whether he was reading Aristotle in translation or in the original Greek. Reading a translation from an incommensurable (untranslatable) original would, by his own lights, be the height of sophistry.

predecessors of Galileo and Newton had known about the subject, and preliminary inquiries soon led me to the discussions of motion in Aristotle's *Physica* and to some later works descended from it. . . . When dealing with subjects other than physics, Aristotle had been an acute and naturalistic observer. In such fields as biology or political behavior, his interpretations of phenomena had often been, in addition, both penetrating and deep. How could his characteristic talents have failed him so when applied to motion? How could he have said about it so many apparently absurd things? And, above all, why had his views been taken so seriously for so long a time by so many of his successors? . . .

One memorable (and very hot) summer day those perplexities suddenly vanished. I all at once perceived the connected rudiments of an alternate way of reading the texts with which I had been struggling. For the first time I gave due weight to the fact that Aristotle's subject was change-of-quality in general, including both the fall of a stone and the growth of a child to adulthood. . . . Though drastically incomplete and far too baldly stated, those aspects of my new understanding of Aristotle's enterprise should indicate what I mean by the discovery of a new way to read a set of texts. After I achieved this one, strained metaphors often became naturalistic reports, and much apparent absurdity vanished. I did not become an Aristotelian physicist as a result, but I had to some extent learned to think like one.[6]

Kuhn returned to his epiphany in 1992, when he and Weinberg spoke at the University of Padua, on the occasion of the four hundredth anniversary of Galileo's first lecture there. Kuhn once again described how he came to admire Aristotle:

How could his characteristic talent have deserted him so systematically when he turned to the study of motion and mechanics? Equally, if his talents had so deserted him, why had his writings in physics been taken so seriously for so many centuries after his death? Those questions troubled me. I could easily believe that Aristotle had stumbled, but not that, on turning to physics, he had totally collapsed. Might not the fault be mine rather than Aristotle's, I asked myself? Perhaps his words

6. Kuhn, *The Essential Tension* (1977), pp. xi–xii. Strained metaphors become naturalistic reports? How about Aristotle's claim, after reading Hippocrates, that the brain was a radiator for cooling the blood.

had not meant to him and his contemporaries what they meant to me and mine. . . . Suddenly the fragments in my head sorted themselves out in a new way, and fell in place together. My jaw dropped in surprise, for all at once Aristotle seemed to be a very good physicist indeed, but of a sort I'd never dreamed possible.[7]

Alas, there is nothing in any of Kuhn's accounts to tell us much about the nature of his epiphany. About all we know is that it was jaw-dropping. Could it have been a religious conversion (as suggested by Weinberg)? Something else?[8] Weinberg wrote to Kuhn for an explanation but got little in return. Kuhn wrote back, "What was altered by my own first reading of [Aristotle's writings on physics] was my understanding, not my evaluation, of what they achieved."[9] Weinberg was unimpressed. Wasn't the phrase "a very good physicist indeed" an *evaluation*?[10]

I guess a true epiphany cannot be explained. It is ineffable. It just *is*.[11] And yet, I had (and still have) this nagging feeling that it *is* possible to compare Aristotle's physics with current modes of explanation. And, further, to make the claim that there has been progress during the last two thousand or so years—say, in the field of dentistry. To again quote Weinberg: "the world acts on us like a teaching machine, reinforcing our good ideas with moments of satisfaction."[12] Reality is there to tell us whether to turn left or right—or not to turn at all, as in the presence of a stop sign. Bertrand Russell, fascinated by Aristotle's antipathy to empirical methods, wrote, "Aristotle maintained that women have fewer teeth than men; although he was twice married, it never occurred to him to verify this statement by examining his wives' mouths."[13] Or the variant from Russell I prefer: "Aristotle could have avoided the mistakes of thinking that women have fewer teeth than men, by the simple device of asking Mrs. Aristotle to keep her mouth open while he counted."[14]

———

The debate about Whiggishness in history of science has been revisited by Steven Shapin, a latter-day sociologist of science. Reviewing Weinberg's 2015 book *To Explain the World* in the *Wall Street Journal*, Shapin expressed his outrage:

7. Kuhn, "Remarks on Receiving the Laurea," p. 105.

8. Kuhn's epiphany recalls a statement by R. G. Collingwood, in *The Idea of History*, a posthumous collection of his writings:

> How does the historian discern the thoughts which he is trying to discover? There is only one way in which it can be done: by re-thinking them in his own mind. The historian of philosophy, reading Plato, is trying to know what Plato thought when he expressed himself in certain words. The only way in which he can do this is by thinking it for himself. . . . The history of thought, and therefore all history, is the re-enactment of past thought in the historian's own mind. (p. 215)

Kuhn took an idealist philosophy of history and grafted it on to a philosophy of science. Or perhaps the other way around.

9. Weinberg, "Revolution That Didn't Happen," p. 52.

10. In *To Explain the World*, Weinberg cites an analysis by historian of science David Lindberg:

> On the larger issue of how to judge Aristotle's success, Lindberg added, "It would be unfair and pointless to judge Aristotle's success by the degree to which he anticipated modern science (as though his goal was to answer our questions, rather than his own)." And in a second edition of the same work: "The proper measure of a philosophical system or a scientific theory is not the degree to which it anticipated modern thought, but its degree of success in treating the philosophical and scientific problems of its own day."

> *I don't buy it.* What is important in science (I leave philosophy to others) is not the solution of some popular scientific problems of one's own day, but understanding the world. In the course of this work, one finds out what sort of explanations are possible,

Mr. Weinberg reckons that the history of science is far too important to be left to the historians, and *To Explain the World* is the kind of thing that might tempt academic historians to lose their cool. They'd remind him that the great thinkers of 17th-century science commonly considered themselves to be reforming natural knowledge to be Christianity's handmaid. Figures like Newton and Boyle discerned divine purpose throughout nature, and not, as Mr. Weinberg implies, just because they were taking an unfortunate detour from properly scientific behavior. . . .

The historians might also thump the table, insisting that searching for anticipations and foreshadowings is both wrong and illogical—"ahistorical" as they'd say. They'd wonder that a history written by a working scientist should be so little concerned with the messy day-to-day practices of getting experiments to succeed, getting calculations right, and persuading others of their truth and accuracy. They'd express bemusement at Mr. Weinberg's insistence that science advances by rejecting teleology, even as he depicts its history as a triumphal progress from dark past to bright present.

Table-thumping isn't interesting—whoever does it.[15]

Ironically, it is Shapin thumping the table. To express a belief in progress is not to express a belief in teleological explanation. A belief in progress doesn't tell us where we're going. It merely tells us that where we are *now* is a little bit better than where we were *before*. Just ask a student of glyptodont mitochondrial DNA. Weinberg's reply to Shapin's table-thumping, in the *New York Review of Books*, did not address Shapin by name:

It is Butterfield's injunction against presentism, "the study of the past with one eye, so to speak, upon the present," that still represents a serious challenge to whiggish historians of science. In laying out maxims for a history of science that emphasizes its internal development, Thomas Kuhn in 1968 argued that "insofar as possible (it is never entirely so, nor could history be written if it were), the historian should set aside the science that he knows." A more uncompromising stand against using present

and what sort of problems can lead to those explanations. The progress of science has been largely a matter of discovering what questions should be asked. (p. 29; emphasis mine)

Weinberg has often been criticized for offering a simplistic version of history of science. As if he is at war with historical context. This mischaracterizes his view. He is at war with the denial of truth and with the denial of scientific progress.

11. "You won't be able to understand it." "It doesn't make sense." "Just take our word for it." Two stories. The first isn't really an epiphany. Both involve the slavish acceptance of the inexplicable. In the early 1970s I was driving from Berkeley to San Francisco. I picked up a hitchhiker. People did that sort of thing in those days. It was someone who had just read *Chariot of the Gods*, a book that argues for extraterrestrial visitors to earth thousands of years ago. He asked me, "How do you explain the existence of electric toaster ovens that are thousands of years old found in the Gobi Desert?" My answer? "I can't." (I resisted the temptation to say, "Well, there are no ancient electric toaster ovens.")

Years ago, I was a teaching assistant in a philosophy of science course offered at Berkeley. A student had just handed in a term paper titled "The Philosophy of Kung Fu." He had written, "I have personally seen things you wouldn't believe." I said to him, "OK, just what are those things I wouldn't believe?" He sternly replied, "Well, you wouldn't believe them." "But, but . . . ," I said, "you have to trust me on this. My credulity is relatively unfettered. Take a chance and tell me what I wouldn't believe. Anyway, I can't evaluate your claim without knowing what it is."

12. *To Explain the World*, p. 255.
13. Russell, *The Impact of Science on Society*, p. 7.
14. Russell, "An Outline of Intellectual Rubbish," in *Unpopular Essays*, p. 115.
15. Shapin, "Why Scientists Shouldn't Write History."

knowledge was taken by several sociologists who study science as a social phenomenon, including the well-known Sociology of Scientific Knowledge group at the University of Bath.

Meanwhile, whiggery in the history of science has not lacked defenders. They are found especially among those, like Edward Harrison, Nicholas Jardine, and Ernst Mayr, who have worked as scientists. I think that this is because scientific history with an eye to present knowledge is needed by scientists. We don't see our work as merely an expression of the culture of our time and place, like parliamentary democracy or Morris dancing. We see it as the latest stage in a process, extending back over millennia, of explaining the world. We derive perspective and motivation from the story of how we reached our present understanding, imperfect as that understanding remains.

Certainly history should not ignore those influential past figures who turned out to be wrong. Otherwise we would never be able to understand what it took to get things right. But the story makes no sense unless we recognize that some were wrong and some right, and this can be done only from the perspective of our present knowledge.[16]

16. Weinberg, "Eye on the Present," p. 82.

My question: Why does it have to be A or B? Why is it presentism, or whatever it is, that is the opposite? Can't it be both?

Why can't the history of science be both Whiggish and something else—presentist and otherwise? We are trapped in the present, but the past intrudes in our lives as a mystery story. How did we get here? Part of the annoyance many contemporary historians of science feel with Weinberg may be that he seemingly deprives them of the mystery of the past. I don't see it that way. Moreover, I see the imprint of the heavy paw of Thomas Kuhn. If science can only be understood sociologically, then the first order of business, perhaps the only order of business, is to examine the social milieu of science. If it's Lavoisier, look to the milieu of the French Revolution. If it's Einstein, the patent office in Bern. But don't look to the empirical content of science. To quote *Structure*:

Like the choice between competing political institutions, that between competing paradigms proves to be a choice between incompatible modes of community life. . . . When paradigms enter, as they must, into a debate about paradigm choice, their role is necessarily circular. Each group uses its own paradigm to argue in that paradigm's defense.[17]

17. Kuhn, *Structure* (1962), p. 93.

What a passage. Paradigms come to life! They enter into debates, into arguments. And their role is "necessarily circular." Whatever that means. Could it mean that one paradigm contradicts another? But if they're incommensurable, how could they? Or could it mean that paradigms are devoid of content? (One could argue that the Kuhnian paradigm, whatever it might be, leads to intolerance. Intolerance toward any conception of science that is *not* sociological.)

Let me provide an example from Weinberg's book. Eratosthenes is credited with having determined the circumference of the earth—in modern measurement approximately twenty-five thousand miles. For those familiar with flat-earth cosmologies, it comes as a surprise.[18]

Eratosthenes (ca. 275–195 BCE) saw the earth as a sphere and believed he could determine its size. His demonstration, first reported in extant sources by Cleomedes some five centuries later (none of Eratosthenes's own writings survive), is taken as one of the hallmarks of ancient science. Here's an oversimplified version: At noon on the summer solstice, you could look up from the recesses of a well at Syene and see the Sun directly overhead. (No one knows the exact location of the well. There are a couple of candidates, one

18. Matthew Lund directed me to Stephen Jay Gould's essay "The Late Birth of a Flat Earth," "in which he argues that the idea that anyone ever believed in a flat earth was a product of the late nineteenth century. Indeed, the argument seems to have been invented in order to castigate the benighted views of disbelievers in evolution." Lund, email to author, January 10, 2017.

on the Elephantine, an island in the Nile.) At Alexandria, due north of Syene, on the summer solstice a sundial showed the sun to be 7.12 degrees from the vertical. If we know the distance from Syene to Alexandria, and we know that 7.12 degrees is roughly $^1/_{50}$ of a circle, we can calculate the circumference of the earth. Take the distance from Syene to Alexandria and multiply by 50.

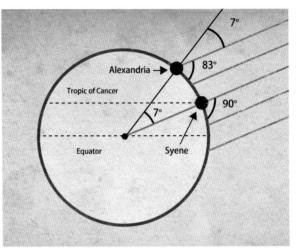

Weinberg, in his analysis of Eratosthenes's method, qualifies his assessment of the result:

> We don't know the length of the stadion as used by Eratosthenes, and Cleomedes probably didn't know it either, since (unlike our mile or kilometer) it had never been given a standard definition. But without knowing the length of the stadion, we can judge the accuracy of Eratosthenes' use of astronomy. The Earth's circumference is actually 47.9 times the distance from Alexandria to Syene (modern Aswan), so the conclusion of Eratosthenes that the Earth's circumference is 50 times the distance from Alexandria to Syene was actually quite accurate, whatever the length of the stadion. In his use of astronomy, if not of geography, Eratosthenes had done quite well.[19]

So Eratosthenes's concept is sound, but there were numerous possibilities for error. The bematists sent out to measure distance by counting paces could have over- or underestimated the distance to Alexandria.[20] Syene and Alexandria might not be on the same

19. Weinberg, *To Explain the World*, pp. 75–76.

20. P. M. Fraser argues that the distance would have been determined by pacers sent by Euergetes or Philopater, the Ptolemaic kings. *Ptolemaic Alexandria*, vol. 1, pp. 414–15.

meridian. (Indeed, Syene turns out to be about 3 degrees east of Alexandria. Another major city, Pelusium, lay more nearly north of Syene,[21] but as far as we know, Eratosthenes did not consider taking his second measurement there.) And Syene is not directly on the Tropic of Cancer, which in 230 BCE would have passed twenty-four miles to the south.[22] The sun could not have shone *straight* down the famous well on the solstice. Nonetheless, Weinberg

21. Pelusium, on the Nile delta, was captured by the Persians in 525 BCE, almost three centuries before Eratosthenes's calculations. Second-century rhetorician Polyaenus describes the siege of the city in his *Stratagems of War*, pp. 268–69: "The Egyptians with great resolution defended it: advancing formidable machines against the besiegers; and from their catapults throwing darts, stones, and fire. Against the destructive showers thus discharged upon him Cambyses [the Persian emperor] ranged before his front line, dogs, sheep, cats, ibises, and whatever animals the Egyptians hold sacred. The fear of hurting the animals, which they regard with veneration, instantly checked their operations: Cambyses took Pelusium; and thus opened himself a passage into Egypt."

22. Nicholas Nicastro, *Circumference*, p. 119.

23. "What Eratosthenes had really measured," he explains, "was the ratio of the circumference of the Earth to the distance from Alexandria to the Tropic of Cancer (called the summer tropical circle by Cleomedes), the circle on the Earth's surface where the noon Sun at the summer solstice really is directly overhead. Alexandria is at a latitude of 31.2°, while the latitude of the Tropic of Cancer is 23.5°, which is less than the latitude of Alexandria by 7.7°, so the circumference of the Earth is in fact 360°/7.7° = 46.75 times greater than the distance between Alexandria and the Tropic of Cancer, just a little less than the ratio 50 given by Eratosthenes." Weinberg, *To Explain the World*, p. 76.

concludes, "Eratosthenes was lucky. Syene is not precisely due south of Alexandria (its longitude is 32.9° E., while that of Alexandria is 29.9° E) and the noon sun at the summer solstice is not precisely overhead at Syene, but 0.4° from the vertical. The two errors partly cancel."[23]

We now know that Eratosthenes's method—measuring shadows and distances—was correct, a valid way of measuring the size of the earth. We also know that many of his assumptions were wrong. But the interplay between assumptions and methods can only be appreciated in hindsight. That is, it can only be appreciated Whiggishly. How else could we appreciate the irony of false assumptions in science? The irony that Eratosthenes got the correct result because his errors canceled each other out? As Weinberg writes, "Eratosthenes was lucky." Maybe so. But appreciating that luck is based on a retrospective knowledge of the correct result.

———

Norton Wise was a postdoctoral student while I was a graduate student at Princeton. Eventually he became the director of the Program in the History and Philosophy of Science (from 1991 to 2000), the program Kuhn had directed in the 1970s. I had spent many, many evenings talking with him and, yes, complaining about Kuhn. I hadn't talked to him in forty years, but when I called him in California, it was as if no time had passed. Norton is much nicer than I am. In our conversation, I was reminded of his openness and sincerity.

NORTON WISE: Do you remember the mode of smoking a cigarette, where Kuhn would start drawing on a newly lit cigarette? He would start a sentence, break off in the middle of the sentence, start drawing on the cigarette, and take a drag that would exhaust half the cigarette. Just an amazing drag. And then start again in the sentence. That's such a clear image to me.

ERROL MORRIS: I remember the mountain of butts and ash.

WISE: Within one seminar.

MORRIS: Oh yes.

how many pounds = 1 ton
2000

Circumference of earth 25,000 miles

science is progressing

W	Y	Tur G	dark P	R	B
Blue B	dark Y	By	Tu	B	W

pg 91. The Arbitrary
The Difference between forcing someone to
state an Untruth and Getting them to believe it.
Fear drives belief

Denying the rationale bz of Truth
Agreement
Forms of life changes and contingent (Witt)
do we create Truth or Discover it?

Hi: Once in a while I pick up a Scottsdale Life magazine when in the Appaloosa library. Amazing to me the many activities that abound here. I am planning on trying out a hiking trail in the McDowell-Sonoran Preserve near The Mustang Library off of Thompson Peak Rd. I went there last week just to get acquainted with the place. It is close enough to here. I frequently use Thompson Peak when doing some errands in the vicinity. I am excited to read that there are guided hikes as well as lectures at Mustang which I would love to attend. "If Rocks Could Talk."

I do walk here daily but need a new environment. When I saw picture of "Love Returns" I had to share it. Thanks for returning the rafting photo.

Mom

WISE: That's what I remember, too. I never saw anyone smoke like that before or since. Of course, the emphysema nearly killed him.

MORRIS: I often think of the attraction of smoking, that it simplifies the world into three parts. There's you, there's the cigarette, and everything else is the ashtray.

WISE: Well, the smoking is to me expressive of the intensity of the seminars. Everyone was on edge. That was from early on, and then continuing through successive seminars. The most apparent thing is that intensity that Kuhn somehow brought, along with the thorough preparation he brought to it, and then expected of everyone else. Of course very few people—no one in the seminar—would have read and analyzed the material in the very focused, intense way that he had done. A kind of adversarial relationship was explicit. You were challenged to be saying anything or offering an opinion. And an opinion immediately evoked maybe agreement, but usually not. Usually some kind of challenge. For me that meant that the relationship, while close and intense over the years, was always adversarial. I found it extremely stimulating but sometimes disturbing. Sometimes *very* disturbing. Right up until the end, shortly before he died, he and I were carrying on this kind of contest of interpretation—

A "contest of interpretation"? An odd expression. But it so aptly characterizes Kuhn.

WISE: I wonder if it was in *that* seminar that I first became aware of his adversarial nature. I was giving an interpretation of William Thomson's [Lord Kelvin's] early electromagnetic mathematical work. Kuhn sharply disagreed with my interpretation and said that it couldn't possibly be right because it didn't follow the steps through which Thomson had developed his argument. It was, instead, a physicist's way of going at things—as an overview, or as a reinterpretation based on later knowledge. It was the kind of thing he was constantly hammering against. The next week I came back with a new interpretation. And again he attempted to shoot that down. But this time I had done a great deal more homework and really had it down in a pretty focused, pretty detailed way. And that maybe was the basis of the respect we gained for each other. All of his students needed to show him that they could stand up to that adversarial mode of interaction, and challenge his own understanding. For some people that worked out pretty well; for others it was a complete disaster.

MORRIS: Your use of the word "adversarial"—I experienced it differently. I would say that it went beyond adversarial. There was a threatening element.

WISE: Yes.

Our discussion turned to Kuhn and "Whiggishness."

MORRIS: Although you didn't use the word, I know it was on the tip of your tongue because you studied with him. It was the supreme accusation—Whiggishness. "This is Whiggish history." I see the argument—and I would love to know the details of the argument about Thomson—that you were Norton Wise, a recent PhD in physics, thinking like a physicist and not like a historian. And that you were providing some kind of anachronistic account.

WISE: That's precisely correct.

MORRIS: There seemed to be a kind of weirdness at the heart of all of it. I don't know how else to express it. The accusation of Whiggishness was a cudgel.

WISE: Yes, it certainly was used in that way. I saw that I had to learn to work in a different mode. I had to learn to write sentences differently. I had to learn to interpret the way in which a text flowed from one line to the next in the course of a page.

MORRIS: But aren't you just talking about close reading?

WISE: Yes.[24]

Who would argue with that? Close reading is entirely commendable. But close reading isn't about Whiggishness or the opposite. It tells us that by carefully studying a passage we can understand it. Incommensurability tells us that unless we inhabit the paradigm

24. Wise sent a follow-up email: "You were interested in two particular features of Tom's mode of working. The first concerns the ability to qualify his statements so as to almost make a strong claim without actually making it. An example appears in his classic article on energy conservation (p. 100 in *The Essential Tension*), where he says, 'Unless the *Naturphilosophie* indigenous to the educational environment of these seven men had a productive role in the researches of some, it is hard to see why more than half of the pioneers should have been drawn from an area barely through its first generation of significant scientific pro-

in which the passage was written, we can *never* understand it. It's an argument not so much about history as about whether history is even possible.

———

Which brings me back to Kripke. And to *Naming and Necessity*. Why is Kripke relevant to any of this? Because his work is an attempt to create new links—between words *and* things and between the present *and* the past. Although he is rarely described in this way, he is among other things, a philosopher of history. One of Kripke's first essays as an undergraduate at Harvard was a series of criticisms of the British idealist historian R. G. Collingwood, well known for his somewhat elliptical statement that history is about the process of *reenacting* the past in the mind—about the idea of projecting oneself into the past with the purpose of reenacting it. Kripke effectively ridicules this notion. What about the historian who tries to *reenact* the thought of Hitler?

> Suppose a historian wishes to penetrate the mind of Adolf Hitler. Does he re-think Hitler's thoughts, in the coldly rational sense of thought intended by Collingwood? If so, he gets nowhere; for example, he rethinks, "The Jews have produced Germany's present decline," and perhaps (since Collingwood believes the historian must rethink *critically*) observes that actually Hitler was quite mistaken on this count. But the real question lies within the sphere of emotion, which Collingwood denies to history: what motivated Hitler's anti-Semitism, where was its popular appeal? The answers to this question are not intellectual, but largely emotional. Nor will it do to modify Collingwood's theory by admitting emotional revivals; a historian who re-enacted Hitler's emotions would thereby cease to be a historian and would, in a vigilant society, become a proper object of public surveillance.[25]

Could it be that some version of this infected Kuhn's mind? As Kripke writes, "This idealist conception is supposed to solve the problem of contemporary knowledge of past events." But he is unconvinced. "The theory that history consists solely of the present

ductivity. Nor is this quite all. If proved, the influence of *Naturphilosophie* may also help to explain why this particular group of five Germans, a Dane, and an Alsatian includes five of the six pioneers in whose approaches to energy conservation we have previously noted such marked conceptual lacunae.' In other words, 'I have not done the research to find actual evidence for this role of *Naturphilosophie*, but it is true nonetheless, unless of course it turns out not to be.' I have never mastered this mode of writing, though I recognize its effectiveness. Second, I cited an example of my own experience in working on the electrical theory of William Thomson, Lord Kelvin, in order to show why Kuhn's critique of Whiggish interpretation had great power in the detailed reading of texts. I was presenting in seminar Thomson's mathematical result on how electrical force F changes to F' across the boundary of an insulator of inductive capacity k, so that $F'/F = 1/k$. This presented problems because Thomson claimed to be reasoning on the basis of a flow analogy to conduction of heat across a surface where the conductivity changed and his equation for the effect did not seem to follow from this view. I gave an account of his thinking which was based (implicitly) on a modern physicist's understanding of electrostatic induction. Tom insisted (strenuously and adversarially) that my account could not be correct because it did not preserve the relation between Thomson's verbal statements and his equation. It was Whiggish, which is the basic lesson here. The story continues, however, with its characteristically adversarial nature. He asserted an interpretation of his own, which I in turn thought could not be right and said so. I then spent a great deal of time and effort on the problem and returned the next week to show why he was wrong and to present yet another account, which turned out to solve the difficulties and to give considerable insight into Thomson's mode of analysis. The Whig story and the adversarial story are about equally important in my perception of the simultaneously intellectual and psychological struggle in working with Tom." Email to author, January 2009.

25. Kripke, "History and Idealism," p. 16.

reenactment of past thoughts seems so implausible on its face as hardly to be worth considering."[26]

A robust *reductio ad absurdum* of Collingwood's view can be found in David Hackett Fischer's *Historians' Fallacies*. Fischer provides a quotation from Rudyard Kipling's *Captains Courageous*:

> When Disko thought of a cod he thought as a cod. . . . So Disko Troop thought of recent weather, and gales, currents, food, supplies, and other domestic arrangements, from the point of view of a twenty-pound cod; was in fact, for an hour, a cod himself, and looked remarkably like one.[27]

Is Kuhn Disko Troop? And Aristotle Troop's twenty-pound cod? Fischer continues:

> To require a historian to rethink Brutus's thought before he killed Caesar is to require him to become Brutus. And this he cannot do, any more than Disko Troop could convert himself into a twenty-pound cod. For Brutus did not merely think different things than Collingwood thought—he thought them differently. The whole idea is antihistorical, antiempirical, and absurd.[28]

We can believe strange things about the past, but we can still refer to *things in the past*.[29] The beliefs of sixth-century BCE mathematicians might be inaccessible to us (or at least, difficult for us to understand), but when Hippasus or one of his contemporaries refers to $\sqrt{2}$, they are *referring* to the same thing we are.[30] There is reality. There is truth. And there is history.

Cervantes wrote (and Samuel Putnam translated), ". . . truth, whose mother is history, rival of time, depository of deeds, witness of the past, exemplar and adviser to the present, and the future's counselor." When we refer to Cervantes, we are tracing a chain of evidence that leads us back into the past. (Just as when we name Cervantes we are setting up a causal chain that leads us into the future. Since it involves the future, I hesitate to call it a *historical* chain.) Reference is like a deed to a plot of land. The world isn't instantly knowable by us, but we can investigate. As the world

26. "History and Idealism," pp. 11, 2.

27. *Captains Courageous* (1897), pp. 50, 108.

28. Fischer, *Historians' Fallacies*, pp. 196–97.

29. It is still possible to be *skeptical* about Kripke's claim, namely, that a historical chain of intentions *guarantees* that we can refer to things in the past. But it is, at least, an *attempt* to show how we can refer to things.

30. $\sqrt{2}$ refers to the same thing pre-Hippasus as it does post-Hippasus, even though our *beliefs* about $\sqrt{2}$ may have changed.

evolves in time it secretes evidence. We can use anything and every-thing in our bag of tricks. DNA evidence, carbon-14 dating, bal-listics, fingernail scrapings, trichology, birth records, photographs, diary entries, eyewitness testimony, oral histories, whatever—this is *investigative realism*. We can trace and retrace our steps like Theseus in the labyrinth. And if we're lucky, find our way back to reality out of our labyrinth of false beliefs.

———

Go back to Goldie. We can believe that Goldie is golden or green or some other color, but we still refer to Goldie. As time goes by, our ideas about Goldie (and history) may change, but that doesn't mean that we no longer refer to Goldie. Nor does it mean that reference is contingent on a paradigm—or on a conceptual scheme or disci-plinary matrix. I imagine one of those very bad elementary school arguments. Some kid says that the earth is flat. I say that the earth is an oblate spheroid. We argue. It's flat. No, it isn't. Yes, it is. No, it isn't. Yes, it is. No, it isn't. Stalemate. We have reached an impasse. Kuhn steps in to adjudicate. He tells us that there is no fact of the matter. You come from different paradigms: the flat earth paradigm and the oblate spheroid paradigm. The name "earth" *means* some-thing different to each of you, and you can't compare the meanings. There is no common reference. But wait. What about the earth? *The earth!* There is that physical thing floating out in space. Is it flat, or is it an oblate spheroid? Or if it's neither, tell me just *what* it is. It must be something.

I suppose the kid in elementary school, if he gets angry enough, could strangle me. When all else fails, there's Humpty Dumpty's reply to Alice. (" 'When *I* use a word,' Humpty Dumpty said, in rather a scornful tone, 'it means just what I choose it to mean—nei-ther more nor less.' ")[31] And there's the Ashtray Argument. With Kuhn's blinkered cosmologies there *really* is no way to resolve these questions. Fisticuffs may be required.[32]

One more parable. For those who truly believe that truth is subjective or relative, ask yourself this question: Is ultimate guilt or innocence of a crime a matter of opinion? Is it relative? Is it subjec-tive? A jury might decide you're guilty of a crime that you haven't committed. Yet you're innocent. (It's possible. The legal system is

31. Please remember Alice and Humpty Dumpty's initial exchange:

> 'And how exactly like an egg he is.' she said aloud, standing with her hands ready to catch him, for she was every moment expecting him to fall. 'It's *very* provoking,' Humpty Dumpty said after a long silence, looking away from Alice as he spoke, 'to be called an egg—*very*!'
> 'I said you *looked* like an egg, Sir,' Alice gently explained. 'And some eggs are very pretty, you know,' she added, hoping to turn her remark into a sort of compliment. (Carroll, *Annotated Alice*, pp. 207–8)

Now, admittedly, Humpty Dumpty is a fictional character. But he's a fictional character shaped like an egg. Yes, he can decide what words mean—at least that's his opinion—but can a fictional egg-shaped character truthfully deny that he looks like an egg?

32. Arthur Schopenhauer wrote about this in one of my favorite essays, "The Art of Controversy." Schopenhauer's great gift is bringing cynicism to a new level. He points out that there are two ways to win an argument, *logic* and *dialectic*. He then tells us that you can never win an argument with logic, and so he passes on quickly to dialectic and provides

thirty-six ways to win an argument *any way you can*. Particularly, number thirty-six, which culminates in a version of the Ashtray Argument:

> A last trick is to become personal, insulting, rude, as soon as you perceive that your opponent has the upper hand, and that you are going to come off worst. It consists in passing from the subject of dispute, as from a lost game, to the disputant himself, and in some way attacking his person. It may be called the *argumentum ad personam*, to distinguish it from the *argumentum ad hominem*, which passes from the objective discussion of the subject pure and simple to the statements or admissions which your opponent has made in regard to it. But in becoming personal you leave the subject altogether, and turn your attack to his person, by remarks of an offensive and spiteful character. It is an appeal from the virtues of the intellect to the virtues of the body, or to mere animalism. This is a very popular trick, because every one is able to carry it into effect; and so it is of frequent application. Now the question is, What counter-trick avails for the other party? for if he has recourse to the same rule, there will be blows, or a duel, or an action for slander. (In *The Art of Controversy, and Other Posthumous Papers*, pp. 45–46)

33. I am not interested in *recherché* possibilities: someone held a gun to my head; the victim fell on a knife that I was holding. I am interested in a clear-cut example. Take the case in *The Thin Blue Line*. Randall Dale Adams's account—I was home in bed—versus the prosecutor's account: Adams was in the car and shot the cop. This is an example that, like Kripke's analysis of proper names, does not involve things in the head. It's *not* about *mens rea,* the definition of manslaughter, involuntary or otherwise, versus murder. It's *not* about this jurisdiction or that jurisdiction. It's about the real world. Was Adams in the car or home in bed?

rife with miscarriages of justice.) But we believe there is a fact of the matter. You either did it or you didn't. Period.[33]

If you were strapped into an electric chair (now a lethal injection gurney) in the Texas Death Chamber, there would be nothing relative about it. Suppose you are innocent. Suppose you were never at the crime scene. Suppose you were home in bed. Would you be satisfied with the claim that there is no definitive answer to the question of whether you're guilty or innocent? No such thing as absolute truth or falsity? Or would you be screaming, "I didn't do it. I didn't do it"? I doubt you would take much comfort in the claim made by the postmodernist priest who comes to administer last rites (perhaps it's Thomas Kuhn with a clerical collar): "It all depends on your point of view, doesn't it?" Or "what paradigm are you in?"

When I was investigating the murder of Robert Wood, a Dallas police officer, and the prosecution and conviction of Randall Dale Adams for that murder, would it have made sense to describe my viewpoint as one paradigm and the viewpoint of the Dallas police as another? Surely, we had different ways of looking at the evidence, different interpretations of the eyewitness testimony, different ways of looking at the crime. Suppose someone said, there's no way of comparing these two paradigms. They're *incommensurable.* Or, even if they can be compared, you can't say one is true and the other false. Or even that one is *more* true than the other. There is no *absolute* truth. Perhaps they could gussy up the claim by citing police procedures and practices. A different puzzle set or disciplinary matrix. Different traditions of looking at crime scene evidence. Or to make it more contemporary, different trading zones. The social construction of the ashtray.

For me, Kuhn's ultimate crime is not the espousal of nonsense. We're probably, in varying degrees, all guilty of that. No, to me, there is a worse crime. The history of his endless textual revisions and supposed clarifications is a history, among other things, of moral and intellectual equivocation. Several commentators have argued that Kuhn was aware of my criticisms long before I made them. To me, that exacerbates the situation; it does not mitigate it.

Philosopher John Burgess told me in our interview:

Kuhn speaks one way when speaking to historians, and another way when speaking to philosophers. The trouble begins when he starts talking about things being socially constructed—As far as I'm concerned, the stars can't be socially constructed. The stars are billions of years old, and human society is *not* billions of years old. And so the latter cannot have constructed the former. On the other hand, if you just say astronomy is socially constructed, well, that's a trivial truism. Who would deny that? Before there was human society, there weren't any astronomers, and there wasn't any astronomy. There is some philosophical issue here, but it's these modes—it's just a sloppy way of talking. Throwing around these expressions is in fact concealing issues rather than illuminating anything. It is encouraging a fallacious jump from the thought "astronomy is constructed" to "therefore, the things astronomy is about are constructed"—or something like that. And when speaking with philosophers, Kuhn would deny holding this outrageous belief. But when speaking to historians, he'd go back to using this language.

The difficulty of ascertaining the truth is often confused with the relativity of truth (or the belief that there is no such thing as truth). Two very different concepts. We may have difficulty *knowing* the exact date and location of the Battle of Hastings, but that doesn't mean it didn't happen at a *specific* time and place. "The past," as L. P. Hartley has written, "is a foreign country. They do things differently there."[34] But when Homer speaks of the "sun," is he speaking about a

34. Hartley, *The Go-Between*, p. 17.

different object than T. S. Eliot is? If Newton were to give Einstein a copy of his *Principia* and Einstein were to give Newton a copy of his "Zur Elektrodynamik bewegter Körper" ("On the Electrodynamics of Moving Bodies") would they be *unable* to understand each other and their respective theories? I don't think so. There would be discussions, perhaps even disagreements about ideas and principles. Clarifications would be needed. But would they look past each other in numb, dumb stupefaction? Part of the enterprise of science is *translating* the theories of the past into the theories of the present. The past may be a foreign country, but I do not believe the people who live (or, if you prefer, lived) there speak a language we cannot understand.

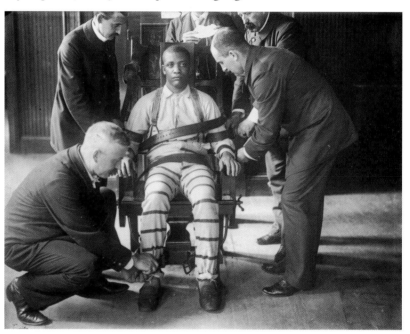

EPILOGUE

PHILOSOPHY, *n.—A route of many roads leading from nowhere to nothing.*
—Ambrose Bierce, *The Devil's Dictionary*

I hadn't been back to Princeton for close to forty years when I was asked to deliver the Spencer Trask Lecture in November 2010.[1] I prepared to write a lecture titled "The Ashtray," about the ashtray that was thrown at me. I started digging through boxes of papers related to my experiences at Princeton. At that time I was very much devoted to rock climbing, and (although this is not well known) Princeton is one of the best places to rock-climb in the world.

1. The faculty member who introduced me before the lecture claimed I had left Princeton because the work was too difficult for me. Alas, I had to interrupt his introduction to assure everyone in the room that the work may or may not have been too difficult for me—but I was thrown out of Princeton because I disagreed with Thomas Kuhn.

The Daily PRINCETONIAN

Vol. XCVI, No. 70   Princeton, N.J., Monday, May 15, 1972   ©   15 Cents

Police arrest 47 demonstrators, reopen IDA

Three-day total rises to 178 arrests; Rutgers students plan to swell ranks

By JAMIE HESS

Police drag away two protesters who were arrested Friday.

Forty-seven more persons were arrested Friday morning as demonstrators returned to blockade the entrances to the Institute for Defense Analyses (IDA) for the third consecutive day.

Undaunted by the mass arrests, protesters have planned a "massive demonstration" for 7 a.m. today involving participants "from all over the Northeast" at the IDA building, located behind the Engineering Quadrangle.

About 20 to 25 Rutgers students and an equal number from New York are expected to participate this morning.

"Chicago Seven" defense lawyer William Kunstler is scheduled to appear at the demonstration at 9:30 a.m., according to the Anti-War Coordinating Committee.

Friday's arrests brought the three-day total at IDA to 178 involving 159 different persons—110 Princeton students, nine professors, four Princeton Theological Seminary students and 36 others, including 19 juveniles.

About 150 persons assembled at IDA's north gate by 8:30 a.m., one-third of whom participated in the blockade. A force of 45 borough township and Mercer County officers arrested every blockader.

IDA security guards consequently were able to open the gate for the first time since Wednesday, making it possible for 25

waiting employes to enter the building through police lines.

Thursday, police arrested only 70 of the approximately 110 persons who linked arms in front of the gate, and the remaining demonstrators prevented the entry of IDA employes into the building.

Forty-six of those arrested were placed in three of four waiting paddy wagons and transported to the Mercer County Court House in Trenton, according to Borough police lieutenant Michael F. Carnevale.

Its "processing procedures and facilities are much better" than those at Borough Hall, he explained.

One juvenile, arrested at 8 for cutting one of the encircling fence's six strands of barbed wire, was taken to Borough Hall and booked.

The 41 non-juveniles were held in a courtroom in Trenton until 2:10 p.m. when they were released on a collective bail of $6750 — $150 for first offenders, up from $100 Thursday, and $250 for repeat offenders. The charge was "interfering with persons lawfully attempting to enter on the premises known as IDA."

The other five juveniles were taken from the courtroom to the Mercer County Youth House also in Trenton, where three males were allegedly beaten and forced to take scalding hot showers. Youth House employes were unavailable yesterday for comment.

To protest the alleged treatment of the juveniles, students have organized a march and motorcade to leave Borough Hall at 6:15 tonight for the Youth House, where a rally is scheduled for 7 p.m.

Photos by Nathan Prichard

Police pull IDA demonstrator away from wire fence

All the juveniles face an as yet unscheduled appearance in Mercer County Juvenile Court on charges of juvenile delinquency. The 41 adults arrested Friday are scheduled to appear in Borough Court at 1:30 p.m. Wednesday, bringing to 139 the total number to appear then.

Two more professors — Associate Professor of Religion Victor S. Preller and Professor of History Stanley J. Stein — were arrested Friday along with Edward B. Meservey, a research assistant at Forrestal.

There were seven repeat offenders, including one triple offender.

Demonstrators did not begin arriving at IDA until shortly after 7 a.m., enabling a few employes who "wanted to see what it was like from the inside" to enter the building at 7.

At 8:29 the police, who had assembled in a parking lot separated from the IDA lot by a line of trees, moved into the lot. They were followed by the paddy

wagons, which drew into a circle on the lawn adjoining the north gate.

The blockaders immediately linked arms and struck up a sustained chant of "IDA must go," as Borough Police Chief Peter J. McCrohan held up his first two fingers and shouted almost inaudibly that the blockaders had two minutes to disperse.

McCrohan then turned to the demonstrators not in the driveway and informed them they must stay off the pavement to avoid arrest. Prosecutor's officers stationed themselves at the pavement's edge, restraining and in some cases pushing the observers

(Continued on page five)

BOOK DONATION

Textbooks, or any other books, especially English-Spanish dictionaries, may be left in a box in the back entry hall of Maclean house. Books are needed for a four-year college program at Leesburg State Prison.

Judicial Committee dismisses Rudenstine disruption charge

By LAIRD HART

The Judicial Committee decided May 5 to dismiss charges of "serious violations of University policy on protests and demonstrations" brought against Dean Rudenstine by two undergraduates.

The committee voted 6-1 not to further examine charges of Douglas R. Noll '72 and Thomas C. Greiner Jr. '72, that "Dean Rudenstine's conduct was disruptive of the rights of peaceable assembly and free inquiry."

Noll and Greiner's charges referred to Rudenstine's statements at the Woodrow Wilson School lobby occupation April 21 warning of possible disciplinary and court action if demonstrators remained in the building past closing time, which Rudenstine believed to be midnight.

Noll and Greiner charged that Rudenstine ought to have been aware that people could stay in the building beyond midnight, and that, by his statements, Rudenstine both intimidated the demonstrators and "forced the discussion" to "issues other than those [the demonstrators] came to discuss."

Noll and Greiner explained in the charges that "whether the presentation by Dean Rudenstine of false information was delib-

erate or an honest mistake does not lessen the gravity of its effect."

The majority opinion of the Judicial Committee found that "in issuing a warning to the participants, [Rudenstine] was acting within the reasonable bounds of his authority."

The committee determined that "the information given in this case provided no basis for believing the charges could be sustained" against Rudenstine, because he "has an obligation to issue warnings of possible disciplinary action in order to protect the rights of individuals."

An administrative officer, the committee concluded, "must be left sufficient latitude of action, and complaints about his choice of action within this latitude are not within the purview of the Judicial Committee, but should be made to his superior.

"On these grounds, the Committee can find no way to justify its acceptance of the charges made."

Minority opinion

M. Duncan Grant '72, the lone dissenter in the committee's 6-1 vote, explained in a three page minority opinion that "a lot of questions remain unanswered, and should be answered in a formal hearing."

Grant urged the committee to accept jurisdiction for four reasons.

First, Grant felt "other members of the committee have misunderstood the function of the pre-hearing conference . . . it appears to dissenter that the ma-

(Continued on page four)

CORRECTION

The Princetonian erroneously reported in Friday's edition that Aaron S. Kaufman '72 was charged with assault and battery in Thursday's anti-war protest at the Institute for Defense Analyses. He was actually charged with resisting arrest. The Princetonian apologizes for the error.

475 persons crowd McCosh 50

Dellinger attacks Nixon policy

By GEORGE KRYDER

A relentless drizzle forced yesterday's "Mothers' Day Rally/ Teach-In For Peace" to be moved from the Borough Hall Green indoors to McCosh 50, where over 475 persons listened to speeches by David Dellinger, Princeton faculty, students and townspeople.

Chicago Seven defendant Dellinger cautioned the audience not "to become innoculated into thinking this latest escalation will be the last.

"Right now we are facing the greatest crisis of the Vietnam war and one of the greatest crises in the history of the American people," said Dellinger.

He castigated Nixon's "ineffective gesture" in blockading North Vietnamese ports as well as the President's refusal to negotiate without the release of POWs and without the assurance that U.S. troops being withdrawn would be safe.

Dellinger called on the American people to "reassert democracy at the roots" by militant protest at "the army bases where people are refusing to fight and at draft centers where people refuse to be inducted."

He called for a march on Washington May 22 culminating in a sit-in at the Pentagon and at

David Dellinger

Congress in a "massive response to not only deny Nixon troops but also the funds for making war."

Dellinger urged the audience to take "committed action" either in Washington or in Princeton.

Next Richard A. Falk, Milbank professor of International Law and Practice, termed the Nixon administration's mining and blockading effort "a diversionary action for the intensification of bombing," and "an atrocity of the first magnitude."

Falk said the "persistent illegality of Nixon's war policies

undermines any legitimacy the government may have," and criticized Congress and the courts for not implementing action to stop the President.

"Our only recourse is citizens' militant action to save constitutional government in this country," he said.

Falk called upon everyone to "stop IDA's aid to war crime," and "to use the Vietnamese people as a model of perseverence in our effort to stop the insane criminality of our leaders."

Professor of History Stanley J. Stein read a statement to the Princeton community from Amherst president John W. Ward.

Ward, who was arrested last week while blockading the entrance to a military base, said in his statement that he was at first torn between his role as college president and his role as a private citizen whose actions were separate from his college. However, in making the decision to protest, "even though you may be wrong," Ward concluded, "at least you will not have lost your own respect for yourself."

Borough Councilman Martin Lombardo demanded that "Nixon stop this craziness" and said he had asked the mayor to call an emergency meeting Tuesday evening to condemn the escalation.

The gothic ornamentation on the buildings made them ideal for climbing. And I was in the best shape I have ever been.

In May 1972 Richard Nixon had ordered the mining of Haiphong harbor and had launched Operation Linebacker. It was the first continuous bombing campaign against North Vietnam since the end of Rolling Thunder in 1968. In 1968, Lyndon Johnson was still president, and Nixon was elected on a peace platform. Today, it seems like a grim joke. Then, it was a betrayal. I was arrested at a demonstration at the Institute for Defense Analysis (IDA), a major defense contractor. I was taken in a paddy wagon to Trenton.

While waiting to be booked, I walked over to a window and realized it would be a very easy matter to just climb out the window and climb down the side of the building and leave, which I did. I always felt a little bit ashamed of myself. I thought, "I should've been formally booked and fingerprinted. There's probably no record of the fact that I was arrested in this demonstration."

Recently, I found an old issue of the *Princetonian* online. My name was in the paper, and it felt good—there *was* a record of the demonstration and of my participation. I heard that the then-president of Princeton, Robert Goheen, had said about the demonstrators, "This isn't Princeton."[2] Later, he backpedaled and insisted he wasn't talking about the demonstrators, but rather about the fact that the IDA was not *geographically* located on the Princeton campus. Clearly, a practitioner of the art of "it depends what you mean by 'x.'" A philosopher might conclude that his remark shows that there

Police break IDA blockade

(Continued from page one)

back from the blockade.

To a chant of "Racist cops, racist war, we won't take it any more," the police advanced in double file up to the blockade. McCrohan announced, "If you walk out, you'll have it easy," and about ten persons complied and marched into the paddywagon.

During the next few minutes, several more unlinked their arms and walked out; more · than a dozen dropped to the pavement and were dragged away. As others walked away, the last seven offered some resistance.

Several of the seven had to be grabbed around the neck to be separated, and once separated they began kicking. The final student to be arrested required four policemen to be subdued. After seven minutes had elapsed, every blockader was in one of three paddywagons.

As the fourth waited empty, the gate was unlocked, and 25 employes who had congregated in three groups in the parking lot, filed in through the police massed in the driveway.

University students arrested were Glenn E. Aguiar '74, Scott P. Anderson '72, Martin W. Bachop '73, Edward G. Berenson '71, Lawrence F. Camp '73, Gordon Curtis '73, Bradford R. DeGraf '75, Carolyn J. Douglas '75 and Philip L. Douglas '72.

Also arrested were Mary B. Gibson GS, Eric P. Goosby '74, Michael Gross GS, Robert M. Hamm '72, Jon M. Hobson '73, Lyle P. Hough '74, James E. Kelly '73, Thomas L. Lescault '74, Judith H. Loebl '75, James E. Ludvik '73, John M. McEnany '72, Mark E. McGovern '75, Geoffrey P. Miller '73, Errol M. Morris GS and Kenneth A. Moy '75.

Also arrested were Charles D. Piot '73, R. Andrew Reath '73, Jane E. Rose '74, Wladimiro Scheffer GS, Kathryn L. Shailer GS, W. Lawrence Stanton GS, John J. Tolson '72, Dennis T. Torigoe GS, David B. Wong GS and Ronald Zuckerman GS.

2. Christopher Connell, "Robert Francis Goheen,"*Princeton Alumni Weekly,* May 14, 2008.

is no such thing as reference. I would conclude otherwise. I have often wondered whether philosophical realists were more likely to oppose the war.

These experiences informed what I became as a filmmaker. The things I was concerned with in those days are still very much with me, are still very much part of who I am. Certainly the issue of murder, mass murder, has stayed with me over the years. It's part of the films that I made with Robert S. McNamara, *The Fog of War*, and Donald Rumsfeld, *The Unknown Known*. At Princeton, I would sit in the Firestone Library reading volume after volume of the transcripts of the Nuremberg War Crimes Tribunal. Thirty years later I had the opportunity to travel with McNamara (and Samantha Power, who in 2013 became the United States representative to the United Nations) to the International Criminal Court (ICC) in the Hague. We showed *The Fog of War* to the court.

McNamara and I answered questions following the screening and then visited with the court archivist. McNamara told him, "I wish that they had these statutes governing war crimes back when I was secretary of defense." The archivist soberly replied, "Sir, they did." Another completely bizarre experience, beyond Kafkaesque, was seeing former Serbian president Slobodan Milošević on the stand behind multiple layers of bullet-proof glass. None of the proceedings I watched had much to do with the content of the charges against him. Part of the desuetude of justice. Here was a mass murderer, but it was as if the crimes were invisible or at least had faded away. It was all procedural—procedures about procedures about procedures, epicycle upon epicycle upon epicycle. And yet, the knowledge that Milošević's crimes were being confronted, even if only in a vague and uncertain way, represented progress. Recording history, requiring people to give an account of what happened, holding them *accountable* for what they had done.

In 1962 *The Structure of Scientific Revolutions* was first published. In 1963 John F. Kennedy was assassinated. Many people were emotionally torn apart. What did it mean that there was no clear answer as to what had happened, or who had done it? It was the *zeitgeist* of the times. And in the years since, the ambiguities only deepened. It was as if the concept of truth itself was being challenged. Could we ever know? Was there something to know? Recently, I was interviewed by the granddaughter of Abraham Zapruder, the Zapruder of the Zapruder film. She was writing about her grandfather's film, her family, and the world around her. About how we retreated into a world without answers, instead of doggedly pursuing solutions to the puzzles of history.

In 1972 there was, of course, a debate raging about the Vietnam War. But many years later, I've come to realize there was another debate embodied here, a debate about truth—whether truth is socially constructed or whether truth ultimately concerns the relation between language and reality. I feel very strongly that, even though the world is unutterably insane, there is this idea—perhaps a hope—

that we can reach outside of the insanity and find truth, find the world, find ourselves.

Making *The Thin Blue Line* was one the most important experiences of my life, something that I remain really, really proud of—helping to overturn the conviction of a man who had been sentenced to death for a crime he did not commit. There are endless obstacles and impediments to finding the truth. You might never find it; it's an elusive goal. But here's something to remember. The world is out there—like an undiscovered continent. And it's our job to go out and discover it. It's one of the deepest lessons that I've taken away from my experiences at Princeton and beyond.

Acknowledgments

Charles Silver provided many of the ideas in this essay. I have benefited enormously over the years from our conversations about Kripke, Kuhn, meaning, and reference. And from his book *The Futility of Consciousness*. This book could not have been conceived or written without him.

One of the great mysteries of my life is why my wife, Julia Sheehan, agreed to marry me. But for whatever reason, she said yes, and I will always be grateful. She once told me the main reason to finish your PhD is so that you don't have to spend the rest of your life trying to finish it. She was right, as always. I want to thank my extremely talented son, Hamilton Morris. And my psychiatrist Nancy Rappaport, who taught me that a 10 percent reduction in self-loathing could result in a 30 to 40 percent increase in productivity. This book also could not have been done without the editorial advice and unremitting parental supervision provided by Josh Kearney. No simple sentence could capture the level of suffering he has endured in the preparation of this manuscript. Ron Rosenbaum and John Canaday read a number of drafts and made many helpful editorial suggestions. No list would be complete without mention of my office manager, editor, and researcher Ann Petrone, who tragically died in 2015. I will always miss her.

I would like to thank my office researchers and editors: James Maxwell Larkin, Julie Fischer, Clare Kim, and Zach Arnold. As well as my office manager, Karen Skinner. I'd also like to thank George Kalogerakis (at the *New York Times*), who published an earlier version of this essay, and my editor at the University of Chicago Press Susan Bielstein, whose attempts to understand my ideas spurred me to greater clarity and concision. Laura Lindgren designed the book. I've wanted to work with her ever since I directed her in an Apple commercial. I'm grateful I finally got an opportunity. David Rice provided a translation of Hasse and Scholz, "Die Grundlagenkrisis der griechischen Mathematik." And James Maxwell Larkin provided a translation of Hans Freudenthal's essay "Y avait-il une crise des fondements des mathematiques dans l'antiquite?"

I would like to thank my interview subjects: Walter Burkert, M. Norton Wise, John Burgess, Andrew Hurley, Stanley Cavell, Hilary Putnam, Steven Weinberg, Ross MacPhee, and Noam Chomsky. I have benefited from conversations with Maria Tatar, Louis Menand, Lawrence Weschler, Brian Leiter, Charles Rosenberg, Peter Galison, James Conant, Marc Hauser, David Kaiser, Michael Nedo, David Wootton, Rebecca Lemov, Natasha Nicholson, Brian Skyrms, Leslie Dunton-Downer, Matthew Lund, Andrew Berry, David Hackett Fischer, Lynda Obst, Sandy Cohen, Melissa Franklin, Romina Padro, Arthur Fine, and Barry Lam. And of course, Saul Kripke. This essay would not have been possible without his work. (Kripke might not agree with this assessment. Perhaps there is a possible world where another philosopher came up with his ideas. It may be possible, but it's not likely. And whoever it might be, it wouldn't be Kripke.)

I am also grateful for the support of Homi Bhabha, the Mahindra Center at Harvard, Harvard Library and its terrific staff, the Saul Kripke Center at the Graduate Center of CUNY, and Springer Publishing. I would like to thank Tom Levin and the other Princeton faculty members who invited me to give the Spencer Trask Lecture at Princeton in November 2010. And finally, the anonymous readers for the University of Chicago Press. It is ironic that the manuscript was originally sent to several post-Kuhnian historians of science, proving that a little bit of Kuhn is like a little bit of arsenic. (My wife once made this point: you can't use Hitler as a spice, nor as a flavoring. The minute you put Hitler in the soup, it becomes Hitler Soup. The same could be said for Kuhn. Post-Kuhnians may not entirely believe in his philosophy, but they have been poisoned by it.)

Cast of Characters

E. T. BELL: One of the early historians of mathematics. Indeed, I got interested in the history of mathematics through reading Bell's *Men of Mathematics*. Too bad he turned out to be an anti-Semite. I wrestled with whether to mention this. But it's important to be reminded from time to time that anti-Semitism is real. In the first edition of *Men of Mathematics*, Bell wrote, "The aggressive clannishness of Jews has often been remarked, sometimes as an argument against employing them in academic work, but it has not been so generally observed that there is no more vicious academic hatred than that of one Jew for another when they disagree on purely scientific matters or when one is jealous or afraid of another."

GEORGE BERKELEY: The originator of the phrase *esse est percipi*. I could never really find anything wrong with solipsism, from Berkeley or others, except it still allows for *something* rather than *nothing*.

AMBROSE BIERCE: My favorite American writer, next to Poe. His *Tales of Soldiers and Civilians* has a running theme—all of life is a dream rudely interrupted by death. And then there's *The Devil's Dictionary*, supposedly a compendium of ironic, sarcastic innuendo, but really far more accurate than the *OED*. Bierce provides a definition of logic: "The art of thinking and reasoning in strict accordance with the limitations and incapacities of the human misunderstanding."

JORGE LUIS BORGES: A genius among geniuses. After all, he imagined a language (and a world) without nouns. Late in life, Borges, completely blind, was standing in front of a very busy and broad intersection in Buenos Aires. He was hoping that someone would come and guide him across. Finally, someone took his hand, and together they made their way to the other side. The man said, "Thank you. I was really worried about crossing this road. You see, I'm blind."

WALTER BURKERT: What could be more invigorating than a history based on a paucity (or even an absence) of evidence? History with an invisible, unknowable past.

HERBERT BUTTERFIELD: The Whiggish critic of Whiggishness. Could it be that Butterfield invented himself so that historians could scold each other endlessly into the future?

LEWIS CARROLL: A writer of limericks, fantasies, and seeming gibberish. Turns out to be one of the most profound thinkers of the nineteenth century. The French philosopher Gilles Deleuze wrote extensively about Carroll. Deleuze turned literature into word salad; Carroll, on the other hand, turned word salad into literature.

R. G. COLLINGWOOD: In *The Idea of History*, Collingwood promoted the idea that history is a reenactment of the past in the mind. If you want to know what Julius Caesar was thinking, think like Julius Caesar. (Easier said than done.) Often described as a British idealist philosopher, to my way of thinking, he seems a version of Thomas Kuhn. If you want to know what Aristotle was thinking, think like Aristotle. It remains to be seen how successful one can be at this kind of enterprise or whether practitioners are buying a one-way ticket to the nuthouse.

DAVID DEUTSCH: A realist voice of reason. A lover of Popper, Dawkins, and the multiple-worlds view of quantum mechanics. He allows Schrödinger to have his cat and eat it too.

PHILIP K. DICK: Latter-day Cassandra. Never saw a paranoid idea he didn't like. If there is a form of paranoid ideation Dick did not express, it has eluded me. The belief that the world might be a simulacrum didn't originate with the Wachowski siblings. Dick had his hand in that cookie jar long before. Still, my favorite Dick-nightmare is in *Ubik*. You think you're alive, but you're really dead. Hear, hear.

JOHN EARMAN: A rarely read philosopher of science who has suffered from being just too good at what he does. I learned from him how ordinary language could deeply confuse philosophical issues in history and philosophy of science. For example, just because special relativity is called special relativity doesn't mean there's anything relative about intervals in Minkowski spacetime.

ALBERT EINSTEIN: The gold standard for being smart. He's the one person to whom the comment "he's no Einstein" clearly doesn't apply.

PAUL FEYERABEND: Miserabilists or incommensurabilists—which is worse? I went from Princeton to Berkeley. Out of the frying pan, into another frying pan. I may not be able to talk meaningfully about incommensurability, but I can certainly talk about the people who believed in it—or putatively believed in it. Feyerabend was probably chief among them. And he alone had a defensible position, if only because he never chose to defend it. Call it utter whack-job philosophy: nothing makes sense, nothing is rational, nothing is reasonable—just believe what you want to believe. He's legendary for having asked a "professional" witch to deliver lectures in his name.

DAVID HACKETT FISCHER: A historian's historian, and the author of many popular books on history. My favorite, *Historical Fallacies*, at first seems an argument about the impossibility of doing history. It comes close. But it is nothing of the sort. It's a book on the dangers of doing history.

P. M. FRASER: How can I express the joy of having on my bookshelf Fraser's three-volume excursion into *Ptolemaic Alexandria*? Like the claim made in the old AT&T phone ads, it's the next best thing to being there. (Or so I imagine.)

NORWOOD RUSSELL HANSON: You've been bitten by a postmodern pit viper. You've been told the poison is fast-acting, invariably fatal. What to do? If the pit viper is Thomas Kuhn, I suggest reading Norwood Russell Hanson immediately. He's the perfect antidote. The idea that observation is theory-laden is important in and of itself. But the idea that observations, informed by different theories, are incommensurable is errant nonsense.

THOMAS HOBBES: An early progenitor of a nondescriptive theory of the denotation of names, but best known for his "progressive" theory of man: namely, man left to his own devices will destroy himself and everything around him. I always wished there was a mnemonic to help me remember Hobbes's phrase about human existence, but the lack of vowels makes it difficult. Solitary, poor, nasty, brutish, and short: SPNBS. Thomas Pynchon in *Gravity's*

Rainbow provided a slightly different version: a law firm named Salitieri, Poore, Nash, De Brutus, and Short.

JORIS-KARL HUYSMANS: Were I to list the greatest misanthropic novels ever written, there would certainly be room for Céline, Nathanael West, and others of a similar disagreeable disposition. But Huysmans's *À Rebours* would be near the top. Here's my favorite line: " 'It is all a matter of syphilis,' reflected Des Esseintes [the novel's protagonist]."

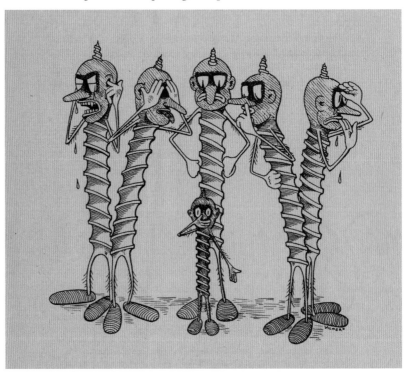

ALEXANDRE KOYRÉ: Old-school history and philosophy of science. A history of ideas beautifully written. I loved Koyré so much, particularly his *Newtonian Studies* and *Études galiléennes*, that I naively thought that's what history and philosophy of science would be about. Silly me.

SAUL KRIPKE: One of the great philosophers. What would we do without him? Like Chomsky's review of B. F. Skinner and the behaviorist school of language acquisition, Kripke's takedown of Searle's cluster-theory of descriptions is a model of philosophical demolition. From his early work on modal logic and his undergraduate paper on Collingwood, through to his

Cast of Characters

more recent work on philosophical logic, he is, like Russell, an exceptional prose stylist. A mixture of film noir and Twain—it is a short jump between Gödel stealing Schmidt's incompleteness proof in Kripke's fable, and Chambers and Tom in *Pudd'nhead Wilson*.

THOMAS KUHN: Ambrose Bierce defined November as "the eleventh twelfth of a weariness." My weariness with Kuhn started long before November.

GOTTFRIED LEIBNIZ: One of the originators of the calculus (in fact, we use Leibniz's notation, not Newton's). Also known for windowless monads. But probably most famous for the principle that this world is the best of all possible worlds. When God created the world, the infinitude of possibilities was subject to one constraint: the world He created had to be the best. Unfortunately, He neglected to specify the best of *what*. Leibniz speculates on His thinking in his *Theodicy*: "It is certain that God sets greater store by a man than a lion; nevertheless it can hardly be said with certainty that God prefers a single man in all respects to the whole of lion-kind. Even should that be so, it would by no means follow that the interest of a certain number of men would prevail over the consideration of a general disorder diffused through an infinite number of creatures."

ROBERT McNAMARA: My favorite war criminal. I came to love the man. How could you not love a man so tortured by guilt? And so aware of the reasons for that guilt.

MATTHEW MESELSON: A scientist who believes in reality. I could never understand why he had not won the Nobel Prize for the Meselson-Stahl experiment, which established the "semiconservative" replication of DNA—the first important result after Watson-Crick. So I asked him. "How come you didn't win the Nobel for the Meselson-Stahl experiment?" He said, "Because I wasn't on the committee that awarded the prize."

ROBERT MUSIL: Author of *The Man without Qualities*, one of my very favorite novels. Ulrich may say that his aim is to abolish reality, but Musil was clearly interested in investigating reality and the nature of consciousness. My interest in mass murderers, still ongoing, owes much to Musil's character Moosbrugger, a demonic killer. Moosbrugger is vexed by questions of his own culpability and, on hearing his death sentence, says, "I am satisfied, even though I must confess to you that you have condemned a madman." Ulrich, reflecting on the trial, says: "If mankind could dream as a whole, that dream would be Moosbrugger."

ISAAC NEWTON: Often preoccupied with a theory of universal gravitation, as well as other sundry things, when he proposed marriage to his putative beloved, he took her hand, essentially forgot what he was doing, and used her thumb to tamp down the ash in his pipe. Needless to say, he ended life as a bachelor. (This much repeated story, like that of Newton's dog Diamond, may be apocryphal. Nonetheless, both deserve to be repeated.)

KARL POPPER: One of the great philosophers of science of the twentieth century. Best known for his books *The Logic of Discovery* and *Conjectures and Refutations*. Popper showed that truth depends on the possibility of falsehood—you can't have one without the other. And that truth is only provisional. Another way of thinking about it: falsity is everywhere. Here are two of my favorite examples. Notoriously bad at multiplication, Ernst Kummer, one of the great algebraists of the nineteenth century, asked his students, What is 9×7? One student said 61; another, 69. Kummer replied, "Come now, gentlemen, it can't be both. It must be one or the other." And a variant on the theme: The last living inhabitant of Zoar, an Ohio utopian community, said, on her deathbed, "Think of it. All those religions. They can't all be right. But they could all be wrong."

HILARY PUTNAM: A philosopher's philosopher, and an uncommonly decent human being. He told me it was a loss to American philosophy my not being in the profession. I don't think he was right, but it was nice to hear. He was legendary for constantly changing his mind. We had a discussion about photography— does it record just the surface of things, or does it "go deeper"? I proposed a thought experiment: Alexander Gardner takes a picture of Abraham Lincoln, who has just been given a face transplant, a Jefferson Davis face transplant. Who is Gardner's picture of? Lincoln? Or Davis? I argued it was still a picture of Lincoln. Putnam disagreed. A year later, he told me I was right.

BERTRAND RUSSELL: When given the Nobel Prize for literature, Russell wondered, Why for literature?! Wasn't he a famous logician and philosopher? Indeed, he was. But he was also a truly great writer. And incredibly funny. Even at the end of his life, he was writing and thinking far more clearly than anybody else. In his mid-eighties, he skillfully disintegumented Strawson's criticism of his theory of descriptions. "I am totally unable to see any validity whatever in any of Mr. Strawson's arguments. Whether this inability is due to senility on my part or to some other cause, I must leave readers to judge."

It's hard to pick my favorite Russell line. In "On Denoting": "By the law of excluded middle . . . either 'the present King of France is bald' or 'the present King of France is not bald' must be true. Yet if we enumerated the things that are bald, and then the things that are not bald, we should not find the present King of France in either list. Hegelians, who love a synthesis, will probably conclude that he wears a wig." Or, wrestling with the mind-body distinction as a child: "What is mind? No matter. What is matter? Never mind." In his obituary for Wittgenstein, Russell had the temerity to wonder whether his student might be insane or a charlatan: "Quite at first I was in doubt as to whether he was a man of genius or a crank, but very soon decided in favor of the former alternative. Some of his early views made the decision difficult. He maintained, for example, at one time that all existential propositions are meaningless. This was in a lecture room, and I invited him to consider the proposition: 'There is no hippopotamus in this room at present.' When he refused to believe this, I looked under all the desks without finding one; but he remained unconvinced." Donald Rumsfeld would be proud.

ARTHUR SCHOPENHAUER: No one thinks of Schopenhauer as a stand-up comedian, and indeed, *The World as Will and Representation* is not a laugh riot. But for me, Schopenhauer is one of the funniest writers ever. His essay on how to win an argument is spot-on. It's important, every now and again, to remember that logic always takes a back seat to dialectic. Logical arguments that are effective are few and far between. What's left, namely, everything else, is for the most part a disaster.

WILLIAM SHAKESPEARE, PLATO, ARISTOTLE: When Hamlet says, just before his O-groans, "The rest is silence," he is offering a grotesque misrepresentation. The rest is not silence. The rest is commentary. From ca. 1600 to the present time we have a plethora of accounts of what the line means. A heap of expository language that dwarfs "the rest is silence." (Like a gnat compared to the Milky Way.)

A similar problem exists for Plato and Aristotle, except in their case, the commentary has been piling up for a couple of millennia. I leave the reader with one thought: if the Athenian Stranger rang your doorbell, would you invite him in to dinner?

CHARLES SILVER: Charlie Silver got his PhD from Berkeley. I was tossed out. He always considered me the lucky one. I have a limited ability to understand philosophy, but I have no understanding of philosophy departments. Charlie was one of the most brilliant and competent people I have known in philosophy, and almost everything I know about philosophy I've learned from him.

STEVEN WEINBERG: One of the great physicists of the twentieth century. Weinberg pioneered the electroweak unification theory—but made the unpardonable error of believing in truth and physical reality. The Kuhnians would never forgive him.

LUDWIG WITTGENSTEIN: A notorious book, *The Jew of Linz* by Kimberly Cornish, reprints a picture of students at the *Realschule* in Linz, Austria, at the beginning of the twentieth century. The picture is said to include two famous, or, if you prefer, infamous, figures: Ludwig Wittgenstein and Adolf Hitler. Is it really them? Arguments have gone back and forth, and I don't know. But they were both enrolled at the *Realschule* around the same time, ca. 1903. I often ask the seemingly rhetorical question, when showing people the photograph, "Which of these two did the greater damage in the twentieth century?" OK, OK, it was Hitler. But think about it.

Bibliography

Altman, W. H. F. "A Tale of Two Drinking Parties: Plato's Laws in Context." *Polis: The Journal for Ancient Greek Political Thought* 27, no. 2 (2010): 240–64. doi: 10.1163/20512996-90000169.

Anscombe, G. E. M. "The Question of Linguistic Idealism." In *The Collected Philosophical Papers of G. E. M. Anscombe*. Vol. 1, *From Parmenides to Wittgenstein*, 112–33. Minneapolis: University of Minnesota Press, 1981.

Augustine. *City of God*. Volume 5, *Books 16–18.35*. Translated by Eva M. Sanford and William M. Green. Loeb Classical Library 415. Cambridge, MA: Harvard University Press, 1965.

Austin, J. L. *Sense and Sensibilia*. Edited by G. J. Warnock. New York: Oxford University Press, 1964.

Ayer, A. J., and Rush Rhees. "Symposium: Can There Be a Private Language?" *Proceedings of the Aristotelian Society*, Supplementary Volumes 28 (1954): 63–94. doi: 10.1093/aristoteliansupp/28.1.63.

Barrow, John D., and Frank J. Tipler. *The Anthropic Cosmological Principle*. New York: Oxford University Press, 1986.

Bartley, W. W., III. "Lewis Carroll's Lost Book on Logic." *Scientific American* 227, no. 1 (1972): 38–47. doi: 10.1038/scientificamerican0772-38.

Beckford, William. *Vathek*. Edited by Roger H. Lonsdale. Translated by Samuel Henley. London: Oxford University Press, 1970.

Bell, E. T. *The Development of Mathematics*. 1937. Facsimile of 2nd ed. New York: Dover, 1992.

Bentham, Jeremy. *The Panopticon Writings*. Edited by Miran Božovič. London: Verso, 1995.

Berkeley, George. *Principles of Human Knowledge*. Edited by Colin Murray Turbayne. Indianapolis: Bobbs-Merril, 1970.

Berlinski, David. *Infinite Ascent: A Short History of Mathematics*. New York: Modern Library, 2008.

Biletzki, Anat, and Anat Matar. "Ludwig Wittgenstein." In *Stanford*

Encyclopedia of Philosophy. Stanford University, 1997–. Article published November 8, 2002. https://plato.stanford.edu/entries/wittgenstein.

Bird, Alexander. "Kuhn on Reference and Essence." *Philosophia Scientae*, no. 8-1 (2004): 39–71. doi: 10.4000/philosophiascientiae.588.

Borges, Jorge Luis. *Collected Fictions*. Translated by Andrew Hurley. New York: Penguin, 1999.

———. "Un Film Abrumador." *Sur* 2, no. 83 (August 1, 1941): 88–89.

———. *Selected Non-Fictions*. Edited by Eliot Weinberger. Translated by Esther Allen, Suzanne Jill Levine, and Eliot Weinberger. New York: Penguin, 1999.

Bowlby, John. *Charles Darwin: A New Life*. New York: W. W. Norton, 1992.

Branch, Taylor. "New Frontiers in American Philosophy." *New York Times Magazine*, August 14, 1977.

Brown, Roger. *Words and Things*. Glencoe, IL: Free Press, 1958.

Burgess, John P. "The Origin of Necessity and the Necessity of Origin." Presented as the Second Annual Saul Kripke Lecture, Saul Kripke Center, CUNY Graduate Center, November 13, 2012. https://youtu.be/1L-tWQzL344.

———. "Saul Kripke: Naming and Necessity." In *Central Works of Philosophy*. Vol. 5, *The Twentieth Century; Quine and After*, edited by John Shand, 166–86. Montreal: McGill–Queen's University Press, 2006.

———. *Saul Kripke: Puzzles and Mysteries*. Cambridge: Polity, 2013.

Burkert, Walter. *Lore and Science in Ancient Pythagoreanism*. Translated by Edwin L. Minar Jr. Cambridge, MA: Harvard University Press, 1972.

Burnet, John. *Early Greek Philosophy*. 2nd ed. London: Adam and Charles Black, 1908.

Butterfield, Herbert. *The Englishman and His History*. Cambridge: Cambridge University Press, 1944.

———. *The Origins of Modern Science, 1300–1800*. 1949; London: G. Bell, 1957.

———. *The Whig Interpretation of History*. 1931; New York: W. W. Norton, 1965.

Carr, Edward Hallett. *What Is History?* 1961; New York: Vintage, 1967.

Carroll, Lewis. *The Annotated Alice: The Definitive Edition; Alice's Adventures in Wonderland and Through the Looking-Glass*. Original illustrations by John Tenniel. Introduction and notes by Martin Gardner. New York: W. W. Norton, 2000.

Cavell, Stanley. *Little Did I Know: Excerpts from Memory.* Stanford, CA: Stanford University Press, 2010.

Cedarbaum, Daniel. "Paradigms." *Studies in History and Philosophy of Science* 14, no. 3 (1983): 173–213. doi: 10.1016/0039-3681(83)90012-2.

Cervantes, Miguel de. *Don Quixote.* Translated by Samuel Putnam. New York: Modern Library, 1998.

Chesterton, G. K. *The Club of Queer Trades.* New York: Harper, 1905.

———. *Orthodoxy.* Chicago: Moody, 2009.

———. *The Wisdom of Father Brown.* New York: John Lane, 1915.

Chomsky, Noam. *Cartesian Linguistics: A Chapter in the History of Rationalist Thought.* 3rd ed. Cambridge: Cambridge University Press, 2009.

———. "The Dewey Lectures 2013: What Kind of Creatures Are We?" *Journal of Philosophy* 110, no. 12 (December 2013).

———. "Notes on Denotation and Denoting." In *From Grammar to Meaning: The Spontaneous Logicality of Language,* edited by Ivano Caponigro and Carlo Cecchetto, 38–45. Cambridge: Cambridge University Press, 2013.

———. *Of Minds and Language: A Dialogue with Noam Chomsky in the Basque Country.* Edited by Massimo Piattelli-Palmarini, Juan Uriagereka, and Pello Salaburu. Oxford: Oxford University Press, 2009.

———. *Reflections on Language.* New York: Pantheon, 1975.

———. "A Review of B. F. Skinner's Verbal Behavior." In *Readings in the Psychology of Language,* edited by Leon A. Jakobovits and Murray S. Miron, 142–43. Englewood Cliffs, NJ: Prentice Hall, 1967.

———. *The Science of Language: Interviews with James McGilvray.* Cambridge: Cambridge University Press, 2012.

———. *Syntactic Structures.* Janua Linguarum. Series Minor, 4. The Hague: Mouton, 1969.

Chomsky, Noam, Gary A. Olson, and Lester Faigley. "Language, Politics, and Composition: A Conversation with Noam Chomsky." *Journal of Advanced Composition* 11, no. 1 (1991): 1–35. http://www.jstor.org/stable/20865759.

Clegg, Brian. "The Dangerous Ratio." http://nrich.maths.org/2671

Collingwood, R. G. *The Idea of History.* Rev. ed. Edited by Jan van der Dussen. Oxford: Oxford University Press, 1994.

Conant, James F. "On Wittgenstein." *Philosophical Investigations* 24, no. 2 (April 2001): 96–107. doi: 10.1111/1467-9205.00138.

Connell, Christopher. "Robert Francis Goheen '40 ★48: Memories of a Leader Who Mastered the Art of Listening." *Princeton Alumni Weekly*, May 14, 2008, 28–29.

Darwin, Charles. "Letter to Asa Gray," May 22, 1860. University of Cambridge Darwin Correspondence Project. https://www.darwin-project.ac.uk/letter/DCP-LETT-2814.xml.

———. *On the Origin of Species: The Illustrated Edition.* Edited by David Quammen. New York: Sterling Signature, 2011.

———. *The Voyage of the Beagle: The Illustrated Edition of Charles Darwin's Travel Memoir and Field Journal.* Minneapolis: Zenith, 2015.

Davidson, Donald. *Inquiries into Truth and Interpretation.* Oxford: Clarendon Press, 1984.

———. "On the Very Idea of a Conceptual Scheme." *Proceedings and Addresses of the American Philosophical Association* 47 (1973): 5–20. doi: 10.2307/3129898.

Davis, Lydia. "Loaf or Hot-Water Bottle: Closely Translating Proust." *Yale Review* 92, no. 2 (2004): 51–70. doi: 10.1111/j.0044-0124.2004.00804.x.

———. "Why a New Madame Bovary?" *Paris Review* (blog), September 15, 2010. https://www.theparisreview.org/blog/2010/09/15/why-a-new-madame-bovary/

Debroy, Bibek. *Sarama and Her Children: The Dog in Indian Myth.* New Delhi: Penguin, 2008.

Delsuc, Frédéric, Gillian C. Gibb, Melanie Kuch, Guillaume Billet, Lionel Hautier, John Southon, Jean-Marie Rouillard, et al. "The Phylogenetic Affinities of the Extinct Glyptodonts." *Current Biology* 26, no. 4 (2016): R155–56. doi: 10.1016/j.cub.2016.01.039.

Deutsch, David. *The Fabric of Reality: The Science of Parallel Universes—and Its Implications.* New York: Penguin, 1998.

Dick, Philip K. "How to Build a Universe that Doesn't Fall Apart Two Days Later." In *The Shifting Realities of Philip K. Dick: Selected Literary and Philosophical Writings*, edited by Lawrence Sutin, 259–80. New York: Pantheon, 1995.

Donne, John. *The Complete Poetry and Selected Prose of John Donne.* Edited by Charles M. Coffin. New York: Modern Library, 1994.

Dudley, Underwood. "Legislating Pi." *Math Horizons* 6, no. 3 (1999): 10–13. http://www.jstor.org/stable/25678199.

Dyson, Freeman. *The Sun, the Genome, the Internet: Tools of Scientific Revolutions*. New York: New York Public Library, 1999.

Earman, John. "Carnap, Kuhn, and the Philosophy of Scientific Methodology." In *World Changes: Thomas Kuhn and the Nature of Science*, edited by Paul Horwich, 9–36. Pittsburgh: University of Pittsburgh Press, 2010.

———. "Who's Afraid of Absolute Space?" *Australasian Journal of Philosophy* 48, no. 3 (1970): 287–319. doi: 10.1080/00048407012341291.

Earman, John, and Arthur Fine. "Against Indeterminacy." *Journal of Philosophy* 74, no. 9 (1977): 535–38. doi: 10.2307/2025796.

Edleston, J. *Correspondence of Sir Isaac Newton and Professor Cotes: Including Letters of Other Eminent Men*. London: J. W. Parker, 1850.

Epstein, Angela. "Believe It or Not, Your Lungs Are Six Weeks Old and Your Taste Buds Just Ten Days. So How Old Is Your Body?" *Daily Mail*, October 13, 2009.

Falkner, Thomas. *A Description of Patagonia, and the Adjoining Parts of South America: Containing an Account of the Soil, Produce, Animals, Vales, Mountains, Rivers, Lakes, &c. of those Countries; the Religion, Government, Policy, Customs, Dress, Arms, and Language of the Indian Inhabitants; and Some Particulars Relating to Falkland's Islands*. Hereford: C. Pugh, 1774.

Fariña, Richard A., Sergio F. Vizcaíno, and Gerardo de Iuliis. *Megafauna: Giant Beasts of Pleistocene South America*. Bloomington: Indiana University Press, 2012.

Fernicola, Juan Carlos, Sergio F. Vizcaíno, and Gerardo de Iuliis. "The Fossil Mammals Collected by Charles Darwin in South America During His Travels on Board the HMS Beagle." *Revista de La Asociación Geológica Argentina* 64, no. 1 (2009): 147–59. http://www.scielo.org.ar/pdf/raga/v64n1/v64n1a16.pdf.

Feyerabend, Paul. "Consolations for the Specialist." In *Criticism and the Growth of Knowledge*, edited by Imre Lakatos and Alan Musgrave, 197–230. Cambridge: Cambridge University Press, 1970.

Fideler, David R., ed. *The Pythagorean Sourcebook and Library: An Anthology of Ancient Writings Which Relate to Pythagoras and Pythagorean Philosophy*. Translated by Kenneth Sylvan Guthrie. Grand Rapids, MI: Phanes Press, 1987.

Fischer, David Hackett. *Historians' Fallacies: Toward a Logic of Historical Thought*. New York: Harper & Row, 1970.

Floyd, Juliet. "Wittgenstein on Philosophy of Logic and Mathematics." In *The Oxford Handbook of Philosophy of Mathematics and Logic*, edited by Stewart Shapiro, 75–129. Oxford: Oxford University Press, 2005. doi: 10.5840/gfpj200425215.

Fowler, David. *The Mathematics of Plato's Academy: A New Reconstruction*. 2nd ed. Oxford: Clarendon Press, 1999.

Fraser, P. M. *Ptolemaic Alexandria*. 3 vols. Oxford: Clarendon Press, 1972.

Frege, Gottlob. "On Sense and Reference." In *Translations from the Philosophical Writings of Gottlob Frege*, edited and translated by Peter Geach and Max Black, 56–78. Oxford: Basil Blackwell, 1952. Originally published as "Über Sinn und Bedeutung," *Zeitschrift für Philosophie und philosophische Kritik* (1892): 25–50.

García Márquez, Gabriel. "The Art of Fiction No. 69." Interview by Peter H. Stone. *Paris Review* 82 (Winter 1981): 44–73.

Ginsberg, Allen. "The Terms in Which I Think of Reality." In *Collected Poems, 1947–1997*, 58. New York: Harper, 2006.

Godfrey-Smith, Peter. *Theory and Reality: An Introduction to the Philosophy of Science*. Chicago: University of Chicago Press, 2003.

Goldfarb, Warren. "Kripke on Wittgenstein on Rules." *Journal of Philosophy* 82, no. 9 (1985): 471–88. doi: 10.2307/2026277.

Gould, Stephen Jay. "The Late Birth of a Flat Earth." In *Dinosaur in a Haystack: Reflections in Natural History*, 38–50. New York: Harmony, 1995.

Greenside, Henry. "Creation and Conservation of Charge during Electron-Positron Particle Production from a Photon." Course materials for Physics 162, "Electricity, Magnetism, and Light," Spring semester, 2015. http://www.phy.duke.edu/~hsg/162/images/electron-positron-production-by-photon.html.

Hacking, Ian. "Putnam's Theory of Natural Kinds and Their Names Is Not the Same as Kripke's." *Principia: An International Journal of Epistemology* 11, no. 1 (2007): 1–24. https://periodicos.ufsc.br/index.php/principia/article/view/14845/13562.

———. *Representing and Intervening: Introductory Topics in the Philosophy of Natural Science*. Cambridge: Cambridge University Press, 1983.

Hanson, Norwood Russell. "An Anatomy of Discovery." *Journal of Philosophy* 64, no. 11 (1967): 321–52. doi: 10.2307/2024301.

———. "A Note on Kuhn's Method." *Dialogue* 4, no. 3 (1965): 371–75. doi: 10.1017/S0012217300035976.

———. *Patterns of Discovery: An Inquiry into the Conceptual Foundations of Science.* Cambridge: Cambridge University Press, 1958.

Harris, Randy Allen. *Rhetoric and Incommensurability.* West Lafayette, IN: Parlor Press, 2005.

Hartley, L. P. *The Go-Between.* Reprint; New York: NYRB Classics, 2002.

Hasse, Helmut, and Heinrich Scholz. "The Foundation Crisis of Greek Mathematics." Translated by David Rice. Originally published as "Die Grundlagenkrisis der griechischen Mathematik." *Kant-Studien* 33, no. 1 (1928): 4–34.

Heath, Thomas L. *A History of Greek Mathematics.* Vol. 1, *From Thales to Euclid.* New York: Dover, 1981.

Hickey, Lance. "Hilary Putnam." In *American Philosophers, 1950–2000,* edited by Philip Breed Dematteis and Leemon B. McHenry, 226–36. Dictionary of Literary Biography, vol. 279. Detroit: Gale Group, 2003.

Hobbes, Thomas. *Elements of Philosophy the First Section, Concerning Body / Written in Latine by Thomas Hobbes of Malmesbury ; and Now Translated into English; to Which Are Added Six Lessons to the Professors of Mathematicks of the Institution of Sr. Henry Savile, in the University of Oxford.* London: R. & W. Leybourn, 1656.

Hoberman, Ruth. *Museum Trouble: Edwardian Fiction and the Emergence of Modernism.* Charlottesville: University of Virginia Press, 2011.

Holmes, Frederic Lawrence. *Meselson, Stahl, and the Replication of DNA: A History of "the Most Beautiful Experiment in Biology."* New Haven, CT: Yale University Press, 2001.

Horwich, Paul. "Kripke's Wittgenstein." In *Meaning without Repre-sentation: Essays on Truth, Expression, Normativity, and Naturalism,* edited by Steven Gross, Nicholas Tebben, and Michael Williams, 359–76. Oxford: Oxford University Press, 2015. doi: 10.1093/acprof: oso/9780198722199.003.0017.

———, ed. *World Changes: Thomas Kuhn and the Nature of Science.* Pittsburgh: University of Pittsburgh Press, 2010.

Hume, David. *The History of England: From the Invasion of Julius Caesar to the Revolution in 1688.* Chicago: University of Chicago Press, 1975.

Huysmans, Joris-Karl. *À Rebours.* Paris: Fasquelle, 1972.

Iamblichus. *Iamblichus' Life of Pythagoras; or, Pythagoric Life: Accompanied by Fragments of the Ethical Writings of Certain Pythagoreans in the Doric Dialect and a Collection of Pythagoric Sentences from Stobaeus and Others.*

Translated by Thomas Taylor. Rochester, VT: Inner Traditions International, 1986.

Jardine, Nick. "Whigs and Stories: Herbert Butterfield and the Historiography of Science." *History of Science* 41, no. 2 (2003): 125–40. http://adsabs.harvard.edu.ezp-prod1.hul.harvard.edu/abs/2003HisSc..41..125J.

Kafka, Franz. *Metamorphosis and Other Stories*. 1915. Translated by Michael Hofmann. New York: Penguin Classics, 2008.

Kant, Immanuel. *Critique of Pure Reason*. Translated by Norman Kemp Smith. London: Macmillan, 1964.

Khayyam, Omar. *Ruba'iyat of Omar Khayyam*. Berkeley: Asian Humanities Press, 1991.

Kindi, Vasso P. "Kuhn's *The Structure of Scientific Revolutions* Revisited." *Journal for General Philosophy of Science* 26, no. 1 (1995): 75–92. doi: 10.1007/BF01130927.

Kipling, Rudyard. *'Captains Courageous': A Story of the Grand Banks*. New York: Macmilllan, 1897.

———. *The Collected Poems of Rudyard Kipling*. Wordsworth Poetry Library. Hertfordshire: Wordsworth, 1999.

Kline, Morris. *Mathematics: The Loss of Certainty*. New York: Oxford University Press, 1980.

Koestler, Arthur. *The Sleepwalkers: A History of Man's Changing Vision of the Universe*. New York: Macmillan, 1959.

Koyré, Alexandre. *Études galiléennes*. Paris: Hermann, 1939.

———. *From the Closed World to the Infinite Universe*. Baltimore: Johns Hopkins University Press, 1957.

———. *Metaphysics and Measurement: Essays in the Scientific Revolution*. London: Chapman & Hall, 1968.

———. *Newtonian Studies*. London: Chapman & Hall, 1965.

Kripke, Saul. "Frege's Theory of Sense and Reference: Some Exegetical Notes." In *Philosophical Troubles: Collected Papers*. Vol. 1, 254–91. New York: Oxford University Press, 2011.

———. "History and Idealism: The Theory of R. G. Collingwood." *Collingwood and British Idealism Studies* 23 (2017): 9–29.

———. "Identity and Necessity." In *Philosophical Troubles: Collected Papers*, vol. 1. New York: Oxford University Press, 2011.

———. *Naming and Necessity*. Cambridge, MA: Harvard University Press, 1980. Originally published as "Naming and Necessity," in

Semantics of Natural Language, 2nd ed., edited by Donald Davidson and Gilbert Harman (Synthese Library 40), 253–355. Dordrecht: D. Reidel, 1972.

———. *Philosophical Troubles: Collected Papers*. Vol. 1. New York: Oxford University Press, 2011.

———. *Wittgenstein on Rules and Private Language: An Elementary Exposition*. Cambridge, MA: Harvard University Press, 1982.

Kuhn, Thomas S. *Black-Body Theory and the Quantum Discontinuity, 1894–1912*. Oxford: Clarendon Press, 1978.

———. "Dubbing and Redubbing: The Vulnerability of Rigid Designation." *Minnesota Studies in the Philosophy of Science* 14 (1990): 298–318.

———. *The Essential Tension: Selected Studies in Scientific Tradition and Change*. Chicago: University of Chicago Press, 1977.

———. "Reflections on My Critics." In *The Road since Structure: Philosophical Essays, 1970-1993, with an Autobiographical Interview*, 123–75. Chicago: University of Chicago Press, 2000.

———. "Remarks on Receiving the Laurea." In *Galileo a Padova, 1592–1610: Celebrazioni del IV centenario, 7 dicembre 1991–7 dicembre 1992*, vol. 1, *L'Anno Galileiano*, 103–6. Trieste: Edizioni LINT, 1995.

———. *The Road since Structure: Philosophical Essays, 1970–1993, with an Autobiographical Interview*. Edited by James Conant and John Haugeland. Chicago: University of Chicago Press, 2000.

———. *The Structure of Scientific Revolutions*. Also issued as *International Encyclopedia of Unified Science*, vol. 2, no. 2. Chicago: University of Chicago Press, 1962.

———. *The Structure of Scientific Revolutions*. 2nd ed. Chicago: University of Chicago Press, 1970.

———. *The Structure of Scientific Revolutions: 50th Anniversary Edition*. With an introductory essay by Ian Hacking. Chicago: University of Chicago Press, 2012.

———. "The Trouble with the Historical Philosophy of Science." In *The Road since Structure: Philosophical Essays, 1970-1993, with an Autobiographical Interview*, 105—20. Chicago: University of Chicago Press, 2000.

———. "What Are Scientific Revolutions?" In *The Road since Structure: Philosophical Essays, 1970–1993, with an Autobiographical Interview*, 13–32. Chicago: University of Chicago Press, 2000.

Kusch, Martin. A *Sceptical Guide to Meaning and Rules: Defending Kripke's Wittgenstein*. Montreal: McGill–Queen's University Press, 2006.

Lakatos, Imre. "Falsification and the Methodology of Scientific Research Programmes." In *Criticism and the Growth of Knowledge*, edited by Imre Lakatos and Alan Musgrave, 91–196. Cambridge: Cambridge University Press, 1970.

Lakatos, Imre, and Alan Musgrave, eds. *Criticism and the Growth of Knowledge*. Cambridge: Cambridge University Press, 1970.

Leibniz, Gottfried Wilhelm. *Theodicy, Abridged*. Edited by Diogenes Allen. Translated by E. M. Huggard. Library of Liberal Arts. Indianapolis: Bobbs-Merrill, 1966.

Levine, Alex, and Steven Weinberg. "T. S. Kuhn's 'Non-Revolution': An Exchange." *New York Review of Books* 46, no. 3 (February 18, 1999): 49f.

Locke, John. *An Essay Concerning Human Understanding*. London: T. Tegg & Son, 1836.

Maier, Dave. "Errol Morris on Wittgenstein, or Someone Like Him in Certain Respects." *3 Quarks Daily*, June 13, 2001. http://www.3quarksdaily.com/3quarksdaily/2011/06/errol-morris-on-wittgenstein-or-someone-like-him-in-certain-respects.html.

Manguel, Alberto. *With Borges*. London: Telegram, 2006.

Martin, Michael F. *Vietnamese Victims of Agent Orange and U.S.-Vietnam Relations*. CRS Report No. RL34761. Washington, DC: Congressional Research Service, 2008. http://handle.dtic.mil/100.2/ADA490443.

Martínez, Alberto A. *The Cult of Pythagoras: Math and Myths*. Pittsburgh: University of Pittsburgh Press, 2012.

Masterman, Margaret. "The Nature of a Paradigm." In *Criticism and the Growth of Knowledge*, edited by Imre Lakatos and Alan Musgrave, 59–90. Cambridge: Cambridge University Press, 1970.

Maxwell, James Clerk. *The Scientific Letters and Papers of James Clerk Maxwell*. Vol. 1, *1846–1862*. Edited by P. M. Harman. Cambridge: Cambridge University Press, 1990.

McDowell, John. "Wittgenstein on Following a Rule." *Synthese* 58, no. 3 (1984): 325–63. doi: 10.1007/BF00485246.

McNamara, Robert S. "The Post–Cold War World: Implications for Military Expenditure in the Developing Countries." *World Bank Economic Review* 5, suppl. 1 (1991): 95–126. doi: 10.1093/wber/5.suppl_1.95.

Meselson, Matthew S. "McGill 2013 Honorary Doctorate Address." Speech presented at McGill University commencement, Montreal, QC, May 27, 2013. Video: https://youtu.be/NQPS6kx-lMaI. Transcript: http://www.belfercenter.org/publication/matthew-meselson-addresses-mcgill-graduates.

Mill, John Stuart. *A System of Logic, Ratiocinative and Inductive: Being a Connected View of the Principles of Evidence and the Methods of Scientific Investigation.* 8th ed. New York: Harper & Brothers, 1881.

Miller, Alexander. "Realism." In *Stanford Encyclopedia of Philosophy.* Stanford University, 1997–. Article published July 8, 2002. https://plato.stanford.edu/entries/realism.

Morris, Errol. *Believing Is Seeing: Observations on the Mysteries of Photography.* New York: Penguin, 2011.

Musil, Robert. *The Man without Qualities.* New York: Alfred A. Knopf, 1995.

Neugebauer, Otto. *The Exact Sciences in Antiquity.* 2nd ed. New York: Dover, 1969.

Nicastro, Nicholas. *Circumference: Eratosthenes and the Ancient Quest to Measure the Globe.* New York: St. Martin's, 2008.

Norton, John D. "Dense and Sparse Meaning Spaces," PhilSci-Archive. May 12, 2012. http://philsci-archive.pitt.edu/9110/.

Orwell, George. *Nineteen Eighty-Four.* Everyman's Library. New York: Alfred A. Knopf, 1992.

Pessin, Andrew, and Sanford Goldberg. *The Twin Earth Chronicles: Twenty Years of Reflection on Hilary Putnam's "The Meaning of 'Meaning.'"* Armonk, NY: M. E. Sharpe, 1996.

Pierre, DBC. *Vernon God Little.* New York: Canongate, 2003.

Pinker, Steven. *The Language Instinct: How the Mind Creates Language.* New York: Perennial, 2000.

Plato. *The Collected Dialogues of Plato, Including the Letters.* Edited by Edith Hamilton and Huntington Cairns. Bollingen Series 71. Princeton, NJ: Princeton University Press, 1971.

Plutarch. *Plutarch's Lives.* Vol. 1, *Theseus and Romulus; Lycurgus and Numa; Solon and Publicola.* Translated by Bernadotte Perrin. Loeb Classical Library 46. Cambridge, MA: Harvard University Press, 1914.

Poe, Edgar Allan. "The Murders in the Rue Morgue." In *The Collected Works of Edgar Allan Poe,* edited by Thomas Ollive Mabbott, vol. 2, pp. 521–74. Cambridge, MA: Belknap Press of Harvard University Press, 1978.

Polyaenus of Lampsacus. *Polyænus's Stratagems of War: Translated from the Original Greek, by Dr. Shepherd, F.R.S.* 2nd ed. London: Printed for George Nicol, 1796.

Putnam, Hilary. "The Development of Externalist Semantics." In *Naturalism, Realism, and Normativity*, edited by Mario De Caro, 199–212. Cambridge, MA: Harvard University Press, 2016.

———. "How Not to Talk About Meaning: Comments on J. J. C. Smart." In *Philosophical Papers*, vol. 2, *Mind, Language and Reality*, 117–31. Cambridge: Cambridge University Press, 1975.

———. "Is Semantics Possible?" In *Philosophical Papers*, vol. 2, *Mind, Language and Reality*, 139–52. Cambridge: Cambridge University Press, 1975.

———. "The Meaning of 'Meaning.'" In *Philosophical Papers*, vol. 2, *Mind, Language and Reality*, 215–71. Cambridge: Cambridge University Press, 1975.

———. *The Philosophy of Hilary Putnam*. Edited by Randall E. Auxier, Douglas R. Anderson, and Lewis Edwin Hahn. Library of Living Philosophers, vol. 34. Chicago: Open Court, 2015.

———. *Reason, Truth and History*. Cambridge: Cambridge University Press, 1981.

Putnam, Samuel. *Paris Was Our Mistress: Memoirs of a Lost and Found Generation*. New York: Viking, 1947.

Quine, Willard Van Orman. *Word and Object*. 1960; Cambridge, MA: MIT Press, 1969.

Read, Rupert, and Wes Sharrock. "Thomas Kuhn's Misunderstood Relation to Kripke-Putnam Essentialism." *Journal for General Philosophy of Science* 33, no. 1 (2002): 151–58. doi: 10.1023/A:1020755503087.

Rescher, Nicholas. *On Leibniz*. Pittsburgh: University of Pittsburgh Press, 2003.

Russell, Bertrand. *The Autobiography of Bertrand Russell*. Boston: Little, Brown, 1967–1969.

———. *The Collected Stories of Bertrand Russell*. Edited by Barry Feinberg. London: George Allen & Unwin, 1972.

———. *The Impact of Science on Society*. New York: Simon & Schuster, 1953.

———. *Introduction to Mathematical Philosophy*. London: G. Allen & Unwin, 1920.

———. *Nightmares of Eminent Persons, and Other Stories*. New York: Simon & Schuster, 1955.

———. "On Denoting." *Mind* 14, no. 56 (1905): 479–93. http://www.jstor.org/stable/3840617.

———. *The Problems of Philosophy*. New York: Oxford University Press, 1997.

———. *Unpopular Essays*. London: Routledge, 1995.

Sandywell, Barry. *Dictionary of Visual Discourse: A Dialectical Lexicon of Terms*. London: Routledge, 2016.

Schalansky, Judith. *Pocket Atlas of Remote Islands: Fifty Islands I Have Not Visited and Never Will*. Translated by Christine Lo. New York: Penguin, 2014.

Schopenhauer, Arthur. *The Art of Controversy, and Other Posthumous Papers*. Translated by T. Bailey Saunders. New York: Macmillan, 1896.

Searle, John. "Proper Names." *Mind* 67, no. 266 (1958): 166–73. http://www.jstor.org/stable/2251108.

Seife, Charles. *Zero: The Biography of a Dangerous Idea*. New York: Viking, 2000.

Seymour-Smith, Martin. *The 100 Most Influential Books Ever Written: The History of Thought from Ancient Times to Today*. New York: Citadel, 1998.

Shakespeare, William. *Hamlet: An Authoritative Text, Intellectual Backgrounds, Extracts from the Sources, Essays in Criticism*. Edited by Cyrus Henry Hoy. 2nd ed. Norton Critical Edition. New York: W. W. Norton, 1992.

———. *1 Henry IV: Text Edited from the First Quarto; Contexts and Sources, Criticism*. Edited by Gordon McMullan. 3rd ed. Norton Critical Edition. New York: W. W. Norton, 2003.

———. *Macbeth: Authoritative Text, Sources and Contexts, Criticism*. Edited by Robert S. Miola. 2nd ed. Norton Critical Edition. New York: W. W. Norton, 2004.

Shapin, Steven. "Why Scientists Shouldn't Write History." *Wall Street Journal*, February 13, 2015. http://www.wsj.com/articles/book-review-to-explain-the-world-by-steven-weinberg-1423863226.

Shipman, G. R. "How to Talk to a Martian." *Astounding Science Fiction* 9 (October 1953): 112–20.

Siegel, Daniel M. *Innovation in Maxwell's Electromagnetic Theory: Molecular Vortices, Displacement Current, and Light*. Cambridge: Cambridge University Press, 2003.

———. "The Origin of the Displacement Current." *Historical Studies in the Physical and Biological Sciences* 17, no. 1 (1986): 99–146. doi: 10.2307/27757576.

Silver, Charles. *The Futility of Consciousness: An Investigation*. Self-published, Amazon Digital Services, 2012. Kindle.

Singer, Mark. "Profiles: Predilections." *New Yorker* 64, no. 51 (February 6, 1989): 38.

Spender, Stephen. *World within World: The Autobiography of Stephen Spender*. Berkeley: University of California Press, 1966.

Strauss, Leo. *The Argument and the Action of Plato's Laws*. Chicago: University of Chicago Press, 1983.

Suskind, Ron. "Faith, Certainty, and the Presidency of George W. Bush." *New York Times*, October 17, 2004.

Sutton, Paul L. "The History of Agent Orange Use in Vietnam: An Historical Overview from the Veteran's Perspective." Presented at the United States–Vietnam Scientific Conference on Human Health and Environmental Effects of Agent Orange/Dioxins, Hanoi, Vietnam, March 3–6, 2002.

Thackeray, William Makepeace. *Vanity Fair: A Novel without a Hero*. Boston: Estes & Lauriat, 1882.

Tolstoy, Leo. *The Sebastopol Sketches*. Translated by David McDuff. New York: Penguin Classics, 1986.

von Fritz, Kurt. "The Discovery of Incommensurability by Hippasus of Metapontum." *Annals of Mathematics* 46, no. 2 (1945): 242–64. doi: 10.2307/1969021.

Ward, Laurence. *The London County Council Bomb Damage Maps, 1939–1945*. London: Thames & Hudson, 2016.

Weinberg, Steven. *Dreams of a Final Theory*. New York: Pantheon, 1992.

———. *To Explain the World: The Discovery of Modern Science*. New York: Harper, 2015.

———. "Eye on the Present—The Whig History of Science." *New York Review of Books* 62, no. 20 (December 17, 2015): 82–84.

———. *The First Three Minutes: A Modern View of the Origin of the Universe*. New York: Basic Books, 1977.

———. "The Revolution That Didn't Happen." *New York Review of Books* 45, no. 15 (October 8, 1998): 48–52.

———. "Sokal's Hoax." *New York Review of Books* 43, no. 13 (August 8, 1996): 11–15.

Whorf, Benjamin Lee. *Language, Thought, and Reality: Selected Writings of Benjamin Lee Whorf.* Cambridge, MA: MIT Press, 1956.

Wilson, Edmund. "The Triple Thinkers." In *Literary Essays and Reviews of the 1930s and 40s,* 7–276. New York: Library of America, 2007.

Wisconsin Historical Society. "Vietnam and Opposition at Home." In *Turning Points in Wisconsin History.* http://www.wisconsinhistory.org/turningpoints/tp-040.

Wittgenstein, Ludwig. *The Blue and Brown Books: Preliminary Studies for the "Philosophical Investigations."* Oxford: Basil Blackwell, 1958.

———. *On Certainty.* Edited by G. E. M. Anscombe and G. H. von Wright. Translated by Denis Paul and G. E. M. Anscombe. With corrections and indices. Oxford: Basil Blackwell, 1969.

———. *Philosophical Investigations: The German Text, with an English Translation.* Rev. 4th ed. Translated by G. E. M. Anscombe, P. M. S. Hacker, and Joachim Schulte. 1953; Oxford: Wiley-Blackwell, 2009.

———. *Philosophical Occasions: 1912–1951.* Edited by James Klagge and Alfred Nordmann. Indianapolis: Hackett, 1993.

———. *Remarks on the Foundations of Mathematics.* Edited by G. H. von Wright, Rush Rhees, and G. E. M. Anscombe. Translated by G. E. M. Anscombe. Rev. ed. Cambridge, MA: MIT Press, 1978.

Wootton, David. *The Invention of Science: A New History of the Scientific Revolution.* New York: Harper, 2015.

Yeats, W. B. *The Collected Poems of W. B. Yeats.* New York: Macmillan, 1964.

Zweig, Stefan. *Messages from a Lost World: Europe on the Brink.* Translated by Will Stone. London: Pushkin, 2016.

Index

Wayne, John, 84
Weinberg, Steven, 12, 12n13, 26n36, 27, 149, 149n1, 150–51, 153–54, 154–55n10, 155–60, 185
West, Nathanael, 180
Whiggishness, 10–12, 12n13, 160, 178; and Kuhn, 162; science, history of, 154, 156
Whig Interpretation of History, The (Butterfield), 10–11
Whigs, 10n9
Whitehead, Alfred North, 64
Whorf, Benjamin Lee, 123, 126; linguistic relativity, 53–54, 54n13
Wilson, Edmund, 36–37
Wise, Norton, 160–62, 162–63n24
Wittgenstein, Ludwig, 2, 15–16, 22, 22n22, 26, 91, 99, 101n32, 108, 108n48, 133n4, 152, 183, 185; and agreement, 92, 97, 97n21, 98, 110; criticism of, 102; family resemblance, 90, 90n3; form of life (*Lebensform*), 90n3, 92–94, 101–2; and Kuhn, 8n6, 36–37n8, 90, 90n3, 92; and language, 93; language games, 90, 90n3, 106n45; mathematical rules, 97n23, 98; paradigm, idea of, 89–90; private language, 94, 94n14, 103, 106; public language, 95, 106; and relativism, 93–94, 94n10, 106, 106n45, 107; Rorschach inkblot, comparison to, 96–97n20; and skepticism, 95–96, 102n36; and truth, 92–93

Wittgenstein on Rules and Private Language (Kripke), 8, 94, 94n13, 97n21, 99n29, 101, 102n36, 107–8
Wood, Robert, 166
Wootton, David, 22n22, 24n29
Word and Object (Quine), 113
Words and Things (Brown), 113
World as Will and Representation (Schopenhauer), 183
World within World (Spender), 89

Xenophon, 79

Yeats, W. B., 23

Zapruder, Abraham, 172–73
Zweig, Stefan, 45–46